Activities for Teaching Science as Inquiry

SEVENTH EDITION

Allyn & Bacon
is an imprint of

Boston   New York   San Francisco
Mexico City   Montreal   Toronto   London
Madrid   Munich   Paris   Hong Kong
Singapore   Tokyo   Cape Town   Sydney

Activities for Teaching Science as Inquiry

JOEL E. BASS
Late of Sam Houston State University

TERRY L. CONTANT
Science Curriculum and Instruction Specialist, LEARN

ARTHUR A. CARIN
Late of Queens College

Vice President and Executive Publisher: Jeffery W. Johnston
Publisher: Kevin M. Davis
Editor: Meredith D. Fossel
Development Editor: Bryce Bell
Editorial Assistant: Maren Vigilante
Senior Managing Editor: Pamela D. Bennett
Project Manager: Mary Harlan
Production Coordination: S4Carlisle Publishing Services

Design Coordinator: Diane C. Lorenzo
Photo Coordinator: Valerie Schultz
Cover Design: Candace Rowley
Cover Image: Fotosearch
Operations Specialist: Susan W. Hannahs
Director of Marketing: Quinn Perkson
Marketing Manager: Erica M. DeLuca
Marketing Coordinator: Brian Mounts

For related titles and support materials, visit our online catalog at www.pearsonhighered.com.

Between the time website information is gathered and then published, it is not unusual for some sites to have closed. Also, the transcription of URLs can result in typographical errors. The publisher would appreciate notification where these errors occur so that they may be corrected in subsequent editions.

Library of Congress Cataloging-in-Publication Data
Bass, Joel E.
    Activities for teaching science as inquiry / Joel E. Bass, Terry L. Contant, Arthur A.
Carin. -- 7th ed.
        p. cm.
    Rev. ed. of: Activities for teaching science as inquiry / Arthur A. Carin. 6th ed. 2005.
    Includes bibliographical references.
    ISBN 978-0-13-615680-2
    1. Science--Study and teaching (Elementary)--Activity programs--Handbooks, manuals, etc.
I. Contant, Terry L. II. Carin, Arthur A. III. Carin, Arthur A. Activities for teaching
science as inquiry. IV. Title.
    LB1585.C267 2009
    372.3'5044--dc22.

                                                                    2008002464

Photo Credits: Helen Bass, p. A-213.

Printed in the United States of America

10 9 8 7 6 5 4 3   EB   12 11 10 09

**Allyn & Bacon
is an imprint of**

PEARSON

Dedication

THIS BOOK IS DEDICATED to the memory of Dr. Joel E. Bass, who passed away after completing this edition. Dr. Bass inspired many science educators during his 35 years at Sam Houston State University, and he touched thousands more through his work on the ninth, tenth, and eleventh editions of *Teaching Science as Inquiry*. Joel, your passion for teaching science lives on in our memories, and in this book.

THIS BOOK IS ALSO DEDICATED to the memory of Dr. Arthur A. Carin, author of the first eight editions of *Teaching Science as Inquiry* (then called *Teaching Science as Discovery*). Through five decades of exemplary writing, teaching, research, and service, Dr. Carin had a significant, positive impact on science education. Art, you are remembered and honored.

Preface

THE RAPID ADVANCE of cognitive learning theories in the past few years has led educators to realize the need for students to be more actively engaged in their own construction of knowledge. This research tells us that an inquiry approach to science teaching motivates and engages all types of students, helping them understand the relevance of science to their lives, as well as the nature of science itself.

Inquiry is both a way for scientists and students to investigate the world and a way to teach. In this instructional environment, teachers act as facilitators of learning, guiding students in asking simple but thoughtful questions about the world and finding ways to engage them in answering their questions.

Inquiry incorporates the use of hands-on and process-oriented activities for the benefit of knowledge construction while building investigation skills and habits of mind in students. Inquiry encourages students to connect their prior knowledge to observations and to use their observations as evidence to increase personal scientific knowledge and explain how the world works.

But is there a manageable way for new and experienced teachers to bring inquiry into their science classrooms?

Drawing on a solid understanding of inquiry with a teaching framework that builds in accountability for science content learning, and using inquiry-based activities, teachers can create and manage an engaging, productive science classroom. By integrating an inquiry approach, science content, teaching methods, standards, and a bank of inquiry activities, the seventh edition of *Activities for Teaching Science as Inquiry* demonstrates a manageable way for new and experienced teachers to bring inquiry successfully into the science classroom.

The Inquiry Framework

Activities for Teaching Science as Inquiry uses the 5-E instructional model as a framework for all inquiry activities. By keying each activity to the National Science Education Standards, the text further provides new and experienced teachers with a solid foundation for science teaching.

NSES STANDARDS ABOUT ORGANISMS AND CONCEPTS AND PRINCIPLES THAT SUPPORT THE STANDARDS FOR GRADES K–4

NSES Standards

Students should understand:

• Characteristics of Organisms (K–4)
• Life Cycles of Organisms (K–4)

Concepts and Principles That Support the Standards

• Organisms have basic needs. For example, animals need air, water, and food; plants require air, water, nutrients, and light. Organisms can survive only in environments in which their needs can be met.
• Each plant or animal has different structures that serve different functions in growth, survival, and reproduction.
• Plants and animals have life cycles that include being born, developing into adults, reproducing, and eventually dying. The details of this life cycle are different for different organisms.

Source: Reprinted from *National Science Education Standards* by The National Academy of Sciences, with permission courtesy of the National Academies Press, Washington DC.

National Science Education Standards

Many years of work and research in the science education community have provided a coherent, research-based vision for a new era of science education. As a result, the *National Science Education Standards* (NSES) were created to coordinate the goals and objectives for science instruction.

Throughout this edition, you will have an opportunity to become familiar with the *National Science Education Standards* as activities are specifically connected to the *Standards*. This integrated coverage in all activities highlights the importance of using the *National Science Education Standards* to inform instruction.

5-E Model

The text follows, now even more closely, the 5-E model of instruction, which frames each activity in terms of engaging, exploring, explaining, elaborating, and evaluating. This learning cycle model reflects the NSES *Science as Inquiry Standards*, seamlessly integrating inquiry and the *Standards* to create a science teaching framework best suited for engaging students in meaningful science learning while providing accountability opportunities for teachers.

3. How do the seeds in the two bags compare?
4. What do you think is the effect of temperature on germination (sprouting)? Why do you think so? What is your evidence?

10. WHAT SEEDS DO WE EAT? (K–4)

ENGAGE a. Ask: *What seeds or seed products do we eat?*

EXPLORE b. Hold a classroom "seed feast." Provide a variety of seeds for children to eat. Consider some of the seeds and seed products in the accompanying chart for the seed feast.

Safety Precautions Make sure children are not allergic to any food you provide for them to eat, such as peanuts.

EXPLAIN c. Using the chart, conduct a discussion of the various seeds and seed products we eat. Emphasize that rather than the cotyledons providing food for the seeds to germinate and begin growth, they are providing food energy for our survival and growth.

SEEDS AND SEED PRODUCTS WE EAT

Food	Seed or Seed Product
Peas	seeds (and fruit)
Beans	seeds (and fruit)
Corn	seeds
Rice	seeds
Peanuts	seeds
Sunflower seeds	seeds
Chocolate	made from seeds of cacao plant
Coffee	made from seeds of coffee plant
Vanilla	made from seeds of orchid
Cumin (spice)	made from cumin seeds
Flour	made from wheat, barley, or other grass seeds
Pretzels	made from flour
Bread	made from flour
Tortillas	made from flour or corn
Breakfast cereals	made from the seeds of grasses including wheat, rye, oats, and barley

Source: Adapted from National Gardening Association, 1990. *GrowLab.* National Gardening Association, Burlington, VT.

ELABORATE d. As a take-home activity, have the students keep a mini-journal about the seeds they eat for a week. Have a discussion with the class to identify the kinds of information that should be included in their journal. Draft a letter to parents describing the project.

EVALUATE e. Create a checklist, to be included with the parent letter, that students can use to self-evaluate their work. Use the same checklist to assist in your evaluation of the final products.
f. Post the mini-journals so students can view and have discussions about the different kinds of seeds their classmates eat. This is a form of informal peer assessment.

Using Activities for Teaching Science as Inquiry

The *Activities for Teaching Science as Inquiry*

- can be used to illustrate and expand on the science content, and model the 5-E lesson procedures, engaging students in constructivist inquiry;
- provide a comprehensive view of how the NSES *Science Content Standards* can be used to organize curriculum and inform instruction in elementary and middle school science;
- provide an interesting way for readers to learn significant science content that will be important for them to know in teaching science;
- provide a way for readers to prepare for the science portion of state certification exams; and
- become a bank of activities readers can draw on in developing lesson plans to teach during their science methods courses when they move into the schools as professional teachers.

The changes made to this edition help to build a clearer understanding of practical methods for implementing an inquiry approach to science education.

EXPLORE

b. Arrange students in groups. Provide two lenses of different magnifying power to each group. Show students how to support a lens vertically by taping it to the bottom of a Styrofoam cup. Remove the shade from the lamp and place the lamp in the room so that all groups have an unobstructed view of it.

Provide these instructions to students:
1. Tape each of the two lenses to the bottom of cups. Label the cups and lenses A and B.
2. Place lens A, supported by a cup, on the table so that it faces the lamp.
3. Fold a white sheet of paper along two opposite edges so it will stand up.
4. Place the sheet of paper behind the lens and move it back and forth until you see an image of the lamp on the paper.

5. Measure and record the distance from the lens to the image on the paper.
6. Ask: *Is the image inverted or right side up?* (Inverted) *Is the image of the lamp larger or smaller than the lamp itself?* (Smaller) Record your answers on a record sheet or in your science journal.
7. Repeat the procedures for lens B. Is the image formed on the paper inverted or right side up? Is the image larger or smaller than the lamp?
8. Which lens, A or B, formed a larger image? For which lens, A or B, was the lens closer to the paper screen?

Acknowledgments

Science education is a dynamic field. Application of new research findings, technological advances, and state and national initiatives result in a gradual evolution of learning theories, instructional and assessment strategies, state content, and inquiry standards. Application of these current ideas in practice occurs most directly in the classrooms of our nation's schools. Our goal in writing and revising this textbook is to provide you an accurate view of contemporary science education, with specific suggestions, guidelines, and examples as you prepare to teach science to children and early adolescents so they become scientifically literate citizens of the future.

The revisions and modifications incorporated in the seventh edition would not have been possible without insightful reviews of the previous edition and suggestions for improvement from our colleagues. We acknowledge and express our gratitude to the following reviewers: James D. Ellis, The University of Kansas; Wendy Frazier, George Mason University; Violetta Lien, Texas State University, San Marcos; Leann Steinmetz, University of Texas, San Antonio; and Senay Yasar, Arizona State University.

We want to thank the many editors at Pearson who have helped make this edition possible, especially Meredith Sarver Fossel and Bryce Bell, whose amiable advice and support has enriched the efficacy of this text. We are also grateful for our collaboration with Autumn Benson, which led to the on-line components of the text through MyEducationLab. We also wish to thank Mary Harlan, our supportive project manager at Pearson. For their help in bringing the book to production, we appreciate the assistance of Mary Tindle and Amy Gehl at S4Carlisle Publishing Services.

Contents

APPENDIXES AP-1

Activities for Teaching Science as Inquiry

SECTION I

Teaching Inquiry Science Activities

NSES   *Inquiry is a set of interrelated processes by which scientists and students pose questions about the natural world and investigate phenomena; in doing so, students acquire knowledge and develop a rich understanding of concepts, principles, models, and theories. Inquiry is a critical component of a science program at all grade levels and in every domain of science. (National Research Council, 1996, p. 214)*

Terrariums offer a wonderful opportunity for children to investigate the world by questioning and hypothesizing, describing and classifying, manipulating and experimenting, explaining and predicting. Sharon Olson began a series of terrarium lessons with her second graders by asking: *What might you find on a forest floor?* As the class discussed this question, Ms. Olson held up the different materials the students suggested (soil, sand, leaves, seeds, fruit, plants, water, twigs, grass, and so on). She then told the students these were some of the things they would put in a container to make a home for living things. For the next few days, small groups of students built and investigated their own terrariums (Hosoume & Barber, 1994). Using readily available containers, such as large, plastic soda bottles (Ingram, 1993), the children arranged soil in the bottom of the containers, planted plants, sprinkled seeds, added moisture, and introduced earthworms and pill bugs to their new homes. With Ms. Olson's assistance, they asked questions about these organisms and planned and conducted investigations. They also organized the data of observations and used it as evidence to answer their questions. Throughout the terrarium lessons, the teacher observed and assessed the children's inquiry abilities and developing knowedge of the habitats and needs of living organisms.

This scenario draws on activities described in this book. Here, you will find directions for more than 140 inquiry activities in physical science, life science, and earth and space science designed for elementary and middle school students. The activities presented here are consistent with and reflect the *National Science Education Standards* and the standards of most states. They do not comprise a comprehensive science curriculum, but they do represent a large number of examples that will

1. help you connect science in the classroom to national and state science standards in a practical way;
2. provide concrete suggestions for teaching science as inquiry; and
3. provide a bank of activities that you can draw on in teaching science as inquiry.

You do not have to be a science specialist to engage your students in these activities, merely curious and willing to learn along with them.

Let us look more closely at what it means to teach science as inquiry.

When Scientists and Students Inquire

Science is an attempt to understand the natural world. Doing science can be as simple as one individual conducting field studies or as complex as hundreds of people across the world working together on a major scientific problem. Whatever the circumstances or level of complexity, scientists are likely to work from some common assumptions, have some common goals, and use some common procedures. When scientists inquire, they

- ask questions about objects, events, and systems;
- employ a variety of equipment and tools to make observations and measurements in order to obtain data and seek evidence to answer their questions;
- use scientific concepts and principles along with clear reasoning to develop tentative explanations that make sense of collected evidence;
- make predictions to test explanations;
- blend logic and imagination;
- reach conclusions or *not* (American Association for the Advancement of Science, 1993; National Research Council, 1996; Rutherford & Ahlgren, 1990).

Although what scientists do is a model for science instruction, because of developmental differences children may not be able to engage in inquiry as scientists do in professional communities. Thus, elementary and middle school science instruction occurs in a simplified form that enables children to participate with understanding (Lee, 2002).

The key to accommodating scientific inquiry to the level of children is the teacher, who plans, guides, scaffolds, questions, informs, and explains—all in the context of children's hands-on engagement with the objects, organisms, and activities of the real world.

Phases of Inquiry Instruction: The 5-E Model

Inquiry instruction can be thought of in terms of five main components or tasks: *engage, explore, explain, elaborate,* and *evaluate.* You may recognize these five instructional phases as the components of the *5-E model of instruction.*

Engage

Inquiry is initiated at the engage phase. In this phase, teachers probe prior knowledge and conceptions (and misconceptions) of learners and help them generate a question to be investigated. Ideally, inquiry in the classroom should begin with authentic questions developed by students from their own experiences with objects, organisms, and events in the environment (American Association for the Advancement of Science, 1993).

In classroom practice, teachers must be prepared to provide guidance in forming questions that can be investigated scientifically. Students learn from teachers how to ask good questions. Teachers can maintain the spirit of inquiry by focusing on questions that can be answered by collecting observational data, using available knowledge of science, and applying processes of reasoning (National Research Council, 1996).

Explore

The essence of science is to use whatever methods fit to gather evidence that can be used in making sense of the natural world. Scientists and children can use various types of investigations in doing science. Different types of questions call for different forms of investigation.

In the early grades, investigations are largely based on systematic description and classification of material objects and organisms (Lowery, 1997), as in the terrarium lessons. Young children's natural curiosity motivates them to explore the world by manipulating and observing, comparing and contrasting, and sorting simple objects in their environment.

By grade 4 or 5, children begin to engage in experimental inquiry—posing questions, collecting information through experiments, and arriving at logical conclusions. Controlled experiments or fair tests can be important parts of experimental investigations, especially in the upper elementary and middle grades. In controlled investigations, students manipulate one variable at a time, determine its effect on a responding variable, and control all other relevant variables. Carefully guided variations of experiments might also be introduced at earlier grades.

As students engage in these inquiry activities, they develop simple skills such as how to observe, measure, cut, connect, switch, pour, tie, hold, and hook. Beginning with simple instruments, they learn to use rulers, thermometers, watches, spring scales, and balance beams to measure important variables. Students learn to use magnifying lenses and microscopes to see finer details of objects and organisms. They may also begin to use computers and calculators in investigations (National Research Council, 2000).

Explain

This phase of inquiry involves the interpretation of collected data. To interpret is to go beyond the data given and to construct inferences, make predictions, and build explanations that make sense of the world. Interpretations use reasoning processes to coordinate scientific knowledge and observational evidence in order to answer initiating questions.

In children's inquiry, teachers should refrain as much as possible from supplying information and providing explanations that children could attain on their own. Nevertheless, it is often necessary for teachers to directly teach terms and concepts, experimental procedures, and scientific principles. Although inquiry teachers may use expository methods to teach principles, the instruction always builds on children's recent activities, and what is learned is applied to new situations to assist students in comprehending it.

Elaborate

If understanding is to be a result of inquiry, students must have opportunities to transfer or apply their new knowledge to new issues and problems (Bransford, Brown, & Cocking, 1999). In the elaborate phase of inquiry instruction, students identify additional questions to investigate, collect pertinent evidence, and connect their newly constructed knowledge to the evidence through such processes as classifying, relating, inferring, predicting, and explaining. Students communicate their investigations to one another and critique and analyze their work and the work of others. By applying their new knowledge in investigating new situations, students continually build understanding.

Evaluate

Evaluation in inquiry teaching involves use of assessment data to discover what students are learning (or not learning) and to provide feedback to modify lesson plans and teaching methods where needed. Continuous assessment through asking key questions, observing and judging the performances and products of students, and administering assessment tasks of various designs will help you probe your students' understanding, consider how misconceptions and alternative theories are affecting their learning, and determine how they are able to apply what they know in new situations. This informaton will provide you the basis for decision making about next steps in instruction.

Characteristics of Inquiry Classrooms

At every step of inquiry instruction, learning takes place within classrooms characterized by student discourse, cooperative group activities, continuing assessment, and teacher scaffolding.

Discourse

Children love to talk about their experiences. Inquiry science provides a rich context in which to develop language and thought (Rowe, 1973). Confronted with puzzling phenomena and given some freedom to investigate, children work hard at expressing their experiences through language.

Just as communication among scientists is central in the construction of scientific knowledge, students learn by talking among themselves and writing about and formally presenting their ideas. Oral and written discourse focuses the attention of students on *what* they know, *how* they know it, and *how* their knowledge connects to the knowledge of other people, to other subjects, and to the world beyond the classroom (National Research Council, 1996).

Teachers make students' ideas more meaningful by commenting and elaborating on them and asking students to clarify, expand, and justify their own emerging conceptions and those of others. Conversational partnerships with the teacher and classmates allow students to build on and use the thinking processes of others to support their own efforts to think in more flexible and mature ways.

Cooperative learning groups play a vital role in the learning community.

Cooperative Groups

Glenn Seaborg, 1951 Nobel Prize winner in chemistry and formerly the principal investigator for GEMS (Great Explorations in Math and Science) at the Lawrence Hall of Science, reminds us that cooperation is the norm in science:

> In the case of all great "discoveries" it must be remembered that science is a group process. When we devise experiments and research today, we do so on the basis of an enormous body of knowledge contributed by people from all over the world over thousands of years. . . . Research effort is above all a team effort. (Seaborg, 1991)

In the context of inquiry instruction, cooperative learning is an important process that asks students to work together and support one another's learning. It entails students working collaboratively in small groups to

- consider a problem or assignment together;
- share limited supplies and science equipment;

- verbalize what they know and what they want to find out;
- plan investigations;
- collect and compare the data;
- consider the multiple viewpoints of group members; and
- propose group solutions to the problem.

Setting Up Cooperative Learning Groups (CLGs). Initially, you should assign students to teams because they tend to gravitate to friends only. For primary grade students or older students who have not worked previously in CLGs, it is best to start with two students. As students acquire basic cooperative group skills, combine two groups of two as a working team. Generally, CLG teams of three or four are recommended once your classroom is comfortable and knowledgeable about the process.

When you form groups, you will want to integrate students with various abilities, disabilities, and cultural backgrounds. To initiate conversation and encourage team cohesion, provide time for each team to choose its own name. Once you have established a cooperative group routine, keep teams together for 3 to 6 weeks so teammates have time to learn to work with each other. After 3 to 6 weeks, change team membership, so students get to work with other students and to experience the differences in team dynamics.

A specific job is assigned to each CLG team member. The names and functions are quite similar in all CLGs. The following are from Robert Jones's (1990) *Inquiry Task Group Management System:*

- *Principal investigator.* In charge of team operations including checking assignments, ensuring that all team members can participate in activities, and leading group discussions. The principal investigator is also the one group member who communicates with the teacher when questions arise. This enables a more orderly atmosphere and limits the number of questions to which the teacher must respond. Often groups can solve their own problems without consulting the teacher.
- *Materials manager.* Gets, inventories, and distributes materials to the team.
- *Recorder/reporter.* Collects and records data on lab sheets and reports results to whole class orally or in writing on class summary chart posted on chalkboard.
- *Maintenance director.* With the assistance of other team members, cleans up and returns materials and equipment to their appropriate storage space or container. Directs the disposal of used materials and is responsible for team members' safety.

Staff members at research institutions, hospitals, and other entities routinely wear name badges indicating job responsibilities. This is a good practice for inquiry team members as well. *Job badges* (see examples in Figures I-1 and I-2) or ID badges will make it easier for students to remember their responsibilities and for you to spot students who should not be straying away from their group's space. Younger students will especially enjoy displaying an ID badge. Their importance in professional communities may have to be established with older students.

Continuing Assessment

Three assumptions underlie inquiry teaching:

1. Clear standards and indicators (assessment criteria) must be written;
2. Teachers must provide high-quality opportunites for students to achieve standards, including both conceptual understandings and inquiry abilities;
3. Students must demonstrate understandings and abilities through well-designed assessments.

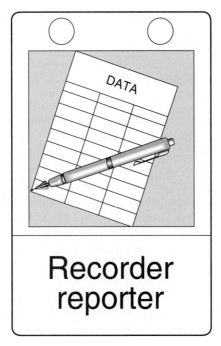

Recorder reporter

Figure I-1   Cooperative learning group (CLG) job badge.
Source: Reprinted by permission from Robert M. Jones, *Teaming Up! The Inquiry Task Group Management System User's Guide.* LaPorte, TX: ITGROUP, December 1990, 55.

Maintenance director

Figure I-2   Cooperative learning group (CLG) job badge.
Source: Reprinted by permission from Robert M. Jones, *Teaming Up! The Inquiry Task Group Management System User's Guide.* LaPorte, TX: ITGROUP, December 1990, 43.

An assessment strategy involving formative and summative assessment is especially compatible with inquiry instruction.

Formative and Summative Assessment.   In formative assessment, informal observations, formal performance tasks, and written work are used during the inquiry lessons to assess students' developing understanding of concepts, principles, theories, and explanations to determine the level and growth of inquiry abilities. For example, through formative assessment, teachers seek to determine:

- What information do students know about an activity before they begin?
- Do students understand that data collected must relate to observations of the real world and provide a basis for predictions, inferences, and explanations?
- Do students use their data to make predictions? How well were students able to provide reasons for their predictions? Are the reasons plausible?
- Are students providing plausible explanations for their observations? Are the students' reasons becoming more detailed? Do students provide more than one reason for their explanations? What do students do to test their predictions and explanations?
- What should they do next to enable students to achieve the planned objectives.

For summative assessment, teachers use application or transfer tasks to determine conceptual understanding. These tasks might be built around the task used in the elaborate phase of inquiry lessons. Be sure to key both formative and summative assessments to standards and objectives. Performance tasks, written tests, and final work products might be used in summative assessment. Scores or grades representing what students know and are able to do can be assigned based on such assignments.

Assessments should always have a clear purpose. The purpose of formative and summative strategies is the continuous improvement of learning and instruction. It is important that both formative and summative assessments are aligned to standards and objectives.

An assessment tool called *performance assessment* is especially compatible with assessing inquiry science learning.

Performance Assessment. Performance assessment is a technique of assessing learning through performance tasks that can be observed or work products that can be examined. Student performances might include measuring, observing, collecting and organizing data, constructing a graph, making a visual or audio presentation, participating in group discussion, presenting an oral defense of work, or presenting a how-to explanation of a procedure. Products presented for assessment could include data tables, graphs, models, reports, and oral or written explanations and problem solutions. Detailed scoring guides, such as checklists and rubrics, are developed and used with performance tasks to judge performance.

The PALS (Performance Assessment Links in Science) website has collected many excellent performance assessment examples from the World Wide Web. Peruse the site at http://pals.sri.com/index.html.

Performance assessment techniques make it possible to gather data on the processes of learning rather than just the outcomes, and to assess *how* students know rather than merely what they know. Performance assessments are often embedded in daily instruction, rather than administered at the end of the week or after a series of lessons.

Student participation is a key component of successful assessment and evaluation systems. If students are to participate successfully in inquiry, they need to be clear about the objectives and criteria for good work, assess their own efforts in light of the criteria, and share responsibility in making judgments and taking action (Atkin, Black, & Coffey, 2001).

Ongoing, formative assessment provides a basis for teacher scaffolding of student understanding.

Scaffolding

In *scaffolding* student learning, the teacher supplies enough external support for students to be successful with the various inquiry tasks. The teacher might help learners at various steps in the inquiry process as they formulate the focus question for an investigation, plan and carry out procedures for data collection, and make sense of the data and answer the question posed. The younger the children and the less experience they have with scientific inquiry, the more scaffolding assistance they will probably need and the more structured the inquiry lessons will need to be. Due largely to language and cultural differences, English Language Learners (ELLs) profit from careful teacher scaffolding.

To scaffold the learning process for students, inquiry teachers might provide suggestions, questions, prompts, or hints. They might also guide students to clarify, elaborate, or justify their investigation procedures and findings. Teachers might even choose to provide necessary terms, concepts, and principles to students through formal, direct instruction. Textbooks, videos, the Internet, and other means might also be used to help students develop knowledge needed to support understanding.

An important skill in the art of teaching is to know when to scaffold a student's learning and when to allow it to take its own course. Just as scaffolds in a building project are designed to be taken down when the building walls are strong, scaffolding support in teaching should be gradually removed or "faded" (Ormrod, 1999) as students develop science knowledge and inquiry processes. In the long run, students should develop their own self-regulated strategies to guide learning.

About the Science Activities in This Book

This book presents for your use a wealth of physical science, life science, and earth and space science activities. Through engaging in these activities, children develop a better understanding of science and how the world works. At the same time, they develop their abilities to inquire—to ask questions about the world around them, to investigate and gather data, and to use their observations as evidence to construct reasonable explanations for the questions posed (see Figure I-3). Furthermore, they develop an understanding of the nature of scientific inquiry (see Figure I-4).

The activities in this book should not be thought of as complete lesson plans; building lesson plans and sequences is something that teachers should do for themselves. Rather, the activities are just that—activities that can be incorporated into lesson plans.

To assist and guide you in the lesson planning process, relevant *Standards and Concepts and Principles That Support the Standards* are given for each activity or for groups of activities on common science topics. Targeted student *Objectives* for building understanding and connecting activities to *Standards* are given. *Relevant Safety Precautions* and *Materials* needed are also provided.

All students should develop abilities to:

- ask questions about objects, organisms, and events in the environment;
- plan and conduct simple investigations;
- use appropriate tools and techniques to gather and interpret data;
- use evidence and scientific knowledge to develop explanations; and
- communicate investigations, data, and explanations to others.

Figure I-3   NSES science as inquiry standards.
Source: Based on the *National Science Education Standards.*

All students should understand:

- Scientific investigations involve asking and answering a question about the world.
- Scientists use different kinds of investigations depending on the questions they are trying to answer.
- Simple instruments, such as magnifiers, thermometers, and rulers, provide more information than scientists obtain using only their senses.
- Scientists develop explanations using observations (evidence) and what they already know about the world (scientific knowledge).
- Scientists make their investigations and results public.
- Scientists review, repeat, and ask questions about the results of other scientists' work.

Figure I-4   NSES standards for understanding the nature of scientific inquiry.
Source: Based on the *National Science Education Standards.*

Using the Science Activities in This Book

The science activities in this book should be thought of as "bare bones" outlines that must be "fleshed out" through lesson planning and instruction. For example, engage activities presented here provide only questions to focus inquiry. You must add activities that arouse motivation and interest and elicit information on students' relevant prior knowledge to expand the basic structure of the engage phase.

Each activity in the book is organized according to the 5-E model of instruction. The activities focus primarily on the first three Es of the instructional model: engage, explore, and explain. In addition, examples of elaborate and evaluate activities are given in some of the activities, which can serve as models as you develop your own elaborate and evaluate activities. Activities that help students understand the nature of science and scientific inquiry are occasionally given within the content of a 5-E activity.

Although the activities in this book may be used individually, most of them are arranged sequentially in clusters to provide a comprehensive view of the phenomena, concepts, and principles of each topic.

Getting Started with Inquiry Science

Following are some suggestions for using the activities in this book for your own classroom inquiry lessons.

Step 1: Preparation

- Organize students into cooperative groups.
- Organize materials needed by teams in small boxes or bags, or on trays.
- Try out activities before they are introduced to students. By trying out activities beforehand, you can anticipate questions and ensure that the activity will work. Finding out in the middle of a lesson that you do not have enough materials or cannot get the equipment to work properly can discourage you or your students.

Step 2: Engage

At the engage phase, you should present an initiating activity that leads to a question students can investigate. The initiating activity should also enhance motivation and interest and provide you with an understanding of the prior knowledge students bring to a lesson. Insofar as possible, you should build on students' prior knowledge at every phase of inquiry.

Remember to:

- Keep the engage portion of the lesson brief and open-ended.
- Ask or help students ask a specific key question that can be investigated.
- Ask questions or use demonstratons and hands-on activities to find out students' prior knowledge and conceptions or misconceptions.
- Tell students they will be exploring this and other related questions.
- Review general and specific safety procedures with students (see Figure I-5).
- Introduce or review pertinent activity information and cooperative group procedures such as, "When we begin, move quickly and quietly into your team. Stay with your team at all times. Speak softly, listen and respond to one another, and take turns. Concentrate on your assigned job."

Safety guidelines for students:
- Always follow the safety procedures outlined by the teacher.
- Never put any materials in your mouth.
- Avoid touching your face, mouth, ears, or eyes while working with chemicals, plants, or animals.
- Always wash your hands immediately after using materials, especially chemicals or animals.
- Always be careful when using sharp or pointed tools. Always make sure that you protect your eyes and those of your neighbors.
- Wear American National Standards Institute approved safety goggles (with Z87 printed on the goggles) whenever activities are done in which there is a potential risk to eye safety.
- Report all accidents, even small ones, to your teacher.
- Follow directions and ask questions if you're unsure of what to do.
- Behave responsibly during science investigations.

Safety guidelines for teachers:
- Examine each of the science activities carefully for possible safety hazards. Eliminate or be prepared to address all anticipated problems.
- Be particularly alert to potential hazards related to children handling and caring for animals. Instruct children in the proper care and handling of classroom pets, fish, or other live organisms used as part of science activities.
- Consider eliminating all activities using open flames. Use hot plates as heat sources, but make sure that the hot plates are not in an area where children might touch them.
- Consider eliminating activities in which students are required to taste substances.

Additional safety suggestions are given in Appendix A.

Figure I-5   Guidelines for safety.

Step 3: Distribution of Science Materials

Do not begin distributing materials until step 2 is completed. Then, have the materials managers collect science materials from the central materials station and deliver them to their team station. This step can make or break the best-planned activity. Make certain that materials managers are reliable and know the specifics of their jobs before they begin.

Step 4: Explore

- Guide students as they consider what data they should collect and what they will do to collect the data.
- As each team begins its work, move from team to team to ensure the proper distribution of materials has occurred and that teams have necessary materials and are proceeding safely. Also check that students understand their goal during the exploration session, how they will collect and record data, why they will do it that way, and how that data connects to the initiating question. Depending on the amount of

scaffolding needed, students might develop their own plan for investigation or they might follow suggestions or a structure provided by their teacher.

- Be careful that you do not give away the "answer" during the explore phase. If students ask questions, respond with a question that will guide them in their exploration. Tell students very little about what can be expected to happen. You want students to make observations, discuss what they observe, and have a chance to make predictions and/or inferences from their observations. Otherwise, they are likely to discover exactly what you have told them they will discover. Part of the joy of exploring is not knowing what to expect!

- Resist presenting science vocabulary during the engage and explore phases. Do not give students the vocabulary words that will describe what they observe before they do the activity. Let students engage in the inquiry and experience the phenomena they observe. It is after exploration that science vocabulary will have more meaning for students.

Step 5: Explain

- Instruct reporter/recorders to report team results to the whole class. In some cases it will be appropriate to post team data on a class summary chart, visible to all. Conduct a discussion of the reported results of the groups. Then ask for students' conceptions of ideas learned and discuss the similarities and discrepancies of team data.

- As students exchange their ideas, listen to how they have conceptualized what they think. Often, they will have developed erroneous beliefs about how something "works." Misconceptions are difficult to change. Simply pointing out alternative and naive conceptions will not generally change what students believe. You can employ several strategies to help students confront and reconsider their alternative conceptions:
  a. Ask questions that challenge students' current beliefs.
  b. Present phenomena that students cannot adequately explain within their existing perspectives.
  c. Engage students in discussions of the pros and cons of various explanations.
  d. Point out explicitly the differences between students' beliefs and "reality."
  e. Show how the correct explanation of an event or phenomenon is more plausible or makes more sense than anything students themselves can offer (Ormrod, 2004; Roth & Anderson, 1988).

- Although the child must do the interpretation work, teachers must be ready to assist in the process. During the explain phase of inquiry, it is appropriate for teachers to supply vocabulary terms, invent relevant concepts and principles, and give hints and even complete explanations to children. But always follow this principle: *Tell only after student explorations.*

Step 6: Elaborate

Suggest questions and activities that allow students to apply what they have learned to new and novel situations. Principal investigators then lead their teams in inquiring into the new questions. Follow up with appropriate class discussion. Also, have students extend their learning with readings, Internet research, or other individualized reinforcement of concepts and principles being learned.

Step 7: Evaluate

Use ongoing, formative assessments at every phase of the lesson as a basis for scaffolding and continued improvement of instruction and learning. All assessments should be directly related to lesson objectives. Vary your methods for assessing understanding of individual team members and the group as a whole. Watching and listening to students, asking them questions, and using performance tasks and traditional assessment items could be used as a basis for evaluation.

Step 8: Team Cleanup

Maintenance directors, with the assistance of team members, should arrange materials so they can be easily reused, return all supplies to designated areas, and ensure that work areas are cleaned. This step might occur at other transition points in the lesson as well, particularly after explore or elaborate. Note that cleanup is a team effort.

The most important element in these inquiry activities is that students can discover the joy and wonder of science. And so can you. Have fun!

REFERENCES

American Association for the Advancement of Science. (1993). *Benchmarks for science literacy.* New York: Oxford University Press.

Atkin, J. M., Black, P., & Coffey, J. (Eds.). (2001). *Classroom assessment and the national science education standards.* Washington, DC: National Academy Press.

Bransford, J. D., Brown, A. L., & Cocking, R. R. (Eds.). (1999). *How people learn: Brain, mind, experience, and school.* Washington, DC: National Academy Press.

Hosoume, K., & Barber, J. (1994). *Terrarium habitats.* Berkeley: Great Explorations in Math and Science (GEMS), Lawrence Hall of Science, University of California.

Ingram, M. (1993). *Bottle biology.* Madison: Bottle Biology Project, Department of Plant Pathology, College of Agricultural and Life Sciences, University of Wisconsin.

Jones, R. M. (1990). *Teaming up! The inquiry task group management system user's guide.* LaPorte, TX: ITGROUP.

Lee, O. (2002). Promoting scientific inquiry with elementary students from diverse cultures and languages. In W. C. Secada (Ed.), *Review of research in education* (Vol. 26, pp. 23–69). Washington, DC: American Education Research Association.

Lowery, L. F. (Ed.). (1997). *Pathways to the science standards: Elementary school edition.* Arlington, VA: National Science Teachers Association.

National Research Council. (1996). *National science education standards.* Washington, DC: National Academy Press.

National Research Council. (2000). *Inquiry and the national science education standards: A guide for teaching and learning.* Washington DC: National Academy Press.

Ormrod, J. (1999). *Human learning* (3rd ed.) Upper Saddle River, NJ: Merrill/Prentice Hall.

Ormrod, J. (2004). *Human learning* (4th ed.) Upper Saddle River, NJ: Merrill/Prentice Hall.

Roth, K., & Anderson, C. (1988). Promoting conceptual change learning from science textbooks. In P. Ramsden (Ed.), *Improving learning: New perspectives.* London: Kogan Page.

Rowe, M. B. (1973). *Teaching science as continuous inquiry.* New York: McGraw-Hill.

Rutherford, F. J., & Ahlgren, A. (1990). *Science for all Americans.* New York: Oxford University Press.

Seaborg, G. T. (1991, Fall/Winter). Some thoughts on discovery. *GEMS Network News.* Berkeley: Lawrence Hall of Science, University of California, p. 5.

Trowbridge, L., & Bybee, R. (2000). *Teaching secondary school science* (7th ed.). Upper Saddle River, NJ: Merrill/Prentice Hall.

SECTION II
Physical Science Activities

....

I. PROPERTIES OF MATTER

The simple activities on properties of matter included here enable children to exercise their natural curiosity as they manipulate, observe, and classify common objects and materials in their environment and continue to form explanations of the world. Consistent with the *National Science Education Standards*, topics studied include describing and classifying properties of material objects and the nature of solids, liquids, and gases (air).

 NSES   Science Standards on Properties of Matter

Students should develop an understanding of

- properties of objects and materials (K–4).
- changes of properties in matter (5–8).

Concepts and Principles That Support the Standards

- Objects have many observable properties (K–4).
- Objects are made of one or more materials (K–4).
- Properties can be used to separate or sort a group of objects or materials (K–4).
- Materials can exist in different states—solids, liquids, and gases (K–4).

 ## A. PROPERTIES OF MATERIAL OBJECTS

▶ *Science Background*

All material objects may be described by their unique properties. By dynamically investigating and classifying properties of different objects, children can function much as research scientists do.

Objectives

1. Define *property* as a characteristic of an object—something you can see, touch, hear, smell, or taste.
2. Develop descriptions and classifications of objects based on their properties.
3. Use description and classification to identify the most significant properties of buttons and how different properties of buttons might be related.

Materials

For each group:

- Collection of 20 to 30 buttons differing in many ways, including color, shape, number of holes, etc.
- One small tray to hold buttons or other objects to be observed and grouped
- Button bingo cards

Safety Precautions

- Caution the students not to put the buttons or other small objects in their mouths, ears, nostrils, or eyes.

1. HOW ARE BUTTONS ALIKE AND DIFFERENT? (K–2)

ENGAGE

a. With the children in a large group, hold up an object, such as a ball. Ask: *What can you tell me about this object? Yes, it is a ball, but what else can you tell me about it? What can you observe about it, using your senses? What is its shape, its color, its texture?* Then hold up a large button. Ask: *Can you use your senses to observe this?* When children recognize that they can make observations about the button, too, tell them: In your groups you will make observations in order to play a game with lots of buttons.

EXPLORE

b. Organize children into cooperative groups. Give each small group of children about 20 different buttons on a tray. Observe the buttons and describe them to one another. Using a gamelike format similar to "I Spy," allow each child to describe a button in sufficient detail (without touching it or otherwise designating it) for the other children in the small group to pick it out. They might describe the button's color, its shape, its texture, the number of holes it has, and other properties.

EXPLAIN

c. Gather children as a whole class and ask: *What words did you use to describe the buttons you observed?* On the board, under the heading *Properties*, make a list of the words suggested by the children.

Discuss with the children the various words that can be used to describe the object. Tell the children that, in science, the term *property* refers to a characteristic of an object or material—things you can observe with your senses. Discuss other uses of the word *property* with the children if they bring them up; be sure to emphasize the way this word is used in science.[1]

---

[1]For a delightful introduction to properties of buttons, see *The Button Box* by Margarette S. Reid (illustrated by Sarah Chamberlain), New York: Dutton Children's Books, 1990.

ELABORATE

d. Ask: *What are buttons for? How are buttons used?* Answers might relate to the function of buttons to fasten garments or the ornamental nature of buttons. Encourage children to find buttons on their clothing or on other children's clothing. You might want to have some extra clothing with buttons on it available for students to examine, as well as books or pictures that show buttons in use. *What properties of buttons relate to how they work? What properties of buttons relate to their ornamental use?* Encourage students to discuss these questions in their small groups, then have groups share their ideas in a whole-class discussion.

EVALUATE

e. Tell each student to select one button. Challenge them to list five properties of their button. Do this orally with very young children. If the class is already writing words, ask students to write the properties on a card with their name written on it and a hole punched in it. Provide 30 cm long pieces of string, wire, or dental floss for students to use to attach their button to their cards. The following rubric could be used to evaluate student's understanding of the term *property*:

Exemplary—successfully lists five properties of the button
Proficient—successfully lists three or four properties of the button
Developing—successfully lists one or two properties of the button
None—unable to list any of the button's properties[1]

2. WHAT ARE SOME DIFFERENT WAYS YOU CAN GROUP BUTTONS? (K–2)

ENGAGE

a. Ask: *How can you group your buttons? How many different ways can you find to group them?*

EXPLORE

b. Tell the children to sort their buttons into groups based on the properties of the buttons. For example, children might make groups of red buttons, blue buttons, green buttons, and multicolored buttons.

c. As children sort their buttons, circulate among them and ask such questions as: *How are the buttons in this group alike? How are they different from one another?*

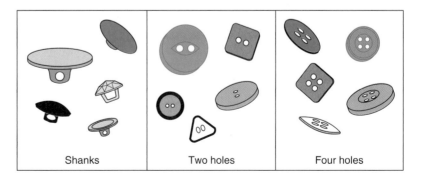

Shanks   Two holes   Four holes

d. Let two cooperative groups come together. Members of one group should study the button classification system of the other group and try to identify the basis of the classification.

EXPLAIN

e. Ask: *How did you sort the buttons? How many different ways was your group able to sort your buttons? Is one way "best"?* Lead the students to the idea that objects can be classified according to various properties and that there is not just one way to sort objects as long as the sorter can explain the property used for sorting.

f. Show the children how to classify their buttons according to two properties. For example, in the first stage of classification they may get a class of all red buttons. In the second stage of classification, they may group the red buttons into two groups, such as round and not round. Thus, they end up with a group of red buttons that are round and a group of red buttons that are not round.

Nature of Scientific Inquiry

g. Tell students that scientists classify (sort, group) trees, leaves, minerals, and other objects and organisms. Ask: *Why do scientists classify things? What is the purpose of classification?* Through discussion, bring out the advantage that through classification, we can simplify our thinking by dealing with a few groups rather than many individual elements.

ELABORATE

h. Let student groups practice multistage classification as you monitor their work. Ask questions like: *How did you sort the buttons first? How did you sort this subgroup of buttons?*

i. For additional practice, prepare several different 9-square (3 by 3) button bingo cards, with button properties named in each square. As in the diagram, include single properties such as red, round, two-holed, wooden, and cloth. Also include some multiple-property squares, such as red and round, or two-holed and plastic. Write different properties of buttons in each square of button bingo cards, as in the diagram.

RED	RED AND ROUND	NOT RED
CLOTH	ROUND	WOODEN
NOT ROUND	TWO HOLES AND PLASTIC	TWO HOLES

SAMPLE BUTTON BINGO CARD

Pass a button bingo card facedown to each pair of children. Give each pair several bingo tokens. Draw buttons from a bag of buttons. Call on children to name different properties of each button you draw. Instruct the children that they are to place a token in each square on their cards that contains a property named. Circulate among the children and interact with them about their understanding of the meaning of properties and classification. If you use a competitive group structure, winners might be the children who are able to correctly place three tokens in a row, column, or diagonally, or the children who are able to place the most tokens on their button bingo card.

EVALUATE

j. Use a digital camera to take pictures of different groupings of buttons. Number the pictures and put them in a slide show for the class to see. For each picture students should write or orally explain the property by which the buttons in the slide were sorted. If the picture shows a multistage classification, they should explain the classification steps that might have been used. Students' understanding of classification can be assessed based on their explanations.

B. PROPERTIES OF LIQUIDS

▶ *Science Background*

Students can conduct simple investigations with water that can be explained through use of an abstract, mental model. In the model of water developed through the activities in this section, water consists of tiny particles or droplets. These particles of water are attracted to each other. Scientists refer to this force of attraction as *bonding*. For children, water drops are *sticky* or *grabby*.

As they develop new understandings of liquids, students also continue to develop their abilities to inquire and their understandings of the nature of scientific inquiry.

NSES   Science Standards

Students should develop an understanding of

- properties of objects and materials (K–4).

Concepts and Principles That Support the Standards

- Objects have many observable properties (K–4).
- Materials can exist in different states—solids, liquids, and gases (K–4).

Objectives

1. Use simple apparatus and tools to gather data and extend the senses.
2. Describe the behavior of water and other liquids under various conditions.
3. Describe and explain the bonding model of liquid particles.
4. Use observational evidence and the model of the bonding of liquid particles to explain the behavior of water and other liquids under different conditions.
5. Set up simple controlled experiment "fair tests" to explore the behavior of water and other liquids.

Materials

Each group will need the following materials:

- Two 30 ml medicine cups
- Beaker for water
- Magnifying lens
- Two medicine droppers (use identical droppers for the whole class)
- 15 cm squares of aluminum foil, wax paper, and plastic wrap
- 30–45 small paper clips

For the teacher:

- Small container of liquid dishwashing soap
- Toothpicks

Safety Precautions

- Caution the students not to taste any liquid substances, unless approved by a responsible adult.
- When children work with water, provide table coverings, such as newspapers, and plenty of paper towels to absorb spills. Clean up spills promptly.

1. HOW MUCH WATER CAN HEAP UP IN A CUP? (2–4)

ENGAGE

a. Pouring water from the beaker, students should fill the medicine cup completely full of water until some overflows. When the children's cups seem completely filled, ask: *How many drops of water from a medicine dropper do you think you can add to your filled cup before it overflows?* Tell the children to make a prediction and record it before they carry out the activity.

EXPLORE

b. Tell your students to hold the medicine dropper about 2 cm above the cup as in the diagram. Slowly drop water into the cup, counting the number of drops needed for the water to overflow. As they count drops, students should observe the shape of the surface of water in the cup and what happens to water drops as they are added to the cup. Instruct them to bend down so that they are eye level with the top of the cup when they observe it.

EXPLAIN

c. Let students chart their predictions and actual counts on the chalkboard or a transparency. Note and discuss variations in the data. If you think there is too much variation among groups, you might ask the groups to repeat their investigation under more common procedures.

Ask: *How many drops did you add before the water spilled over the edge of the cup? How does your tested result compare with your prediction? How would you describe the shape of the water above the rim of the cup? What happens to each drop of water as it hits the surface of water in the cup? What happens to the last drop added to the cup, the one that makes the water overflow?*

Encourage each group to contribute to the discussion of their drop data and their observations.

d. Ask: *What keeps the water from overflowing as water drops are added?*

As children discuss possible answers to this question, begin to develop a mental model of water, with water consisting of particles or drops that are all attracted to one another. Lead children to understand that water heaps up in medicine cups and does not overflow because water particles bond to, stick to, or grab on to one another. This simple model of liquids anticipates and lays a foundation for the introduction of atomic and molecular forces in later grades. If the children mention atoms and molecules of water (H_2O), listen but do not pursue the idea at this time. Rather, continue to focus on the notion that water is made up of tiny droplets that attract one another.

ELABORATE

e. As an extension, ask: *How many drops of water do you think you can place on the surface of a clean penny? Can you add more drops to the head or tail of a penny?*

Lead children to make and record predictions, and then to design and conduct investigations to answer their questions. Chart the results on the board and discuss the results.

EVALUATE

f. To get an idea of your student's mastery level for Objective 5, apply the following rubric to the procedures they develop and use in their groups as you informally monitor their work on the second question.

Exemplary: In addition to the standards for Proficient, multiple trials are used.
Proficient: Except for side of penny, all variables are kept constant (i.e., height of dropper above the penny, angle the dropper is held).
Developing: Students talk about the importance of holding variables constant, but don't actually do it when conducting the experiment.
None: Students proceed without a plan, just add drops to pennies without regard to variables that might affect the outcome.

....

2. HOW MANY PAPER CLIPS CAN YOU ADD TO A CUP OF WATER? (2–4)

ENGAGE

a. Using the beaker, students should fill the 30 ml cup completely full of water again.

Ask: *How many paper clips do you think you can add to the water in the cup before it flows over the rim?* Tell the children to make and test a prediction.

EXPLORE

b. Tell students to gently slide small paper clips one at a time into the water in the cup and count the number of paper clips needed to make the water flow over the rim. Remind them to record their data. Tell them to repeat this activity two more times. Students should discuss what happened in their group while other groups finish collecting data.

EXPLAIN

c. Ask each group to chart results on the board, then discuss similarities and differences. Ask: *How do your predictions compare with actual results? Why do you think you were asked to do three trials in your group? Why do you think so many paper clips could be added to the cup before the water overflowed?* Students should explain that the water did not overflow at first because of the attractive forces between water droplets. Even though putting in more paper clips made the water level rise, the water's surface was still "sticking together" as in the previous investigation.

Nature of Scientific Inquiry

d. As children carry out these investigations of water, occasionally emphasize to them that they are *doing* science and *being* scientists. They are asking questions, gathering evidence, building a model of water drops, and using their model to construct explanations of what they see. Point out that scientists don't do an experiment one time before drawing a conclusion. They conduct many trials.

. . . .

3. CAN YOU GET A PAPER CLIP TO "FLOAT" ON TOP OF WATER? WHY DOES THE PAPER CLIP NOT SINK? (2–4)

ENGAGE

a. Ask: *What can you do to make a paper clip "float" on the surface of water? If you push the paper clip down, will it bob back up?*

EXPLORE

b. Allow students to try to make a paper clip stay on the top of water in a medicine cup or glass. To accomplish this task, bend a second paper clip so that a cradle is formed (see diagram). Place the other paper clip on the cradle and lower it into the water as in the diagram. The paper clip should stay suspended on top of the water.

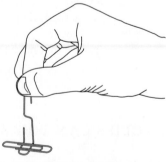

Use wire cradle to place another
paper clip on water.

EXPLAIN

    c. Ask: *Why does the paper clip stay suspended on the top of the water?* (Some students may suggest that it's floating, but it really isn't.) *Did the paper clip stay on the top of the water every time you put it in the cup? Why?* Tell students that to explain why the paper clip stayed on top of the water, we must connect observations to our model of water. Lead students to understand that because of the attractive forces among water drops, the surface of the water acts like a skin. The paper clip does not float in the water, like boats do, but is supported by water's skinlike effect. The paper clip rides on the top of the water's skin. If you push the paper clip down in the water, it breaks the skin and goes to the bottom of the container and will not bob back up. Scientists refer to the skinlike effect of water as *surface tension.*

ELABORATE

    d. Show some images of water striders and other organisms that are walking on the surface of water. Ask: *How do some bugs walk on water?* (Students may suggest surface tension or floating.) Explain that similar to the paper clip, a water strider is able to walk on the "skin" at the surface of the water. Challenge students to find other objects or organisms that stay on the surface of water because of water tension.

....

4. WHAT DOES SOAP DO TO THE SKINLIKE EFFECT OF WATER? (2–4)

ENGAGE

    a. Ask: *How can we break or overcome the skinlike effect on the surface of water?*

EXPLORE

    b. Tell students to use a beaker to fill the 30 ml cup completely full of water again. Tell them to add drops of water to the cup until it is about ready to flow over the rim. Take two toothpicks. Dip one of the toothpicks in a container of liquid dishwashing soap. Go from group to group, touching the end of the clean toothpick and then the soapy end of the other toothpick to the surface of the water in the cups.

EXPLAIN

    c. Ask: *What did you see happen?* (The water flowed over the rim of the cup.) *What do you think was on the second toothpick? Why do you think the water flowed over the rim of the cup when it was touched with the soapy toothpick? Why did we use two toothpicks, a clean one and a soapy one?* (This is a controlled experiment. Using two toothpicks, a clean one and a soapy one, shows that it was not the toothpick, but what was on it that caused the water to overflow.)

    d. Through discussion, lead the students to apply the model of water drops, adding the idea that soap tends to break the bonds that water drops have for one another. When the bonds are broken, the weight of the water causes it to flow over the rim of the cup.

....

5. WHAT HAPPENS TO WATER DROPS ON DIFFERENT SURFACES? (2–4)

ENGAGE

    a. Ask: *Do water drops look and act the same on different kinds of surfaces? How could we investigate to find out?*

EXPLORE

b. Provide each group small squares (about 15 cm by 15 cm) of wax paper, aluminum foil, and plastic wrap. Tell students to use a medicine dropper to place three or four drops of water on the wax paper. Ask: *How would you describe the shape of the water drops?*

c. Tell students to push the drops of water around with a pencil point. Ask: *What happens to the drop when you push on it with a pencil point? What happens when you push several drops near each other?*

d. Tell them to investigate and compare what water drops look like and what they do on each of the three surfaces—wax paper, aluminum foil, and plastic wrap (see diagram). Provide magnifying lenses to enhance student observations.

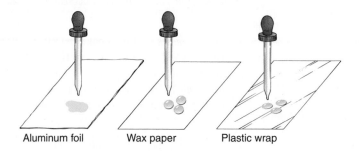

Aluminum foil   Wax paper   Plastic wrap

Ask: *What is the smallest size drop you can make? What is the largest size drop you can make? On which of the three surfaces does water heap up the most? spread out the most? What is the shape of water drops on wax paper? on aluminum foil? on plastic wrap?*

EXPLAIN

e. Ask: *What did you find out? Why do you think the drops were heaped up on wax paper and spread out on aluminum foil?*

Using *evidence* from the children's investigations, invent (directly teach) the terms *cohesion* and *adhesion*. The bonding of a material to the same kind of material is known as **cohesion**. Water drops cohere to one another. The attraction of one material for another material is called **adhesion**. Adhesive tape bonds to different kinds of material, such as skin. Add the notions of cohesion and adhesion to the model of water drops bonding to one another.

Help children understand that the adhesive attraction between water and aluminum foil is greater than the adhesive attraction between water and wax paper. Thus, water drops can bead up more on wax paper because they do not have to overcome a great adhesive force for the surface.

ELABORATE

f. Ask: *Do you think it would be easier to use a toothpick to lead a drop of paper around on wax paper or on aluminum foil? Why do you think so? Try it and see. What differences do you observe for the two surfaces? Why do you think these differences happen?*

Guide children to plan and conduct an investigation and to use their data to answer these questions. With your assistance, children should reason that because there is greater adhesion (greater stickiness) between aluminum foil and water than between wax paper and water, it is harder to lead a drop of water around on aluminum foil than on wax paper. The aluminum foil grabs on to the drop more than the wax paper does.

EVALUATE

g. To determine if the students can apply the two terms introduced in this lesson, have them respond to the following items.

1. Cohesion describes how well a liquid. . .
2. Adhesion describes how well a liquid. . .

You put a drop of water on each of three surfaces. The following drawing shows how the drops look when viewed from the side.

Drops on Different Surfaces

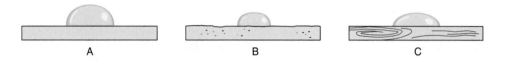

3. To which surface does water have the greatest adhesion? How do you know?
4. On which of the surfaces shown previously would it be easiest to lead around a drop of water with a toothpick? Why?

You put a drop of three different liquids onto the same surface. The following drawing shows how the drops look when viewed from the side.

Different Liquids on Same Surface

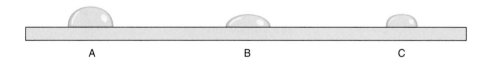

5. Which liquid has the greatest cohesion? How do you know?
6. Which of the drops shown in the previous figure would be the easiest to lead around with a toothpick on this surface? Why?

6. WHEN THE SURFACES ARE SLANTED, WILL WATER DROPS RUN DOWN FASTER ON WAX PAPER, PLASTIC WRAP, OR ALUMINUM FOIL? (3–5)

ENGAGE

a. Ask: *When the surfaces are slanted, on which surface will water drops slide or roll down fastest? What could you do to find out?*

EXPLORE

b. Help students plan a *controlled experiment (fair test)* to determine on which surface the water drops run down more quickly (see the diagram). They might, for example, control the slant of the surface and vary the type of surface (aluminum foil, plastic wrap, or wax paper).

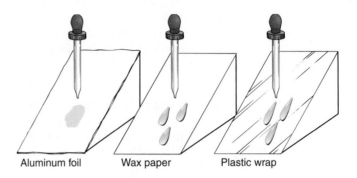

Aluminum foil   Wax paper   Plastic wrap

EXPLAIN

c. Ask: *What were your results? Why do you think the water drops ran more quickly down the wax paper ramp?* With your assistance, children should explain that water drops do not adhere or stick to wax paper as much as they do to aluminum foil and plastic wrap. Thus, the water drops ran down the wax paper ramp more quickly.

Nature of Scientific Inquiry

d. Ask: *What is a fair test or controlled investigation? What question are we trying to answer in the water drop race? Why is the water drop race fair? What is controlled in the investigation? What is deliberately changed or manipulated? Why do scientists use controlled investigations?*

   Discuss the meaning of fair tests or controlled investigations with the children. The question of which type of surface the water drops will roll or slide down fastest is answered through a fair test. The test is fair if none of the surfaces has an unfair advantage, such as being more slanted than the other surfaces. Scientists use fair tests in order to keep clear which variable is making a difference in an investigation.

e. Ask: *What does it mean to explain something? How do scientists develop explanations? How do they know their explanations are correct?*

   Through discussion, lead children to understand that to explain an event means to use observations and science knowledge to show that the event is reasonable and could be expected to occur. Explain that scientific explanations are tentative ideas about the way things are. They can be altered with new observations and new scientific knowledge.

7. WHY DO SEVERAL STREAMS OF WATER COHERE INTO ONE STREAM? (2–4)

ENGAGE

a. About 2 cm apart as shown in the diagram, puncture four very small holes in a horizontal line about 2 cm from the bottom of a 1 gallon plastic jug. Put masking tape over the holes.

   Note: Do not make the holes too large. Also, be sure the holes are very close together.

   Ask: *What do you think will happen when water is poured into this container and the masking tape is removed? How many jets of water will you get coming out of the holes in the bottom of the plastic jug?*

EXPLORE

b. This activity might be conducted as a teacher demonstration with students assisting. Hold the jug over a sink or large tub, pour water into the jug, and remove the tape. Ask: *What do you observe?*

Tell students to pinch the four jets of water together just as if they were going to pinch someone. Repeat this procedure several times to see if it always works the same way.

EXPLAIN

c. Ask: *What do you observe? Why do you think this happened?*
Lead students to use the water drop model and the concept of cohesion (the bonding of water drops) to explain why the four streams of water cohered into one stream.

C. PROPERTIES OF OOBLECK

▶ *Science Background*

Investigating and describing the properties of oobleck can be a fascinating task for students grades 1–8. Oobleck is the name given to a special mixture of cornstarch, water, and food coloring that has some unique properties. The substance flows like liquid when you pour it, but keeps its shape like a solid when you hit it hard and fast.

You may have recognized the name *oobleck* from the Dr. Seuss children's book, *Bartholomew and the Oobleck*. Other books that treat this strange substance or its variations include *Horrible Harry and the Green Slime* by Suzy Kline and *The Slimy Book* by Babette Cole.

NSES Science Standards

All students should develop an understanding of

• properties of objects and materials (K–4).
• changes in properties in matter (5–8).

Concepts and Principles That Support the Standards

• Objects have many observable properties (K–4).
• Materials can exist in different states—solid, liquid, and gas (K–4).

Objectives

1. Conduct simple investigations to determine the properties of oobleck.
2. Describe properties of oobleck and compare them with various properties of solids and liquids.
3. Explain how their investigations of oobleck are like what scientists do when they investigate.

Materials

- Four boxes cornstarch
- Plastic bowls
- Water
- Post-It Notes

▶ *Preparation*

Pour 4¼ cups of water into a large bowl and add four boxes of cornstarch and another 2½ cups of water. Swirl and tip the bowl to level the mixture, mix it well with a large spoon or your hands, and then set the bowl aside.

Safety Precautions

- Oobleck is strange but is safe to handle.
- However, oobleck can be quite messy. Have plenty of newspaper around for children to use as a work surface. Impress on the children that part of doing science is to maintain a clean, orderly laboratory for investigating. Thus, they must be actively responsible for the cleanliness of their own work area.
- To protect their clothing, let the children wear large shirts over their regular clothes, as in art. Or give the children "lab coats" made of plastic grocery sacks with armholes and a neck hole cut in the bottom.
- Do not put oobleck down the sink as it will clog the drain. If oobleck falls on the floor, scoop most of it up and mop up the remainder with a damp sponge. If it falls on a carpet area, scoop up what you can, then vacuum after it dries.

1. WHAT ARE THE PROPERTIES OF OOBLECK? (1–6)

ENGAGE

a. Ask the class if they remember what *property* means in science. If they are are not sure, remind the children that a *property* is a characteristic of something that can be seen, heard, smelled, or felt by the senses or detected by instruments, such as magnifying lenses, that extend the senses. Tell the children that you have a very strange substance that you will call oobleck, after the Dr. Seuss story, *Bartholomew and the Oobleck*. Ask: *What are the properties of oobleck? What can you do to find out?*

EXPLORE

b. Tell children they are to play the role of scientists in investigating the properties of this strange substance. Each group will get a sample of oobleck and a pad of Post-It notes. Instruct them to write down as many properties of oobleck as they can discover, one property per Post-It note. (Suggest that they write darkly with large letters so that the property can be read from across the room.)

c. Pour about a cup of oobleck into each plastic bowl, give a bowl to each cooperative group, and encourage each group to explore this strange substance and record their findings. Some properties children might observe include:

> *It is gooey, sticky, and white; you can squeeze it into a ball but when you release the pressure it seems to melt into a puddle; it is soft when you move your hand through it slowly, and hard when you move your hand fast; it dries out when left on paper for more than 10 seconds.*

When they can think of no more properties to write down, ask each group to sort its pile of Post-Its according to the importance of the property observed. Have them put a star on the two notes they think have the most important properties written on them.

EXPLAIN

d. Ask cooperative group reporters to read one property their group has found and post it on a chart for all to see. If any other groups have that property, they should add it to the chart at this time. Moving from group to group, continue until all properties have been posted. Discuss which of the properties the children think are most important or distinctive for oobleck and why they picked those properties.

e. Show the children a solid object and a liquid in a container.
Ask: *Do these two things have the same properties?* (No) *Are these things the same state of matter?* (No, one's a liquid and one's a solid) *Which is a liquid? How do you know?* (Because of the way it acts; its properties) *What are the main properties of liquids?* (Flowing easily and taking the shape of its container) *Which is a solid? How do you know?* (Because of the way it acts; its properties) *What are the main properties of solids?* (Maintaining its shape) Discuss whether oobleck is best classified as a liquid or a solid. Discuss whether oobleck should be called a solid or a liquid—or do we need a third category? Consider using a graphic organizer such as a three-column chart or a Venn diagram to support this discussion.

Nature of Scientific Inquiry

f. Ask the students to identify and list the ways they acted like scientists during their investigation of oobleck. In their lists they might include *asked questions, talked, searched, planned, used magnifying lenses, experimented, recorded, explained, discussed, argued, defined, criticized, changed ideas, decided, asked more questions.*

Discuss with students how what they did fits within these more formal statements in the NSES Inquiry Standards (see Figure I-3).

Ask students to give specific examples of what they did that is like one or more of these processes of scientists.

 ## D. PROPERTIES OF WHITE POWDERS

▶ *Science Background*

Investigating the physical and chemical properties of materials forms the basis for an exciting inquiry for children. This set of activities involves the study of four common white powders: granulated sugar, table salt, baking soda, and cornstarch. At first, it seems hard to distinguish among the powders; they appear to have closely similar properties. But when observed through a magnifier, powders are found to be quite distinctive. Further, chemical tests reveal that the white powders react differently from one another when drops of water, iodine, and vinegar are added to them.

Objectives

1. Use simple tools and instruments that extend the senses to gather data.
2. Carry out chemical indicator tests to determine how different powders react with water, iodine, and vinegar.
3. Accurately record and analyze data.
4. Use data to draw conclusions.

Materials

For each pair of students:

- Small quantities of salt, granulated sugar, baking soda, cornstarch, and flour
- Medicine droppers
- Plastic spoons
- Zip-lock bag (large enough to hold recording chart)
- Magnifying lenses
- Safety goggles
- Small containers of water, vinegar, and iodine
- Copies of recording chart

Safety Precautions

- Students should wear safety goggles for these investigations with powders.
- Caution children not to taste any of the powders or liquids and to wash their hands after they test each powder.
- Do not put powders in the sink as they may clog drains.

1. WHAT ARE THE DISTINGUISHING PROPERTIES OF COMMON WHITE POWDERS? (3–6)

ENGAGE

a. Ask: *How are sugar and salt different? How are they alike? If you have several white powders, how can you tell them apart?*

Tell the students they will be observing some powders with a magnifier and doing chemical tests, acting like scientists (e.g., forensic chemists) to see what happens when different indicators (water, vinegar, and iodine) are added to different powders.

Prepare data tables like the one in the diagram. Give each team two data tables. Instruct the students to place one of the data table sheets into the plastic bag and seal it, for use as a lab tray. Show the students how to enter data on the other data table.

Explain that the data table provides a record of observations and experiments that we can refer to later. If necessary, remind students how to use a magnifying lens to extend the sense of sight.

DATA TABLE FOR INVESTIGATING WHITE POWDERS

Observations	Powder 1 Granulated Sugar	Powder 2 Table Salt	Powder 3 Baking Soda	Powder 4 Cornstarch
Visual (Magnifying Glass)				
Water Test				
Iodine Test				
Vinegar Test				

Using a Magnifier

To observe an object through a magnifier or magnifying lens, hold the magnifier close to the object, look through the magnifier at the object, then lift the magnifier toward your eye, stopping when the object begins to blur.

Many science classrooms have magnifiers with three lenses. The large lens usually provides a twofold magnification, the medium-sized lens provides a sixfold magnification, and the small lens an eightfold magnification. To provide increased magnification, two or even three magnifiers can be fitted together and used as a single magnifier.

EXPLORE

b. *Visual observation.* Instruct students to use a magnifying lens to visually observe each powder and to write down their observations on the data table.

c. Show students how to use the data table/investigation tray to guide their investigations. Data will be recorded on the other data table.

d. *Water tests.* Students should place a small spoonful of each powder in the water test row on the lab tray (plastic bag with record sheet inside). They should then add several drops of water and mix with a toothpick to see what happens. Observations should be recorded in the data tables.

e. *Iodine tests.* Instruct students to place a small spoonful of each powder in the iodine test row of the lab tray. Then, they should add a drop or two of iodine to each powder and write down the results in their data tables. Caution the students to be careful. Iodine can stain hands and clothing.

f. *Vinegar tests.* Students should place a small spoonful of each powder in each vinegar test row of the lab tray. They should then add a drop or two of vinegar to each powder and write down the results in their data tables.

EXPLAIN

g. *Compare.* Discuss the properties of the four powders that have been revealed through the different chemical tests. Help students to compare the results of their tests with the master chart of properties of white powders shown in the diagram. If necessary, ask students to repeat tests to see what happens.

PROPERTIES OF WHITE POWDERS				
Observations	Powder 1 Granulated Sugar	Powder 2 Table Salt	Powder 3 Baking Soda	Powder 4 Cornstarch
Visual (Magnifying Glass)	White crystals	White box-shaped crystals	Fine white powder	Fine yellowish white powder
Water Test	Dissolves in water	Dissolves in water	Turns milky water	Makes water cloudy
Iodine Test	Turns yellow with iodine	No reaction with iodine	Turns yellow orange with iodine	Turns red, ends black with iodine
Vinegar Test	Dissolves in vinegar	No reaction with vinegar	Fizzes with vinegar	Gets thick, then hard with vinegar

ELABORATE

h. Ask: *If you had a mixture of powders, how could you find out what is in the mixture?*

Give each pair of students small samples of a mixture of two white powders, flour, and one of the original white powders. Be sure to keep track of which mixture each group gets.

Ask: *What powders are these?* Challenge children to determine if each powder is one they have encountered previously, and if so, which one. (Children would not have studied the properties of flour.) Ask: *What is the evidence for your conclusions?*

i. Clean Up. Students should throw away plastic bags and toothpicks, return powders and test supplies to teacher-designated spot, clean and dry anything dirty, including their hands. Caution students not to put any of the powders in the sink since they can clog drains.[2]

EVALUATE

j. Let students present and discuss their procedures and their conclusions. Ask students to explain the basis for their conclusions. Use the following checklist as an assessment tool to monitor the quality of the presentations.
- ☐ Explained their procedure clearly.
- ☐ Conducted tests with the mixture in the same way as with single powders previously.
- ☐ Referred to data table of properties of single powders.
- ☐ Used that data as evidence of conclusion.
- ☐ Stated conclusion clearly.
- ☐ Recognized that the other powder in the mixture must be a powder not yet studied.
- ☐ Correctly identified the powder that they had previously studied that was in their mixture.

Nature of Scientific Inquiry

k. Discuss with the children how their activities in these investigations are like those of scientists. Ask: *What are some of the ways you have acted as scientists in this investigation of powders?* Common activities of children and scientists might include asking questions, talking, searching, planning, using magnifying lenses, experimenting, recording, explaining, discussing, arguing, defining, criticizing, exchanging ideas, deciding, asking more questions.

E. PROPERTIES OF AIR

▶ *Science Background*

Although we cannot see, taste, smell, hear, or feel air (if we reach out our hand to grab it), we know that air is a real substance because of the way it interacts with objects that we can see.

Through the following activities, discussion, and expository teaching, you will help the students begin to develop an understanding of these principles about air:

▶ *Principles About Air*

1. Air, like solids and liquids, is a real material substance (made up of particles too small to see).
2. Bubbles in water indicate the presence of air.
3. Air exerts pressure; it can press or push on things.

---

[2]More information on these activities on white powders can be found at these Internet sites: http://www.csulb.edu/~lhenriqu/mysterypowder.htm, http://etc.sccoe.kiz.ca.us/i98/ii98units/cross/mystery/text/powders.html, http://eduref.org/cgi~bin/printlessons.cgi/virtual/lessons/science/chemistry/chm0200.html.

4. We live at the bottom of an ocean of air that exerts a great pressure on all things on the surface of the earth.
5. Objects tend to be moved from regions of high air pressure toward regions of low air pressure.

Together, these principles can be used to explain evidence gathered about a wide variety of phenomena.

NSES

Science Standards

All students should develop an understanding of

• properties of objects and materials (K–4).
• changes in properties of matter (5–8).

Concepts and Principles That Support the Standards

• Materials can exist in different states—solid, liquid, and gas (K–4).
• Objects (such as gases) have many different properties (K–4).
• The position and motion of objects can be changed by pushing or pulling. The size of the change is related to the strength of the push or pull (K–4).
• Unbalanced forces will cause changes in the speed or direction of an object's motion (5–8).

Objectives

1. Investigate and describe natural events related to air and air pressure.
2. Demonstrate and describe evidence for each of the principles about air and air pressure.
3. Use observational evidence and the principles about air to explain what happens in various investigations and phenomena.

Materials

• Large syringes
• Soda straws
• Several medicine droppers
• Containers for water

▶ *Teaching Suggestions*

We suggest that you use Activities 1–5 as teacher demonstrations in inventing, developing, and applying principles about air. Emphasize that these principles are based on evidence and are useful in explaining phenomena and predicting outcomes. The demonstrations might then be made available later to your students, perhaps at learning stations.

1. IS AIR A REAL MATERIAL SUBSTANCE LIKE SOLIDS AND LIQUIDS? (1–4)

ENGAGE

a. Show the children three sealed plastic food storage bags, one filled with a solid (such as sand), a second with water, and a third with air. Ask: *What is in each bag?*

After children discuss the contents of each bag, ask: *How do you know what is in each bag?*

Some children may say that air is in the third bag. Ask: *Since you cannot see, hear, feel (if you place your hand in the bag), smell (if you open the bag), or taste what's in the bag, how do you know that air is really in the bag?*

Water   Air   Sand

EXPLORE   b. As a demonstration, partially submerge the bag of air in a clear container of water. Use scissors to clip one of the submerged corners of the plastic bag or use a push pin to poke a hole in the plastic bag below the water's surface. Ask: *What do you observe?* (Bubbles in the water)

EXPLAIN   c. Ask: *How can you explain what you see?* Use this activity to introduce and develop Principles 1 and 2 about air. Lead students to note that although we cannot see air, evidence for the existence of air comes from many activities, such as activities with medicine droppers and plastic syringes.

Discuss the meaning of the term *evidence* (observations that we can use to support conclusions). Use the term in story form, such as:

> Two boys came out of the house and noticed that the driveway was wet. One boy said, "It has rained." The other boy said, "No. My Dad washes his car every Saturday."

What *evidence* might have supported the first boy's conclusion? What was the implied conclusion of the second boy? What evidence might have supported the second boy's conclusion?

ELABORATE   d. Ask: *What other evidence can you think of to show that air is a real material substance?* Through discussion, help your students come up with many examples involving interactions with air, such as wind, rustling of leaves in a tree, paper airplanes, kites, balloons, your breath on a cold morning, or a dropped sheet of paper floating down to the floor.

2. DOES AIR TAKE UP SPACE? (1–4)

ENGAGE   a. Ask: *Can air and water be in the same space at the same time?*

b. Push an "empty" glass straight down into a container of water. Ask: *What do you observe?*

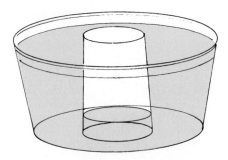

c. Tilt the glass while it is underwater. Ask: *What do you observe?*

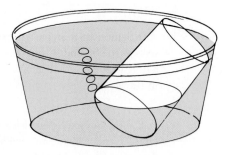

EXPLAIN

d. *How can you explain why the water did not come into the glass?* Through discussion, lead students to apply the principle that air is a real material substance. Air keeps the water from coming into the glass. Although the glass looks empty, we infer that it contains air.

e. Ask: *Why were bubbles seen in the water when the glass was tilted?*
Through discussion and direct instruction, help students use Principle 2 to explain that bubbles show that air is escaping into the water from the glass.

3. HOW CAN AIR KEEP WATER OUT OF A CONTAINER? (1–4)

ENGAGE

a. Will water enter a glass pushed mouth-down into a container of water?

EXPLORE

b. Crumple up a paper towel in the bottom of a dry, empty glass. Push the glass mouth down into a large container of water so that it is completely submerged. Ask: *What do you observe?*

EXPLAIN

c. Ask: *Why do you think that the paper towel remains dry?* Help students use Principle 1 to explain what they see in this demonstration. Air is a real material substance that keeps water from coming up into the glass and wetting the paper towel. Tell the students that large, air-filled, inverted containers, called **diving bells**, have been used in underwater work for centuries. Ask: *Why does water not come into a diving bell when it is submerged?*

ELABORATE

    d. Push an empty glass mouth down into a large container of water until it is completely submerged. Tilt the glass so that it fills with water. Ask: *How can you use a straw to replace the water in the glass with air? When you have emptied the glass of its water using the straw, how can you use the straw to replace the air in the glass with water again?*

        Your students will need Principle 1 to explain their observations. Air is a real material substance. When air is blown into the glass through the straw, it replaces the water in the glass. When the air is removed through the straw, the water comes back in.

4. HOW CAN YOU USE A SYRINGE TO FEEL AIR PRESSURE? (3–5)

ENGAGE

    a. Hold up a syringe and pull back on the plunger. Ask: *What is in the syringe?* (Air) *What evidence would support your answer?* (If you put the tip into water, bubbles come out when you push the plunger.)

    b. In this activity you will make more observations about air in the plunger.

EXPLORE

    c. Distribute small- to medium-sized plungers to the students. Tell them to try the following activity, then demonstrate for them. With the plunger pulled out part of the way, plug the opening of the syringe with your finger. Try to push the plunger in. Ask: *What do you observe?*

EXPLAIN

    d. Ask: *Why do you think the plunger of the syringe is so hard to push in?* Use Principle 1 to help students understand that when you push in on the plunger, the air presses back. This demonstration is another type of evidence that air is a real material substance. The demonstration also shows that air can exert pressure. Building on this experience and the children's discussion of it, teach (invent) Principle 3.

5. HOW DOES A DRINKING STRAW WORK? (3–5)

ENGAGE

    a. Ask: *What do you have to do to drink water with a straw?*

EXPLORE

    b. Have the students work in pairs. Give each student a clear drinking straw and clean paper cup containing fresh water. Have them take turns drinking water through their straw as their partner observes. Ask: *What did you see happen? What did you do to get water up the straw and into your mouth?*

EXPLAIN

    c. Ask: *Why do you think the water rose into the straw?* Your students will likely say that the water was "sucked" into the straw. Help the students understand that, even though the term is commonly used, *suction* is a misconception; liquid is not pulled into the straw by suction.

        Lead the children to understand that when you expand your lungs, some air comes out of the straw and enters your lungs. There is then less air in the straw and it exerts less pressure. According to Principle 4, the outside air pressure is now greater than the pressure in the straw. According to Principle 5, the atmosphere (remember, we live at the bottom of an ocean of air) then pushes liquid up into the straw.

ELABORATE

    d. Ask: *What do you do to get water to come into a medicine dropper?* (You dip the tube of the medicine dropper in water, squeeze the bulb, release it, and water comes into the medicine dropper tube.) *What happens to the air in the medicine dropper tube when you squeeze it?* (Some air comes out of the tube.)

    e. Ask: *In what ways might a medicine dropper be like a drinking straw?* Help students to see that the two systems are similar. When you reduce the pressure in either system, the pressure of the atmosphere surrounding us pushes down on the surface of the water, forcing some liquid up into the dropper or straw.

Nature of Scientific Inquiry

    f. Ask: *What do scientists do when they explain something?* Through discussion, lead students to understand that when scientists explain an event, they connect observations and scientific concepts and principles in a reasonable way to make sense of the observations. When scientists propose an explanation, they use scientific knowledge and observational evidence to support their explanation. Children should check their explanations against scientific knowledge, experiences, and observations of others.

EVALUATE

    g. Refill the students' paper cups from part b of this investigation with water. Using a straight pin, walk around the room and put a tiny hole in each drinking straw above the water line. Challenge the class to drink their water through their straw as before. Ask students to answer the following questions in their science notebooks: *What do you observe?* (When I try to get water to come into my mouth as I usually do, nothing happens.) *Why do you think this happens?* (Because of the hole. Air comes in through the hole so I can't lower the pressure of the air at the top of the straw. Therefore the water isn't pushed up by the water pressure on the rest of the water.) *What evidence supports your explanation?* (My straw worked before the hole, but didn't work after the hole. Or if I cover the hole in my straw tightly, I can use it again to bring water from the glass to my mouth.)

II. MOTION AND FORCES

Forces are needed to change the motion of an object—to start it moving or stop it, to speed it up or slow it down. There are many different kinds of forces in the physical world, such as frictional forces, mechanical forces exerted by simple machines, gravitational forces, magnetic forces, static electric forces, and the bonding forces between water molecules. A force may be direct, as when we push on a lever arm, or it may be indirect, as when a magnet pulls on a piece of iron from a distance.

The study of simple forces in grades K–7 provides concrete experiences on which a more comprehensive study of forces and motion may be based in secondary grades.

 NSES   Science Standards

All students should develop an understanding of

- the position and motion of objects (K–4).
- motions and forces (5–8).

Concepts and Principles That Support the Standards

- The position and motion of objects can be changed by pushing or pulling (K–4).
- The size of the change is related to the strength of the push or pull (K–4).
- Unbalanced forces will cause changes in the speed or direction of an object's motion (5–8).
- Changes in systems can be quantified through measurement (5–8).
- Mathematics is essential for accurately measuring change (5–8).
- Rate involves comparing one measured quantity with another measured quantity (5–8).

A. FRICTIONAL FORCES

▶ *Science Background*

Friction is the result of an interaction between a moving object and the surface on which it moves. Students' everyday experience is that friction causes all moving objects to slow down and stop if they are not being continuously powered. Through experiences in which friction is reduced (by a lubricant or through the use of wheels), students can begin to see that a moving object with no friction would continue to move indefinitely.

Objectives

1. Design and conduct an investigation to demonstrate the friction present as an object moves across a level surface.
2. Ask questions about friction and describe frictional effects as an interaction between an object and a surface.
3. Explain how wheels and lubricants can reduce friction.

Materials

- Screw hook
- Block of wood
- Rubber bands
- Ruler
- Sheets of coarse sandpaper
- Five or six round pencils

1. WHAT IS FRICTION? HOW CAN FRICTION BE REDUCED? (3–6)

ENGAGE

a. Ask: *How can you measure the effects of friction?*

EXPLORE

b. Students should carry out these investigation procedures in cooperative groups.
   1. Turn the screw hook into the end of a block of wood. Attach a rubber band (or a spring scale) to the hook.
   2. With the rubber band on your finger, lift the block into the air and measure the stretch with a ruler, as in diagram (a). Design a data table and record your measurement in it.

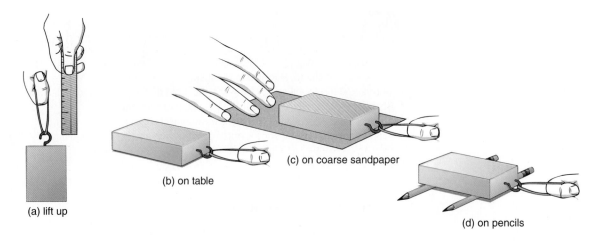

(a) lift up

(b) on table

(c) on coarse sandpaper

(d) on pencils

3. Position the block on a table with the rubber band extended, as in diagram (b). Now drag the block on the table and measure the rubber band's stretch once the block begins to move. Record your measurements.
4. Repeat the procedure in step 3, this time with sandpaper beneath the block, as in diagram (c).

EXPLAIN

c. Invite students to present their procedures and findings. During the discussion ask: *What change did you observe in the stretch of the rubber band when the block is dragged on the table and on sandpaper?* (It stretched more on the sandpaper.) *How does the surface on which the block slides affect the force to move it?* (The rougher the surface, the more force it takes to move the block.) *What is the cause of the increase in force needed to move the object on sandpaper?* (There is more friction.) *What is friction?* Introduce the concept of friction. **Friction** is a force opposing motion that results when two surfaces slide across one another.

ELABORATE

d. Now place two round pencils underneath the block and drag it across the table, as in diagram (d). Measure the stretch of the rubber band just after the block begins to move. Once each group has tried this several times, ask: *What happens to the stretch of the rubber band this time?* (It is less.) *Why?* (The pencils are rolling, reducing the friction.) *In what way do rollers (wheels) help objects to move?* Explain that rollers (wheels) reduce friction.

EVALUATE

e. As an assesment of the student's abilities to understand and apply their knowledge about the concept of friction, ask them to answer these questions in their science notebook:
   1. Your teacher needs help rearranging her new classroom. She asks you to push her desk from the front of the room to the back of the room. You don't want to have to push very hard. *Which kind of floor covering do you hope there is in the classroom: A. Smooth, polished cement; B. Thick carpeting; or C. Rough concrete?* (Surface A) *Why did you select this surface?* (There would probably be less friction since it is smoother.) *What does friction have to do with your choice?* (If the friction between the desk and the floor covering is low, I won't have to push as hard.)

2. In your investigation today, how does the stretch of the rubber band relate to the force of friction between the block and the surface on which it is sliding? (The greater the friction between the block and the surface on which it is sliding, the greater the stretch of the rubber band.)

B. EQUAL-ARM BALANCES

▶ *Science Background*

An equal-arm balance is a system consisting of a crossbar pivoted in the center and weights that can be placed at different positions on each side of the bar, as is shown in the diagram. The amount of each weight and its distance from the central pivot point are the relevant factors in determining balance.

Objectives

1. Use these qualitative rules to predict and explain balance on an equal-arm balance:
   Symmetry rule. Equal weights at equal distances will balance [see diagram (a)].
   Relational rule. Heavier weights close in can balance lighter weights farther out [see diagram (b) and diagram (c)].
2. Demonstrate and explain that balance occurs when the product of weights and distances on one side of the pivot equals the product of weights and distances on the other side of the pivot.

Materials

• Equal-arm balance for each pair of students

(Plastic equal-arm balances, often referred to as "math balances," are sold by Delta Education and other equipment companies. Addresses for equipment companies are given in Appendix E.)

1. WHAT FACTORS AFFECT THE EQUILIBRIUM OF AN EQUAL-ARM BALANCE? (3–6)

ENGAGE

a. Ask: *What affects the balance of an equal-arm balance scale? How can you predict accurately whether a balance will be level?*

EXPLORE

b. Distribute balances to your students. Give the children the following balance problems, one at a time. Allow ample time for students to work on each problem and discuss their findings, before giving the next one. Be noncommittal about patterns they may discover.

1. Place two weights at the second peg from the center on the left side of the balance. Leaving the left side always the same, find at least three different ways to balance the crossbar by adding weights to a peg on the other side. (You can use as many weights as necessary, but be sure to add weights to only one peg at a time on the right side, not to two or three pegs.) Use drawings, words, or data columns to show what you did. Tell your teacher what you did to balance the crossbar.
2. Start with two weights on the left side at the third peg from the center. Find at least four ways to balance the crossbar. (Remember, you can use as many weights as necessary, but be sure to add weights to only one peg on the right side, not to two or three pegs.) Write down what you did and show your work to your teacher.

3. Start with four weights at the third peg on the left side. How many ways can you find to balance the crossbar? (Remember to add weights from only one peg at a time on the other side.)

4. Set up your own combinations of weights and distances on one side of the balance and use your developing knowledge to predict what might be done to the other side to produce balance.

EXPLAIN

c. *Ask: What did you do to balance the crossbar? Can you find patterns in the different ways you found to balance the crossbar? How can you test to determine if the pattern you found is a general one, applying in all cases?*

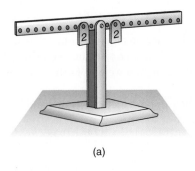

(a)

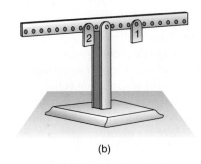

(b)

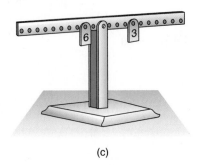

(c)

d. Through discussion, lead your students to understand the following balance patterns or rules:

> *Symmetry rule.* Equal weights at equal distances will balance [see diagram (a)].
> *Relational rule.* Heavier weights close in can balance lighter weights farther out [see diagram (b) and diagram (c)].

Both of these rules are qualitative or nonnumerical rules. They are understood by children from ages 8 or 9, but they may not be stated explicitly.

ELABORATE

e. At some point, older students (from ages 10 or 11) may understand the use of formal mathematics to coordinate weights and distances. Challenge students to work with their data from step *b* to find a mathematical rule for the balance, a rule involving doing something with the actual numbers.

The mathematical rule for the balance is:

$$(W_L) \times (D_L) = (W_R) \times (D_R)$$

where W = weights, D = distances, L = left side, and R = right side of the balance. Thus, the product of the weight and distance on one side is equal to the product of weight and distance on the other side.

Lead older children to try this rule for themselves, using the data from different trials. If the crossbar is balanced, the products of the weights and distances on the left side will always equal the products on the right side for each of these three cases.

Interestingly, this rule applies even if weights are placed on more than one peg on each side. Then, the sum of the weights multiplied by their distances on one side must equal the sum of the weights multiplied by their distances on the other side.

EVALUATE

f. Use these or similar multiple-choice items to assess the students' understanding of the principles related to equal-arm balances.

For students in grades 3 or 4 who only explored the balance qualitatively:

1. If one blue weight is near the pivot on the left side of the balance and one blue weight is near the end of the beam on the right side of the balance:
   A. The beam will be level (balanced).
   B. The right side of the beam will be lower than the left side of the beam.
   C. The left side of the beam will be lower than the right side of the beam.

2. If three blue weights are at the end of the left side of the beam and two blue weights are at the end of the right side of the beam:
   A. The beam will be level (balanced).
   B. The right side of the beam will be lower than the left side of the beam.
   C. The left side of the beam will be lower than the right side of the beam

3. Which of the following is NOT a true statement about the balance?
   A. Equal weights at equal distances will balance.
   B. Equal weights at different distances will not balance.
   C. A heavier weight far out can balance a lighter weight close in.
   D. A lighter weight far out can balance a heavier weight close in.
   E. Different weights at equal distances will not balance.

For students in grades 5 or 6 who investigated the balance quantitatively:

4. On the right side of the balance beam there is a 10 gram weight on the second peg from the pivot point. Where should you put a 5 gram weight to make the beam balance?
   A. On the second peg from the pivot point on the left side of the balance beam.
   B. On the fourth peg from the pivot point on the left side of the balance beam.
   C. On the fifth peg from the pivot point on the left side of the balance beam.
   D. On the 10th peg from the pivot point on the left side of the balance beam.

5. The right side of the balance beam has a 5 gram weight on the 10th peg from the pivot. The left side of the balance beam has a 10 gram weight on the sixth peg from the pivot. Which statement best describes the position of the balance beam?
   A. It is level.
   B. The right side is up.
   C. The left side is up.

Answer Key: (1. B; 2. C; 3. D; 4. B; 5. B)

 C. LEVERS

▶ *Science Background*

The rules governing equal-arm balances are important in science because they also apply to the operation of levers. A lever system has a crossbar, pivoted at a fulcrum. Using a small effort force far out from a fulcrum, a person can lift a heavy load that is nearer the fulcrum. At the lower grades, students can use the symmetry and relational rules of the equal-arm balance to explain and predict actions of a lever. Middle school students might use the balance equation to predict how much force is needed to lift a load of a given weight when the distances involved are known.

Objectives

1. Identify the fulcrum, effort force, and load/resistance of different kinds of levers.
2. Explain how a lever is like an equal-arm balance.
3. Demonstrate and explain that a small effort force far from the fulcrum can lift or move a large load near the fulcrum.

Materials

- Heavy box or other heavy object
- Half-meter stick or 50 cm board

1. WHAT IS A LEVER? HOW COULD YOU USE ONE? (2–6)

ENGAGE

a. Tell students a story about two girls who were climbing a mountain. A rock slide deposited a boulder, trapping the leg of one of the girls. The boulder was too heavy to lift directly. Ask: *What might her companion do to lift the boulder enough so that the girl could get her leg free?*

EXPLORE

b. Lead students to consider getting a tree limb, finding something to use as a fulcrum (pivot), and then using the tree limb to lift the boulder enough for the girl to get her leg free. Model the situation in the classroom using a heavy box to represent the boulder, a half-meter stick for the lever arm, and a book as the pivot.

EXPLAIN

c. Introduce the terms *load*, *force*, and *resistance* as they relate to levers. Ask: *Where was the load (or resistance) for this lever? Where was the fulcrum? Where was the force applied?*

Lead students to understand that a lever can be used to lift a heavy load, if the force on the lever is much farther from the fulcrum than the load is.

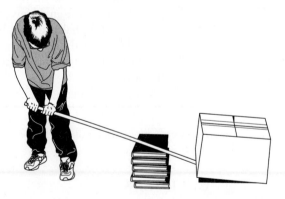

2. HOW IS A LEVER LIKE A BALANCE? (3–6)

ENGAGE

a. Make sure that students have studied the equal-arm balance, following procedures similar to those in the previous section of these activities. Ask: *How is a lever like an equal-arm balance?* Ask the students to identify the fulcrum, effort, and resistance on a balance and on a lever.

EXPLORE

b. Instruct the students to design an investigation to determine how much effort they must exert at different distances on one side of the balance/lever to lift weights at specific positions on the other side. For example, using the balance as a lever, they might place a load of 8 weights at a distance of 10 units from the fulcrum and note that the farther from the pivot/fulcrum they apply the effort force, the easier it is to lift the load.

EXPLAIN

c. Encourage students to discuss their procedures and conclusions. Through this activity, students should realize that a great amount of effort force is needed to move a heavy load when the effort force is much nearer to the fulcrum than is the load.

ELABORATE

d. Ask: *How does the balance and lever principle apply to a seesaw?*

If possible, take your students to a playground seesaw. Or make a classroom seesaw by placing a solid 2 inch by 6 inch board about 6 to 8 feet long on another board under it to act as a pivot. Let the children investigate how a smaller child far out from the pivot of the seesaw can balance a larger child nearer to the fulcrum.

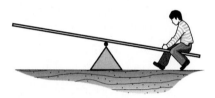

1. If two children are the same weight, where should they sit on a seesaw to make it balance?
   A. Both should sit on board on the same side of the pivot.
   B. One should sit close to the pivot on one side and the other one should sit far away from the pivot on the other side.
   C. They should sit equal distances from the pivot, one on each side of the seesaw.
2. If Joe and Bill are sitting at opposite ends of the seesaw board and Joe's end of the board is on the ground, what do you know about the weights of these students?
   A. Bill weighs more than Joe.
   B. Joe weighs more than Bill.
   C. Joe and Bill each weigh the same amount.
   D. Joe and Bill have gained weight since the beginning of the year.
3. Elizabeth, a first grader, wants to seesaw with her father. Where should they sit so they can make the seesaw go up and down?
   A. Elizabeth should sit on one end of the board and her father should sit on the other end of the board.
   B. Elizabeth should sit near the fulcrum and her father should sit near the end of the board on the other side.
   C. Elizabeth should sit near one end of the board and her father should sit near the fulcrum on the other side.
   D. Elizabeth should sit on her father's lap.

Answers (1. C; 2. B; 3. C)

D. INCLINED PLANES

▶ *Science Background*

An inclined plane or ramp can be used as a simple type of machine to reduce the force needed to move an object up to a given height.

Objectives

1. Describe and demonstrate how an inclined plane can be used to reduce the force needed to move an object up to a given height.
2. Name and describe examples of inclined planes in everyday life.

Materials

- Smooth board, 4 feet long
- Block with screw eye in one end or a rubber band wrapped around it
- Spring scale

1. WHAT IS AN INCLINED PLANE? HOW CAN YOU USE IT? (3–6)

ENGAGE

a. Ask: *What happens to the force needed to move an object up an inclined plane when the angle of the plane is increased?*

EXPLORE

b. Lead students to plan and conduct an investigation similar to this one.
   1. Use the spring scale to find the weight of the block by lifting it straight up, as shown in the diagram. Repeat this several times and find the average reading on the scale. Record the average weight.
   2. Take the 4-foot board and place two or three books under one end so that the end of the board is raised about 10 cm. Place the block with the screw eye in it on the inclined board as shown in the diagram. Slip the hook of the spring scale through the eye of the block.

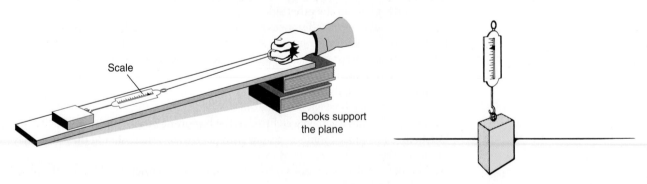

   3. Slowly and evenly pull the scale and block up the board.
   4. Record the amount of force needed to pull the block up the board and the height of the plane. Do this several times and record your observations. Using the data obtained, determine the average force required to pull the weight.
      Ask: *How much force is required to pull the block up each plane? Is the force to move the block up the plane greater than, equal to, or less than the weight of the block? Why?*
   5. Repeat the activity, but this time make the inclined plane steeper by changing the number of support books so that the end of the board is about 20 cm high.
   6. Again, find the average force needed to pull the weight up the board.

EXPLAIN

c. Ask: *How do the forces to move the block up the two inclined planes compare? How is the force needed different when lifting the block straight up than when pulling the block up the board? Why?*

Guide students to understand that inclined planes are used for moving objects that are too heavy to lift directly. An inclined plane is a simple type of machine. Because of the slant of the plane, a smaller force is needed to move an object up an inclined plane than to lift it straight up the same height.

Ask: *What generalization can you make about the amount of force required to move a block as an inclined plane becomes steeper? What is the advantage of having a long inclined plane rather than a short inclined plane if both planes are the same height?*

ELABORATE

d. Ask: *Why do roads not go straight up and down mountains?*
Which of the following examples is an inclined plane?

wheelchair ramp	stairway
hill	vertical cliff
gangplank	head of an ax

Ask: *Where are there examples of inclined planes in the school or on the school campus?*

EVALUATE

e. To assess students' understanding of inclined planes, ask students to respond to this application question.

1. You have a very heavy box to move to the top of a wall. To use the least force to accomplish this task, you should:
   a. Use a smooth board about five times as long as the wall is high as an inclined plane, and push the box up the board to the top of the wall.
   b. Use a smooth board about three times as long as the wall is high as an inclined plane, and push the box up the board to the top of the wall.
   c. Use a smooth board about two times as long as the wall is high as an inclined plane, and push the box up the board to the top of the wall.
   d. Don't bother finding a board; just lift the box onto the top of the wall.

E. PULLEYS

▶ *Science Background*

A pulley also can be used as a simple type of machine to reduce the force needed to lift an object.

Objectives

1. Describe and demonstrate how pulleys can be used to reduce the force needed to lift an object to a given height.
2. Name and describe examples of pulleys in everyday life.

Materials

- Ring stand and clamp for attaching pulleys (or other pulley support)
- Two single pulleys
- String for the pulley
- Spring scale
- 100 g weight
- 50 g weight
- Meterstick

1. WHAT IS A PULLEY, AND HOW CAN YOU USE IT? (3–6)

ENGAGE
a. Ask: *What is a pulley? How do pulleys work? How can pulleys help us lift heavy objects?*

EXPLORE
b. Lead students to conduct this investigation.
1. Obtain a ring stand and a clamp for attaching a pulley (or find another suitable support for the pulley), a single pulley, some string, a spring scale, and a 100 g weight. Assemble your equipment as shown in the diagram.
Ask: *How much do you think you will have to pull on the scale to raise the 100 g weight?*

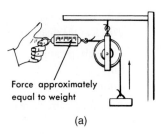

Force approximately
equal to weight

(a)

2. Pull on the scale and raise the 100 g weight. Record the force needed to raise the weight.
3. Repeat this activity several times and record each measurement.
Ask: *What do you think will happen when you use two pulleys to raise the 100 g weight?*
4. In addition to the equipment you have, obtain a second pulley and a 50 g weight. Assemble your equipment as shown in the diagram.

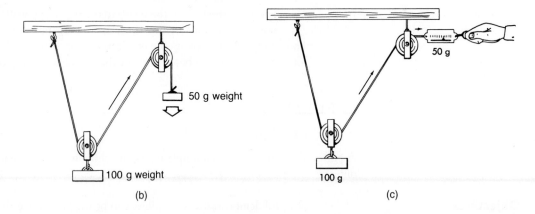

50 g weight

100 g weight

(b)

50 g

100 g

(c)

5. Pull the 50 g weight with the spring balance and record your observations.
6. Remove the 50 g weight and attach the spring scale to the free end of the string, as shown in the following diagram.
Ask: *How much force do you think the scale will show when you raise the 100 g weight?*
7. Raise the weight by pulling on the scale. Ask: *How much is the reading on the scale when you raise the weight?* Repeat the activity several times and record each measurement. Ask: *Why is there an advantage in using this type of pulley system?*

EXPLAIN

c. Ask: *From your investigation, what can you generalize about pulley systems?* Get input from the students. They might first suggest that more pulleys reduce the amount of force needed to lift a heavy weight. Actually, it is not the number of pulleys, but the number of ropes or strings pulling against the resisting weight that makes a difference. In diagram (a), one string pulls upward and the force needed to lift the block is the same as the weight of the block. In diagram (b), two strings pull upward against the load/block and the force needed to lift the load is one-half its weight.

ELABORATE

d. Challenge each group to design a pulley system to lift a piano weighing 300 pounds. Draw a sketch of that pulley system and explain why your group chose that design.

EVALUATE

e. Each group will present their design to the class. They should display and explain their diagram, and give reasons why they think their design is best.

f. The rubric that follows is designed to assess students' understanding of how pulleys change the force needed to lift heavy objects. Distribute this rubric to the students to guide their work and then use it to evaluate their presentations.

Exemplary:
- Includes all of the bullets in the Proficient Level.
- Includes an accurate estimate of the amount of force needed to lift the piano with their pulley system.

Proficient:
- Diagram is neat and legible, and major parts of the system are labeled.
- Explanation of the diagram is clear and relates accurately to the diagram.
- The reasons for their design are clearly stated and based on an accurate understanding of how pulleys make lifting easier.

Developing:
- Only one or two of the three bullets from the Proficient Level are achieved.

Very Little:
- None of the three bullets from the Proficient Level is achieved.

2. HOW CAN A PULLEY ARRANGEMENT HELP YOU USE A SMALL FORCE TO OVERPOWER A LARGE FORCE? (4–6)

Materials
- Two 1¾ inch dowel rods, about 36 inches long
- 20 feet of ½ inch nylon rope

Safety Precautions

Since a large force will be involved, make sure the dowel rods are short and very strong. Safe dowel rods can be cut from a shovel handle purchased from a hardware or building supply store.

ENGAGE

a. Ask: *How can we design a pulley system out of dowel rods and a rope so that a small force can overcome a very large force?*

EXPLORE

b. Tie a strong loop in one end of the rope and loop it over one of the dowel rods. With one person holding one dowel rod in both hands and a second person holding the other dowel rod in both hands, pass the rope back and forth over the dowel rods about four times as in the illustration.

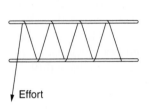

Effort

c. Select four large volunteers and let them hold on to the ends of the dowel rods, with two against two in a tug-of-war. Let a smaller person pull on the free end of the rope.

EXPLAIN

d. Ask: *What happens? Why?* (The force of the smaller person draws the two larger persons together. The rods and rope make up a pulley system with several pulleys. If the rope is looped four times over the rods, there are eight ropes pulling on a dowel. The smaller person will have to pull with one-eighth of the force of the four students trying to hold the rods apart. The effect of this pulley system is dramatic.)

F. BERNOULLI'S PRINCIPLE

▶ *Science Background*

When air rushes over a surface, it has the effect of reducing the air pressure on that surface. This cause-and-effect relationship is called Bernoulli's principle, for Daniel Bernoulli (1700–1782), an important Swiss mathematical scientist who first described the relationship.

Objectives

1. State Bernoulli's principle and use it to analyze a rushing air situation.
2. Use Bernoulli's principle to explain what happens in various rushing air demonstrations.

Materials
- Notebook paper
- Drinking straw

1. WHAT IS BERNOULLI'S PRINCIPLE? HOW CAN YOU USE A PIECE OF PAPER TO INVESTIGATE IT? (4–6)

ENGAGE

a. Conduct this demonstration for students.
   1. Obtain a piece of paper.
   2. Make a fold 3 cm wide along one of the sides of the paper. Make another 3 cm wide fold on the opposite side as indicated in the diagram.
   3. Place the paper on a flat surface, with the folds acting as legs to hold the paper up. Ask: *What do you think will happen if I blow through a straw under this folded paper?*
   4. Using a drinking straw, blow a stream of air under the paper.

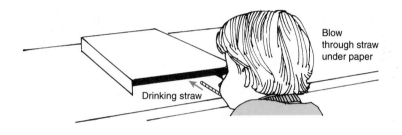

EXPLORE

b. Provide paper and straws to students and allow them to repeat the demonstration.

EXPLAIN

c. Ask: *What do you notice about the way the paper moves?* (The center of the paper moves down.)

   How did the air move under the paper when you blew under it? (The air was moving in a stream under the paper.)

   What can you infer about why the paper went down in the center? Guide students to understand that air pressure pushed the paper down.

   Would the air pressure be greater on the top of the paper or on the bottom of the paper? Help students understand that the air pressure would be greater on the top if the paper was pushed down by the air pressure.

   Why is the air pressure lower on the bottom of the paper? Invent Bernoulli's principle: When air rushes over a surface, the air pressure on that surface is reduced. Make sure that the students can use Bernoulli's principle, along with their observational evidence, to explain the example.

2. HOW WILL A PIECE OF PAPER MOVE WHEN YOU BLOW ACROSS THE TOP OF IT? (3–6)

ENGAGE

a. Ask: *If you were to hold a strip of paper by each corner and blow across the top of the paper, what would happen to the paper? Why do you think so?*

EXPLORE

b. Assist students to conduct this investigation.
    1. Obtain a strip of paper about 5 cm by 27 cm.
    2. Along the 5 cm side, hold the upper left corner of the strip with your left hand and the upper right corner with your right hand.
    3. Blow hard across the top of the paper (see diagram).

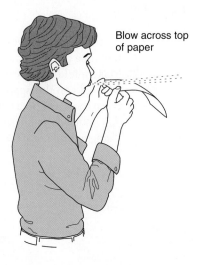

Blow across top of paper

EXPLAIN

c. Ask: *What happens to the paper while you are blowing across it?* (It moves upward.)

    Why does the paper move in this direction? Where does the air move faster, over the top of the paper or the bottom of the paper? Why do you think so?

    Lead students to apply Bernoulli's principle to explain why the paper strip moves upward. The air pressure was reduced as air rushed over the top of the paper. The greater air pressure under the paper pushed the paper upward, overcoming the gravitational forces that tend to bend the paper downward.

ELABORATE

d. Discuss these questions with the class:
    1. *Why is it unwise to stand close to the edge of a platform as a moving train is coming?*
    2. *How does Bernoulli's principle apply to flying planes?*
        If a plane is moving fast enough, the upward pressure on the wings is enough to support the weight of the plane. The plane must keep moving to stay aloft. If the plane's engines cut out in midair, it would glide down immediately.
    3. Look at the following diagram of an airplane wing. *Is the air moving faster at A or B? Why?*

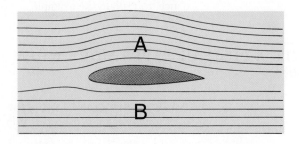

    4. *How do wing slopes vary and why?*

3. WHAT WILL HAPPEN TO A WAD OF PAPER PLACED IN THE OPENING OF A POP BOTTLE IF YOU BLOW ACROSS THE BOTTLE OPENING? (3–6)

ENGAGE

a. Ask: *Using what you know about the effects of rushing air on air pressure, what do you think will happen to a wad of paper placed in the opening of a pop bottle if you blow across the bottle opening? Will the paper go into the bottle or come out of the bottle? Make a prediction. Explain your reasoning.*

EXPLORE

b. Guide students to conduct this investigation.
   1. Wad a small piece of paper so it is about the size of a pea (about 0.5 cm diameter).
   2. Lay the pop bottle on its side.
   3. Place the small wad of paper in the opening of the bottle, next to the edge of the opening. (See diagram.)

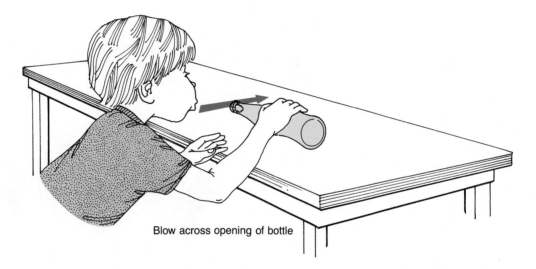

Blow across opening of bottle

   4. Blow across the opening in front of the bottle. Make sure you bend down so that you are level with the bottle.

EXPLAIN

c. Ask: *What happens to the wad of paper?* (It moves out of the bottle.)
   Why is the wad of paper forced to do that?
   What do you infer about the air pressure in the bottle and the air pressure at the opening of the bottle when you blow across it? (Air pressure in the bottle is greater.)

G. PENDULUMS

▶ *Science Background*

Students typically identify three variable factors that might affect the rate of swing of a pendulum: the weight of the pendulum bob, the angle at which it is released, and the length of the pendulum string. Determining which factors are indeed relevant requires that students conduct controlled investigations in which one factor at a time is varied and its effect on the rate of swing of the pendulum is determined, while the other two variables are controlled or left unchanged.

Surprisingly, only the length affects the rate of swing. Varying the weight of the pendulum bob or the angle at which the pendulum is released has no effect on its rate of swing.

Objectives

1. Demonstrate procedures for measuring the rate of a pendulum's swing.
2. Design controlled experiments to test hypotheses about factors that might affect the speed of a pendulum.
3. Record, analyze, and draw accurate conclusions from data.

Materials

Watch with a second hand for each group, or clock with a second hand for the whole class

- Paper clips
- Pennies
- Ball of string
- Tongue depressors or pencils (to support the pendulums)
- Masking tape (to tape the pendulum support to a desk)

▶ *Preparation*

- Tie paper clips to one end of several pieces of long string and insert one or more pennies into each paper clip to make the pendulum bobs (as in the drawing). Wedge the string into the slit of a tongue depressor as in the drawing. Students can adjust the length of string as needed by sliding it along the notch of the tongue depressor.

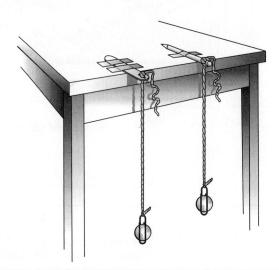

- Determine where teams of students can set up pendulums that can swing freely. To support the pendulums, students should tape or hold the tongue depressor or the pencil securely on the edge of a table.

....

1. WHAT FACTORS MIGHT AFFECT THE RATE OF SWING OF A PENDULUM? (5–8)

ENGAGE

a. Show students a pendulum using pennies as the pendulum bob and a tongue depressor or pencil as the support. Ask: *Do all pendulums swing at the same rate, or do some swing slower or faster? How can you measure how fast a pendulum swings?*

EXPLORE

b. Provide each cooperative group with the materials to make a pendulum similar to the one you demonstrated. Lead the students to count the number of swings of their pendulum in 15 seconds. Explain that this is called the rate of swing of the pendulum. Define a swing as one complete back-and-forth cycle.)

Ask: *How can you get a pendulum to swing faster or slower (more or fewer swings in 15 seconds)?* Challenge the students to identify the things about their pendulum that they could possibly change.

c. After some discussion, ask students to focus on these three separate, measurable *variables* that might make a pendulum swing faster or slower:
   1. Length of the pendulum
   2. Weight or number of pennies that make up the pendulum bob
   3. Angle at which the pendulum is released

d. Instruct students to write down a separate question about each variable (e.g., *How does the rate change when the weight of the pendulum bob is changed?*). Then tell them to design and conduct controlled experiments to answer the questions they have asked.

e. Monitor students' experiments and provide assistance with the procedures, logic, and data interpretation for controlled experiments. Ask the students to record what they do and what they find out.

f. When students have had ample time to explore, help the class to standardize the way they measure weight, length, angle, and rate (number of back-and-forth swings in 15 seconds). At this time you should be ready to introduce the use of a data table like the one illustrated to help students organize their investigations, keep track of their data, and interpret their data to form conclusions.

PENDULUM DATA TABLE					
Does length affect the rate of swing of a pendulum?		**Does weight affect the rate of swing of a pendulum?**		**Does the release angle affect the rate of swing of a pendulum?**	
What variable did you manipulate?		What variable did you manipulate?		What variable did you manipulate?	
What variables did you control?		What variables did you control?		What variables did you control?	
What responding variable did you measure?		What responding variable did you measure?		What responding variable did you measure?	
Length of Pendulum	Rate (number of swings in 15 seconds)	Weight of Pendulum (number of pennies)	Rate (number of swings in 15 seconds)	Angle of Pendulum Release	Rate (number of swings in 15 seconds)
20 cm		1		small	
40 cm		2		medium	
60 cm		3		large	
What can you conclude about length and rate of swing?		What can you conclude about weight and rate of swing?		What can you conclude about the angle of release and rate of swing?	

This data table is not only a place for students to record measurements so they can remember them but also a "think sheet" that facilitates the planning and conducting of investigations, guides the students in recognizing relationships, and assists them in drawing conclusions.

EXPLAIN

g. Instruct students to use their data to answer their questions about the factors that affect the rate of a pendulum.

If students have changed more than one variable at a time (for example, changing length and weight together), discuss with them the importance of experimental design. Ask: *Why must you change only one variable at a time when investigating? Why must other variables be kept constant?* (So you can be sure which of the variables really made a difference)

ELABORATE

h. Challenge students to notice pendulums in the world around them or find examples of pendulums in books or magazines or on the Internet. Grandfather clocks, swings, and trapezes are all forms of pendulums.

EVALUATE

i. Assessment task for cooperative learning groups:
    * Instruct students to create a pendulum that swings from one extreme to the other in one second (7.5 complete back-and-forth swings in 15 seconds). They should record the steps they followed to achieve their goal.
    * Use the following rubric to assess levels of group performance in solving the task.

    Exemplary:
    * Includes all of the bullets from the Proficient Level.

    * The pendulum's rate is exactly 7.5 complete back-and-forth swings in 15 seconds.

    Proficient:
    * The steps they followed were clearly described.
    * They only varied the length of the string, since they knew that the mass of the bob and the angle of release do not affect the rate of the pendulum's swing.
    * They referred to their data table from previous trials to estimate a reasonable string length to try.
    * The pendulum's rate is between 7 and 8 complete back-and-forth swings in 15 seconds.

    Developing:
    * One or two of the bullets from the Proficient Level were not observed.

    Little Understanding:
    * No more than two of the bullets from the Proficient Level were observed.

j. Assessment task for individuals:
    * Ask students to explain in writing: *How would you adjust a grandfather clock that was running too fast? too slow?* (Students should realize that the pendulum must be lengthened for the clock to slow down and shortened for the clock to run faster.)

III. SOUND

Sound is an important part of our lives, enabling us to communicate with one another, be alert to different situations, and enjoy music and the sounds of the world around us. The simple activities included here enable children to begin to understand the basic physics of sound. Consistent with the *National Science Education Standards*, topics studied include sources of sounds, the way sounds travel, and detectors of sound.

NSES Science Standards

All students should develop an understanding of

- position and motion of objects (sound) (K–4).

Concepts and Principles That Support the Standards

- Sound is produced by vibrating objects (K–4).
- The pitch of a sound can be varied by changing the rate of vibration (K–4).
- Sound is a form of energy (5–8).
- Energy is transferred in many ways (5–8).
- Most change involves energy transfer (5–8).
- Vibrations in materials set up wavelike disturbances that spread away from the source. Sound waves and earthquake waves are examples. These and other waves move at different speeds in different materials (*Benchmarks for Science Literacy*, 6–8).

 ## A. SOURCES OF SOUND

▶ *Science Background*

Sounds are produced when objects vibrate or move back and forth rapidly. An object that produces sound is called a *sound source*. Many different objects can generate sounds. For example, musical instruments produce sound when some part of them is made to vibrate.

Characteristics such as pitch and loudness allow us to distinguish one sound from another. Pitch is determined by the frequency, or rate, of a vibration of sound.

Objectives

1. Define *vibration* as the back-and-forth movement of an object.
2. Demonstrate, describe, and explain the generation of sound by various vibrating sources.
3. Define *pitch* as how high or low a sound is. Demonstrate, describe, and explain how the pitch of a sound may be varied.
4. Define *loudness* as the amount, amplitude, or intensity of sound. Demonstrate, describe, and explain how the loudness of a sound may be increased.

1. HOW ARE DIFFERENT SOUNDS PRODUCED? (2–4)

Materials

- Craft sticks (15 cm in length)

ENGAGE

a. Ask: *How can you use a craft stick to create sounds?*

EXPLORE

b. Instruct students to hold a 15 cm craft stick firmly against a desk with one hand. With the other hand, they should pluck the overhanging part of the stick, causing it to vibrate. Remind the students to observe carefully while carrying out this procedure.

EXPLAIN

c. Ask: *What did you hear?* (A sound) *What did you see?* (Part of the craft stick was moving up and down.) *What did you feel?* (Possibly, the end of the craft stick moving up and down) *What is meant by vibration?* (A rapid back and forth motion) *Which part of the craft stick vibrates and produces sound? Were all the sounds produced by the craft sticks the same?* (No, not exactly) *How were they different?* (They were different notes, some high, some lower. Some children may mention the term *pitch* to describe this difference.)

Ask: *What is meant by the pitch of a sound? How can you change the pitch of a vibrating craft stick?*

ELABORATE

d. Challenge students to produce a high-pitched sound by vibrating the stick and to produce a low-pitched sound by vibrating the stick. Then have them try to make pitches that fall in between. Remind students to observe carefully and to pay attention to what they are changing about the craft stick. Then let them discuss their findings.

e. Ask: *What did you do to change the pitch of the vibrating craft stick?* (Change the amount of the craft stick hanging over the edge of the desk.) *How did you make your lowest pitch?* (Hold the craft stick so that most of it hangs over the edge of the desk.) *How did you make your highest pitch?* (Hold the craft stick so that only a little of it hangs over the edge of the desk.) *Does the craft stick vibrate faster or slower when more of it hangs over the edge of a desk?* (It vibrates slower when more of it hangs over the edge of the desk.) *How is the speed of vibration related to the pitch of the sound produced?* (The faster the vibration, the higher the pitch of the sound produced.) Consider asking students to demonstrate their ideas with the craft sticks to support the answers to these questions.

EVALUATE

f. To check for understanding of the relationship among length of vibrating object, speed of vibration, and pitch of the sound produced, have the students respond to the following assessment items.

1. Compete the following table to describe the relationships among variables in this investigation. The words to choose from are:
Fast, High, Long, Low, Short, Slow

Length of craft stick hanging over the edge of the table	Speed of vibration	Pitch of the sound produced

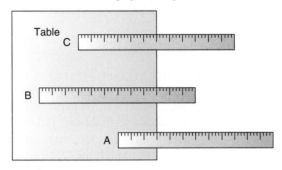

Rulers hanging over edge of table.

2. Which of the rulers shown in the drawing would produce the lowest pitched sound when plucked? (A)
3. Which of the rulers shown in the drawing would vibrate the fastest when plucked? (B)

2. HOW IS SOUND PRODUCED BY A TUNING FORK? (2–4)

Materials
- Tuning forks
- Wood blocks
- Container of water

Safety Precautions
To protect tuning forks from damage, strike them only against a wood surface or the sole of your shoe or with a rubber mallet to produce vibrations and sounds.

ENGAGE
a. Ask: *What is a tuning fork? How does a tuning fork produce sounds?*

EXPLORE
b. Instruct students to observe while you conduct this demonstration:
1. Hold the tuning fork by its stem.
2. Strike a wood block or sole of your shoe crisply with the tip of one of the fork tines.
3. Bring the fork near your ear and listen. Strike the fork again and lightly touch the tip of one of the fork tines to the surface of the water in a container.

EXPLAIN

    c. Ask: *What vibrates in producing sound from a tuning fork? What is your evidence that the fork tines are vibrating?*

3. HOW IS SOUND PRODUCED BY A DRUM? (2–4)

Materials

- Cylindrical container
- Puffed rice or wheat cereal
- Large balloon or sheet rubber
- Strong rubber band
- Drumstick or pencil with eraser

ENGAGE

    a. Ask: *What vibrates in a drum to produce sound?*

EXPLORE

    b. Stretch a large balloon or piece of sheet rubber over the open end of a cylindrical container, such as an oatmeal container. Place a rubber band around that end to hold the rubber sheet securely in place. This makes a simple drum. Sprinkle puffed rice or wheat cereal on the drumhead. Tell students to tap the drumhead softly with a drumstick or eraser end of a pencil and observe what happens. Then tell them to hit the drumhead harder and watch the cereal and observe the sound produced.

EXPLAIN

    c. Ask: *What part of a drum vibrates to produce sound? What is your evidence? What is meant by loudness? How do you vary the loudness of a drum?*

4. HOW IS SOUND PRODUCED BY A BANJO? (2–4)

Materials

- Rubber bands of varying lengths and thicknesses
- Small, open box or plastic cup

ENGAGE

    a. Ask: *What vibrates to produce sound in a stringed musical instrument, such as a banjo?*

EXPLORE

    b. Tell students to make banjos by stretching rubber bands of varying lengths and thicknesses over a small box or plastic cup. Pluck the rubber bands to produce sounds.

EXPLAIN

    c. Ask: *What part of a rubber band banjo vibrates to produce sound? What is your evidence?*
    d. Ask: *What do you think might affect the pitch of the sound from a banjo?* Instruct students to investigate how the pitch of a sound is varied on a rubber band banjo by varying the tension and thickness of the rubber bands. Ask: *What variables can you change to vary the pitch of a rubber band banjo?* (Length, thickness, and tension of the rubber bands) *How do you vary the loudness of the banjo?*

ELABORATE

    e. Ask: *How can you vary the pitch of the sound produced by a stringed musical instrument, such as a guitar or ukulele?* Allow students to observe how strings of differing thickness and different lengths produce different pitches in guitars, ukuleles, or other stringed instruments. Demonstrate how the tension of a string can be varied to produce high- and low-pitched sounds with a guitar or other stringed instrument.

TEACHING BACKGROUND

Each time a guitar player plucks a guitar string, it starts to vibrate. The rate of vibration determines the pitch of the string. Guitars have strings of differing thickness. Thinner strings vibrate more quickly and produce higher-pitched sounds than thicker ones. Strings under greater tension also vibrate more quickly and produce higher pitches than strings under less tension. The musician uses the tuning knobs on the guitar to adjust the tension of the strings. As she increases the tension of a string, that string vibrates more rapidly and the pitch gets higher. As she decreases the tension of a string, the string vibrates more slowly and the pitch gets lower.

Source: Full Option Science System, *Physics of Sound.* Lawrence Hall of Science, University of California, Berkeley.

EVALUATE

f. Challenge students to create a stringed instrument on which they can play a scale of eight ascending notes (eight notes in a row, each with a higher pitch). Each student will explain his or her stringed instrument to the class, then play a scale. Give the following rubric to the students to aid in their preparation, then use it to evaluate their instruments and presentations. Total possible score is 35. If you want an approximate grade on a 100-point scale, just multiply the score from the rubric by 3. A student who was judged Exemplary in all categories would have a grade of 105. A student who was judged Proficient in all categories would have a grade of 84. A student who was judged Developing in all categories would have a grade of 42.

Criteria	Exemplary (5 Points)	Proficient (4 Points)	Developing (2 Points)
Appearance	Very attractive; shows much effort and care in construction	Looks OK; some effort and care in construction is evident	Sloppy; shows little effort; careless construction
Sturdiness	Very sturdy; looks like it will withstand repeated use	Somewhat sturdy; didn't fall apart before or during performance, but looks like it might	Not sturdy; falls apart before or during performance
Safety	Completely safe, all potential safety issues addressed	Seems safe, if instrument used properly	Obvious that someone could be harmed during the use of this instrument
Explanation	Tells (in an interesting, organized manner) their name, name of their instrument, what is vibrating, and how different pitches are produced	Presents most information described in Exemplary; but presentation not very enthusiastic or interesting; or presentation is unorganized	Not informative, not interesting, unprepared, or silly

(continues)

Criteria	Exemplary (5 Points)	Proficient (4 Points)	Developing (2 Points)
Speaking Skills	Presenter speaks clearly and at a proper volume for audience to hear; uses good eye contact; and holds instrument so it is visible to all	One of the desired elements from Exemplary not achieved	Two or more of the desired elements from Exemplary not achieved
Playing of Scale	All 8 notes of scale are played in order from low pitch to high pitch and are all "in key"	8 different pitches are played, they are in order from low pitch to high pitch, but they are not "in key"	Instrument produces fewer than 8 pitches or scale not played in order
Volume of Instrument	All notes produced can be easily heard throughout the classroom	Most notes produced can be heard in the classroom	Can't hear many notes, too quiet

5. HOW CAN YOU MAKE A DRINKING STRAW FLUTE? (2–4)

Materials

- Drinking straws
- Scissors

ENGAGE

a. Ask: *What is a flute? How is sound produced in a flute? How can you vary the pitch of a sound produced by a flute?*

EXPLORE

b. Give each student a drinking straw. Have students use scissors to cut a V-shape at the end of the straw and pinch it closed to produce a reed.

Pinch here　Side view　　　Cut a V　Top view

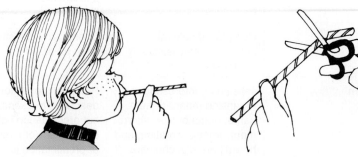

Have students blow on the V cut into the straw flute to produce a sound. (*Note:* They will need to experiment to get the proper lip vibration.) Now, have students cut the straw into different lengths and blow on the straw flute to get different pitches.

EXPLAIN   c. As you circulate among students, or when you return to a whole class structure, ask: *What part of a straw flute vibrates to produce a sound? What can you vary to change the pitch of a straw flute?*

ELABORATE   d. *How do you think clarinets, oboes, and saxophones produce sounds? How could we find out?* Provide the opportunity to do library and/or internet research about how these woodwind instruments make sounds.

....

6. HOW CAN YOU MAKE A BOTTLE PIPE ORGAN? WHAT AFFECTS THE PITCH OF THE SOUND PRODUCED BY A BOTTLE? (2–4)

Materials   For each cooperative group:

- 8 identical glass or plastic soda or water bottles
  Or a test-tube rack with 8 identical test-tubes

- Water

ENGAGE   a. Blow across a bottle that is about three-fourths full of water so that a sound is produced from the bottle. Ask: *How could you vary the pitch of the sound coming from the bottle?*

EXPLORE   b. Fill eight identical bottles with varying amounts of water. Blow across the open ends of the bottles. Explore the sounds they produce. Arrange the bottles to play an ascending scale (pitches that get higher one after another).

EXPLAIN   c. Ask: *What part of a bottle vibrates to produce sound?* (The air) *How is the air in the pop bottle made to vibrate?* (By blowing over the opening in the bottle) *What can you vary to change the pitch of a pop bottle?* (Change the amount of water in the bottle) *How do you think pipe organs and horns produce sounds?* (The air inside them vibrates.)

ELABORATE

d. Challenge student groups to play a simple tune using their bottle organs.

B. TRANSFER OF SOUND

▶ *Science Background*

Sound moves away from a source through a material medium. Air, water, and solids are all good media for carrying sound. Sounds travel through media in waves that are analogous to waves in water. Sound cannot travel through a vacuum because there are no particles to vibrate and carry the sound waves. When sound waves bounce off some solid object in the distance, they return to the source as echoes.

Objectives

1. Define *medium* as the material substance through which sound travels from a vibrating source to a receiver.
2. Demonstrate and describe how sound travels through solid, liquid, and gas media.
3. Describe how sound travels through different media in waves that are analogous to water waves.
4. Demonstrate and describe ways that sound can be directed and amplified.
5. Describe and explain echoes as the reflection of sound waves.

1. DOES SOUND TRAVEL THROUGH AIR, SOLIDS, AND LIQUIDS? (2–4)

Materials

• Lengths of garden hose
• Metersticks
• Pieces of metal or rocks
• Bucket

ENGAGE

a. Ask: *How does sound travel? Does sound travel through all kinds of materials? Can sound travel through the air in a garden hose? Does sound travel through solids? Does sound travel through water?*

EXPLORE

b. Have students listen to sounds through straight and curving lengths of garden hose. Make sure all of the water is drained out of the hose.
c. Have students work in pairs. One student should hold a meterstick to her ear. The partner should scratch the other end of the stick with a pencil. Repeat the activity with the meterstick held away from the ear a few centimeters.

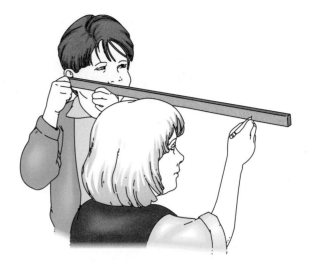

d. Obtain a large bucket of water. Ask students to take two pieces of metal or two rocks and hit them together under the water. Then, tell them to hit the objects together out of water.

EXPLAIN

e. Ask: *How does the garden hose demonstration show that sound travels through air?*
   What do you hear through the meterstick? How do you think the sound of the pencil travels through the meterstick?
   What did you hear when you hit the objects together underwater? Was the sound louder or softer when you hit the objects together out of the water?
   Which seemed to be a better conductor of sound: the solid meterstick, air, or water?

 ## C. RECEIVERS OF SOUND

▶ *Science Background*

Receivers are instruments that detect sound. Sound is one of the many forms of energy. Our ears are marvelously designed receivers of sound that are tuned to keep us in touch with much of our environment.

Objectives

1. Explain how the outer ear and an ear trumpet are similar in gathering incoming sound signals.
2. Explain that in receiving sound, a detector in the receiver is set in vibration by the incoming sound signals.
3. Identify and describe the operation of the sound detectors in the human ear and a stethoscope.

1. HOW CAN SOUNDS BE HEARD BETTER? (2–4)

Materials

* Stethoscope
* Ear trumpet
* Listening tube

ENGAGE

a. Ask: *What part of your body detects sounds? How is your ear specially designed to receive and detect sounds?*

EXPLORE

b. Roll a piece of poster board into a cylinder and fasten it on both ends with paper fasteners. Have students use the listening tube to listen to faint sounds.

c. To make an ear trumpet, curl a fan-shaped piece of cardboard into a cone. Fasten the cone with three brass fasteners. Ask students to place the small end of the ear trumpet to their ears and listen to the faint whispers of partners some distance away from them.

d. Ask students to tap their fingers together and listen to the sound. Have them tap their fingers together again and listen to the sound through a stethoscope. Then, have them tap their fingers underwater and listen to the sound without and with a stethoscope.

Safety Precautions

• Help students to clean earpieces of stethoscopes with alcohol and cotton swabs before and after using them.

• Caution students not to damage the diaphragm of a stethoscope by striking it against hard objects.

• Only use listening tubes, ear trumpets, and stethoscopes to listen to faint sounds. Since these listening devices make sounds louder, listening to loud sounds with them may damage your ears.

EXPLAIN

e. Ask: *How do listening tubes enable sounds to be heard better?*

How does the ear trumpet enhance hearing? How is an ear trumpet similar to the outer ear?

How does the stethoscope work? How does a stethoscope enable you to hear soft sounds better?

In what ways do the rolled cylinder, the ear trumpet, and the stethoscope extend the sense of hearing?

TEACHING BACKGROUND

A sound receiver must be able to detect sound pulses that reach it. The ear is a sound receiver. The outer part of the ear collects sound much like the large end of an ear trumpet when it is used as a listening tube. When sound energy strikes the eardrum, the resulting vibrations initiate the hearing process.

A stethoscope has a diaphragm that vibrates when sound strikes it. Faint sounds can be detected by the diaphragm. The sounds are then conducted from the diaphragm down the air-filled tubes to the ear. In a similar way, a telephone mouthpiece has a diaphragm that vibrates when sound energy strikes it. In a telephone, the vibrations in the diaphragm are converted electromagnetically to electrical energy. Electrical energy is then conducted from one telephone along telephone wires or from a series of towers to another telephone where the diaphram in the earpiece vibrates because of the electrical signals it receives.

D. SOUND CHALLENGES: HOMEMADE TELEPHONES

 Science and Technology Standards

Students should develop

- abilities of technological design, including the ability to
  a. identify a simple problem of human adaptation in the environment;
  b. propose a solution;
  c. implement proposed solutions;
  d. evaluate a product or design; and
  e. communicate a problem, design, and solution (K–4).

Objectives

1. Construct homemade telephones.
2. Explain the operation of a homemade telephone, using the concepts of vibrating source, conducting material, and receiver.
3. Design and carry out investigations to determine the best type of materials for a homemade telephone.
4. Demonstrate abilities of technological design.

1. CAN SOUND TRAVEL THROUGH A STRING? (2–4)

Materials

- Spoon
- String

ENGAGE

a. Ask: *Can sound travel through a long string?*

EXPLORE

b. Loop a length of string around a spoon. Try to tie the spoon at about the middle of the string. Hold the two ends of the string in your ears. Bend over so the spoon hangs freely. Have your partner gently strike the spoon with another spoon.

EXPLAIN

c. Ask: *What do you observe? What is your evidence that the string is a conductor of sound?*

2. HOW CAN YOU MAKE A DEMONSTRATION TELEPHONE? (2–4)

Materials

- String, wire, or nylon fishing line
- Cups of various kinds (Styrofoam, waxed cardboard, plastic, large, small)
- Nail, paper clips, toothpicks

ENGAGE

a. Ask: *How can you design a "telephone" that will enable you to communicate across some distance using a string as a medium?*

EXPLORE

b. Show students how to construct a homemade telephone using plastic cups. In advance, use a small nail to punch a hole in the bottom of each cup. Tell pairs of students to cut a 20 foot (6 or 7 meter) length of string and thread the ends into cups. Tell them to tie a paper clip around each end to hold the string firmly in place inside the cup. Instruct them to try out their homemade telephones with their partners.

EXPLAIN

c. Ask: *What is the original source of sound for your telephones? What is set in vibration in the mouthpiece of the telephone? What is the conductor of sound? How is the sound detected at the other end of the telephone?*

ELABORATE

d. Challenge students to improve the quality of their homemade telephones by investigating the effects of different string or wire media, different types of cups, and different ways to hold the string or wire against the bottom of the cups. Tell students to come up with standard ways to test their telephones so they can decide which parts are most effective. If you have a microphone probe to use with CBL software, this would be a great time to introduce that technology.

TEACHING BACKGROUND

A homemade telephone is a human-constructed product that connects well to scientific principles. Many concepts introduced in the activities on sound are used in this activity. The voice of one partner sets particles of air in vibration. The cup/mouthpiece of the string telephone is then set in vibration. The sound energy produced by the vibrating cup is conducted along the string to the other cup. Thus, the second cup is set in vibration. This vibrating cup sets the air in vibration, producing sound. The sound is then carried to the ear. Designing, constructing, and evaluating homemade telephones provides a good introduction to the technological design cycle.

▶ *Evaluate*

To demonstrate mastery of Objective 2, ask each pair of students to create a labeled drawing and brief explanation of the homemade telephone they constructed that they think worked best.

Distribute the following checklist to guide their work then use it to evaluate their products.

Your explanation of your best homemade telephone should:

☐ Fit on one page.
☐ Include first and last name of both partners.
☐ Include a neat sketch of your homemade telephone in use.
☐ Label the following parts of your homemade telephone on the sketch: vibrating source, conducting material, and receiver.
☐ Indicate the length of the conducting material (in centimeters).
☐ Identify the materials used to make each part of your homemade phone.
☐ Include a description of how your phone works.
☐ Include an explanation of why this phone was the best one you designed.

IV. TEMPERATURE AND HEAT

▶ *Science Background*

Heat, like light, sound, and electricity, is a form of energy. Energy is one of the few concepts in science that children talk about accurately before they can define it. Children's ideas about energy—getting "quick energy" from a candy bar or turning off lights so as not to "waste energy"—may be imprecise but are reasonably close to the concept of energy that we want children to learn (*Benchmarks for Science Literacy*, American Association for the Advancement of Science, 1993).

Technically, energy is the ability to do work. More intuitively, something has energy if it can bring about a change in another object or in itself. Heat can bring about many changes. For example, it can change the state of a substance from liquid to gas (evaporation) or from solid to liquid (melting); it can change the temperature of a substance; it can cause most things to expand; and it can change the rate of a reaction, such as how fast a substance dissolves.

Science Standards

All students should develop an understanding of

- light, heat, electricity, and magnetism (K–4).
- transfer of energy (5–8).

Concepts and Principles That Support the Standards

- Heat can be produced in many ways, such as burning, rubbing, or mixing one substance with another (K–4).
- Energy is a property of many substances and is associated with heat (5–8).
- Energy is transferred in many ways (5–8).
- Heat moves in predictable ways, flowing from warmer objects to cooler ones, until both reach the same temperature (5–8).

Objectives

1. Name and describe sources of heat and activities that produce heat.
2. Design, conduct, and interpret experiments to determine the effects of the color of a material on the amount of radiated heat absorbed by the material.
3. Design and conduct experiments to determine the final temperature of water mixtures.
4. Explain that heat flows from warmer substances to cooler substances until an equilibrium temperature is reached.

1. WHAT MAKES THINGS GET HOTTER? (3–5)

Materials

- 6 inch piece of wire coat hanger
- Mineral oil
- Brass button

- Wool cloth
- Piece of metal
- Pencil eraser
- Notebook paper

ENGAGE

a. Hold up the piece of wire coat hanger. Ask the class: "*If you touched this, how do you think it would feel?*" If its temperature is not mentioned, lead them to also consider that property. Let several students feel the wire before you start and report their observations, especially about temperature, to the class. Bend a 6 inch piece of wire hanger back and forth 10 times as shown. Let the students quickly touch the wire at the point where you bent it.

Ask: *How does the wire feel now?* (The wire got hotter.) *What do you think will happen if I bend the wire more times, for example, 20, 25, 30, 35 times?* (Each time the wire gets hotter.)

Safety Precautions

Try out this activity first to find out how many bends will make the wire too hot for students to safely touch.

EXPLORE

b. In cooperative groups, have students explore actions that cause materials to heat up. For example, rub your hands together very fast and hard, or rub a brass button on a piece of wool, metal on paper, or a pencil eraser on paper and quickly touch it to your upper lip or the tip of your nose (sensitive parts of your body).

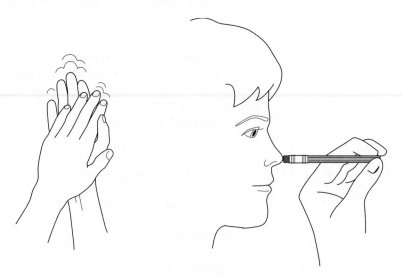

c. Have groups each complete an *I Notice/I Wonder* chart about their observations and the questions they generate.

If temperature probes and CBL software is available for student use, students could use this technology to make their observations quantitative rather than just qualitative.

EXPLAIN

d. Ask: *What did you observe in each case? How was heat produced in these activities?* Guide students to understand that bending things and rubbing things produces heat.

ELABORATE

e. Try rubbing your hands together again, but put a few drops of oil or water on your hands first. Ask: *How do you think the second rubbing will feel different from the first rubbing?*
Ask: *What did you observe? Why do you think it happened?*

2. HOW CAN YOU HEAT UP THE SAND IN A JAR? (5–8)

Materials
- Baby food jar with screw top or small plastic food storage container with secure lid
- Sand
- Thick towel
- Thermometer or temperature probes with CBL software on computers

ENGAGE

a. Hold up a baby food jar three-fourths full of sand. Ask: *What do you think will happen to the sand in a baby food jar if you shake it many times?* Hint: *Think back to the previous activity.*

EXPLORE

b. For each cooperative group, fill a baby food jar three-fourths full of sand, screw on the jar top, and then wrap it with a thick towel. Each person should take a turn doing the following things:
   1. Measure the initial temperature of the sand, then shake the sand vigorously for 5 minutes.
   2. Measure the temperature of the sand.
   3. Write your findings on a record sheet like the one shown.

Person	Minutes of Shaking	Temperature in °C
1	5	
2	10	
3	15	
4	20	
5	25	

4. Pass the jar to the next person.
5. When everyone has had a turn, compare the temperature of the sand from the first to the last reading.
6. How were they different? (The temperature was higher after each shaking.)
7. Set up a graph like the one shown, then graph the data from the record sheets.

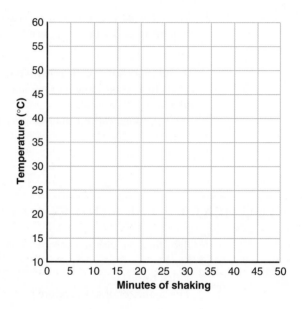

EXPLAIN

c. Ask: *What did you observe? What do your data indicate? What was the source of the heat energy in the sand?* Explain that shaking something is a form of energy (mechanical energy; kinetic energy). Heat is also a form of energy. When you shook the sand, the energy of the sand's motion was transferred to heat energy when the sand grains struck one another and the container. The heat energy in the sand caused its temperature to go up.

3. WHAT IS THE EFFECT OF HEAT ON AIR IN A CONTAINER? (1–4)

Materials

For each group:

- Liquid soap solution in a wide-mouthed container or pie pan
- Ice water in a deep container
- Test tube, medicine vial, small juice can

ENGAGE

a. Ask: *What can we do to change the shape of a soap bubble on the mouth of a container?*

EXPLORE

b. Squirt some liquid soap into a large container of water with a wide opening at the top. Stir the water. Dip the open end of a test tube, medicine vial, or small juice can into the soapy water so that a soap film forms across the end of the container. Challenge students to get the soap film to expand. One way to get the soap film to expand is for students to wrap their hands around the container (without squeezing) so that their hands cover as much of the container as possible.

Ask: *What do you observe?*

c. Get a soap bubble on a small container, such as a test tube or medicine vial. Put the container in the container of ice water. Ask: *What happens to the soap bubble?*

EXPLAIN

d. Ask: *Were you able to change the shape of the soap film? How? Why did the soap bubble expand when you held the container in your hands? Why did the soap bubble go down into the container when you placed the container in ice?*

Through their explorations, the students should note that when they hold the container in their hands, the air in the container is heated and the soap film expands, becomes dome-shaped, and eventually pops. Lead students to understand this principle about heat and air pressure:

Air expands (takes up a greater volume) when it is heated. Thus, air in a closed container exerts more pressure on its container when it is heated. Air contracts (takes up a smaller volume) when it is cooled. Thus, air in a closed container exerts less pressure on its container when it is cooled.

ELABORATE

e. Obtain a large can, such as a vegetable can from the school cafeteria. Dip the open end of the can into soap solution in order to form a soap film over the open end of the large can. Let several students wrap their hands around it to see if they can get the soap film to expand. Ask children to describe what they see and to explain why it happens.

EVALUATE

f. To assess if students can apply the principles they have been investigating to a new situation, have them answer the following question.

1. You blow up a red balloon so that it is 40 cm around its widest part. Then you put the balloon into the freezer for an hour. What do you predict will be true about the balloon immediately after it is taken out of the freezer compared to before it was placed in the freezer?

For each pair of answers below, circle the answer you predict to be true.

The balloon will be blue.	The balloon will be red.
The air in the balloon will be colder.	The air in the balloon will be warmer.
The balloon will be larger.	The balloon will be smaller.
The balloon's circumference will be less than 40 cm.	The balloon's circumference will be more than 40 cm.
The air in the balloon is exerting more pressure on the balloon.	The air in the balloon is exerting less pressure on the balloon.

Then write an explanation of why you expect the changes you have circled.

4. WHAT AFFECTS THE TEMPERATURE CHANGE OF WATER HEATED IN SUNLIGHT? (5–8)

Materials

- Three tin cans of same size
- Small can of shiny white paint
- Small can of dull black paint
- Two small paintbrushes
- Styrofoam covers for cans
- Three thermometers or temperature probes with CBL software
- Lamp with 150 to 300 watt bulb (to use in place of sunlight)

ENGAGE

a. Ask: *If something is left in sunlight, does its color affect how hot it gets? How could you investigate to find out?*

EXPLORE

b. Guide students to plan and conduct a controlled experiment to determine the effect of color on heating in sunlight. These activities may be done in cooperative groups or as a whole class demonstration. Based on the experience of your class with inquiry you might give them the following instructions (structured inquiry) or allow them to design their own investigation to answer the question.

1. Obtain three identical-sized cans and remove all labels. Paint one can dull black and another can shiny white; leave the third can unpainted, shiny metal.
2. Fill each can with the same amount of regular tap water.
3. Put a Styrofoam cover on each can and insert a thermometer through each cover.
4. Set the cans in direct sunlight or at equal distances from a 150 to 300 watt light bulb. (See diagram.)
5. Prepare a table for data collection and record the temperature of the water in each can at 1-minute intervals. (Do not move the thermometers when you record the temperature each time.)

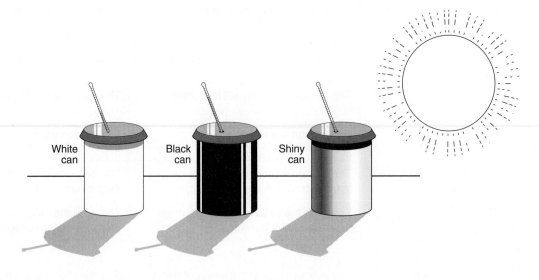

EXPLAIN

   c. Ask: *What happens to the water temperature in the three different cans after being in the sun or near light bulbs for a while? If they are different temperatures, how would you explain that?* Explain that heat energy is transferred from the sun to earth. Lead students to understand that the shiny surface of the unpainted can and the shiny white paint reflect radiant energy, whereas the dull black paint absorbs most of the radiant energy which then heats the water.

ELABORATE

   d. Ask: *How would you relate the unequal heating in the tin cans to different land and water surfaces of the earth?* Guide students to understand that dark patches of ground absorb more radiant energy than do shiny water surfaces or lighter-colored land surfaces. The unequal heating of the earth contributes to climate and weather changes.

   e. Ask: *What color space suits do astronauts wear? Why?*

EVALUATE

   f. Use the following item to check student understanding about this concept.

     1. You are planning to camp in a sunny area during the summer. You want to be able to stay cool in your tent during the hottest part of the day. All of the tents are identical except for their color. What color tent do you want? Why? (Students should select a white or very light colored tent, so that most of the sun's rays are reflected rather than absorbed. This tent should remain cool longer than a dark tent.)

. . . .

5. WHAT AFFECTS THE FINAL TEMPERATURE OF A WATER MIXTURE? (3–6)

Materials

   • Styrofoam cups (at least 250 ml)
   • Graduated cylinders or measuring cups
   • Thermometers or temperature probes with CBL software
   • Stirring spoons

ENGAGE

   a. Ask: *What happens to the temperature of bath water when you add hot water to cold water? Does the amount of hot water and cold water matter? How could you predict the new temperature when hot and cold water are mixed?*

EXPLORE

   b. Tell students to plan an investigation to determine the final temperature when hot and cold water are mixed. Students could plan and conduct the following activity in cooperative groups:

     1. Pour the following volumes of water at the indicated temperatures into separate Styrofoam cups:

       • 100 ml of hot water
       • 100 ml of cold water
       • 50 ml of hot water
       • 50 ml of cold water
       • 150 ml of hot water
       • 150 ml of cold water

2. Measure and record the temperature of the 100 ml samples of water in a copy of the prepared data table (see illustration). If possible, make all temperature measurements in degrees Celsius.
3. In a third cup, carefully mix and stir the two 100 ml samples of water.
4. Measure and record the final temperature.
5. Repeat steps 2, 3, and 4 for the following mixtures:
   * 150 ml of hot water and 50 ml of cold water
   * 150 ml of cold water and 50 ml of warm water

c. Instruct cooperative group recorders to record their data on the class master data table.

TEMPERATURE OF WATER MIXTURES			
	Amount of Water in Each Container	**Initial Temperature of Water**	**Final Temperature of Mixture**
Mixture 1	100 ml		
	100 ml		
Mixture 2	150 ml		
	50 ml		
Mixture 3	50 ml		
	150 ml		
Mystery Mixture			Predicted _____
			Measured _____

EXPLAIN

d. Ask: *What patterns do you see in the class data? In what ways do these patterns help you predict the final temperature of the mixtures?* Lead students to notice that if the volumes of two samples of water are the same, the final temperature will be halfway between the two initial temperatures. If the volumes of the two samples are different, the final temperature will be nearer the initial temperature of the larger sample.

ELABORATE

e. Tell students you are going to give them a new water mixing problem, but they will need to predict the final temperature before they mix the water samples and take data.
f. Prepare a large container of cold water at near freezing temperature (but with no ice). Prepare another large container of water at room temperature. Give materials managers a cup of cold water and a cup of room temperature water.
g. Instruct groups they are going to mix 175 ml of cold water with 50 ml of warm water. Ask groups to make a prediction of the final temperature and then to conduct the investigation. Predictions do not need to be exact. For example, a group may just predict that the final temperature will be halfway between the temperatures of the two samples or very near the temperature of the larger sample.
h. Instruct recorders to record the predicted and final temperatures of their mixtures on a class chart. Invite students to present and discuss their predictions, the basis of the predictions, and the final temperatures obtained.

Explain that the final temperature of a mixture depends on both the initial temperatures and volumes of the samples. When a large volume of water is mixed with a smaller volume of water, the final temperature will be nearer the initial temperature of the large volume. There are actually mathematical ratios here that can be dealt with at upper grades.

Nature of Scientific Inquiry

i. Ask: *What have you done in this investigation that is like what scientists do?*

Lead students to understand that they have formulated a problem, planned and conducted an investigation, used a thermometer and graduated cylinder to collect data, recorded data in a table, interpreted the data and formed an explanation for experimental results, and tested the explanations through a prediction. These are some of the things scientists do.

EVALUATE

j. Use the following item to check student understanding of the principle presented in this lesson:

1. The water that comes from your cold faucet is 10°C. The water that comes from your hot faucet is 72°C. If you mix equal parts of water from each faucet in the bathtub, what will be the initial temperature of your bath water? How do you know? (41°—Since I put in equal amounts of the two temperatures of water, the resulting temperature is halfway between the two temperatures.)

V. LIGHT

▶ *Science Background*

Visible light is a form of energy. In empty space, light travels at a speed of 186,000 miles per second.

Because our eyes are light detectors, light is an especially important part of our lives, enabling us to see the world around us. We see objects when light that is either emitted or reflected from an object reaches our eyes. Further, light is the energy source for photosynthesis and the growth of plants that sustain both human and animal life. Thus, light is at least indirectly essential for most forms of life.

NSES   Science Standards

All students should develop an understanding of

• light, heat, electricity, and magnetism (K–4).

Concepts and Principles That Support the Standards

• Light can be reflected by a mirror, refracted by a lens, or absorbed by an object (K–4).
• Light travels in straight lines until it strikes an object (K–4).

A. SOURCES AND RECEIVERS OF LIGHT

Objectives

1. Distinguish between sources and reflectors of light.
2. Identify and describe human-constructed sources of light (e.g., lightbulbs) and natural sources of light (e.g., the sun).
3. Explain that our eyes are detectors of light and that we can "see" an object only if light is emitted or reflected from the object.
4. Identify materials that are transparent, translucent, and opaque, and explain what we "see" when each of these materials is placed over an object.

1. HOW DO WE SEE THINGS? (1–5)

Materials

- Flashlights
- Shoe boxes
- Assorted small objects

Safety Precautions

As they study light, impress on students the importance of protecting their eyes at all times. Students should never look directly into the sun or any other bright light source. Also, they should never look into a laser light source or shine a laser toward someone else.

ENGAGE

a. Darken the room completely and write this statement on the chalkboard: "We cannot see without light." Tell students to read what you have written. Illuminate the sentence with a flashlight and tell students to read it. Ask: *Why did the words on the chalkboard appear? Is light needed in order for us to see?*

EXPLORE

b. Cut two small holes in a shoe box, one for students to look into the box and the other to illuminate the inside of the box with a flashlight. Place an object in the box, cover the flashlight hole, and put the top on the box. Tell students to look into the box and describe the object. Illuminate the object with the flashlight and tell students to describe the object again.

c. Build a small electric circuit consisting of a bulb in a bulb holder, a battery in a battery holder, a switch, and wires. Place the circuit inside another shoe box with only one hole cut in the end of it. Arrange the circuit so the switch is outside the box and place the top on the box. Tell students to look into the box and describe the objects in it. Tell them to activate the switch and describe the objects again.

EXPLAIN

d. Ask: *How did light enable you to see the statement on the chalkboard? How did the flashlight enable you to see the object in the shoe box?* Lead students to understand that the eye is a receiver of light, like the ear is a receiver of sound. We see things only when light from them reaches our eyes. *Why were you able to see the bulb in the box?* (Light coming from the bulb reached our eyes and enabled us to see it.) Explain that there are natural sources of light, such as a flame, and artificial, human-constructed sources of light, such as the lightbulb.

ELABORATE

e. Tell the student groups that they have 5 minutes to make a list of the objects/things they can see in the classroom or outside now. When the 5 minutes are up, encourage them to discuss in their small groups: *What enables you to see these objects?* Then have them indicate which of the things on their list produce their own light and which only reflect light. Have a whole class discussion about their conclusions.

f. Ask: *Why are you able to see the sun?* (It produces light.) *Why are you able to see the moon?* (It reflects light from the sun.)

EVALUATE

g. To assess student understanding about the effect of light on what we see, ask students to respond to the following.

1. Imagine you are exploring a cave when your yellow flashlight goes out. No one else in your group has a source of light. No light is entering the cave from outside. It is completely dark.

   Which of the following statements best describes what you see in the the dark cave?

   A. I can't see my flashlight at all, even after my eyes are adjusted to the dark cave.
   B. After my eyes are adjusted to the dark cave, I can see my yellow flashlight.
   C. After my eyes are adjusted to the dark cave, I can see my flashlight but I can't see its yellow color.
   D. After my eyes are adjusted to the dark cave, I can only see a faint outline of my flashlight.

2. Explain why you selected the answer you did.

2. WHY CAN WE SEE CLEARLY THROUGH SOME MATERIALS AND NOT OTHERS? (K–2)

Materials

- Transparent materials (clear plastic wrap, clear glass)
- Translucent materials (wax paper, cloudy plastic, tissue paper)
- Opaque materials (cardboard, aluminum foil, wood)

ENGAGE

a. Allow students to examine a small object placed underneath a sheet of wax paper or a piece of cloudy plastic. Ask: *What do you see? Why is the object not easily seen?*

EXPLORE

b. Give each group of students some samples of transparent, translucent, and opaque materials. Ask the students to place one kind of material at a time over a printed page. For each material, have students fill in a chart with one of these choices: (1) can see through it easily; (2) can see through it but not very clearly; (3) cannot see through it.

EXPLAIN

c. Ask: *Through which of the materials could you see the print on the page easily? Through which of the materials could you tell there was print on the page but it could not be seen clearly? Through which of the materials was it impossible to see the print on the page?* List the student responses in three columns on the board. Introduce the terms *transparent*, *translucent*, and *opaque* by adding them as headings to the three column chart on the board. Guide students to understand that light is transmitted through transparent media, such as air, water, and glass, so the print was clearly visible. Translucent materials transmit some light, so the print was not so clear. Opaque materials do not transmit any of the light energy striking them, so the print was not possible to see.

ELABORATE

d. Using the same materials as before, let the students look through them at the lights on the ceiling of the classroom. Ask: *In terms of how much light comes through, what is the difference between the transparent, translucent, and opaque materials?*

e. Have them classify other objects/materials in the room according to their ability to transmit light as transparent, translucent, or opaque.

EVALUATE

f. To check student understanding about this concept, ask them to complete this chart in their science notebook.

Type of material		Translucent	
How much light is transmitted	Nearly all		
Example			Aluminum foil

B. HOW LIGHT TRAVELS

▶ *Science Background*

Light travels in straight lines until it is absorbed, reflected, or refracted by an object. Unlike sound, light cannot ordinarily bend around corners. Evidence that light travels in straight lines is apparent in our daily lives: beams of sunlight streaming through windows, not being able to see around corners, looking straight at objects to see them. The inverted image that is formed on the screen of a pin-hole camera is also evidence that light travels in straight lines.

Objectives

1. Demonstrate that light travels in straight lines unless it is absorbed, refracted, or reflected by an object.
2. Construct a pin-hole camera and demonstrate how it works to form an image.
3. Describe the pathway of light as it passes through a hole in the end of a pin-hole camera and forms an inverted image on a wax paper screen in the camera.
4. Investigate how the size and number of holes affects the image produced in a pin-hole camera.

1. WHAT TYPE OF PATH DOES LIGHT TAKE AS IT TRAVELS? (3–6)

Materials

- Flashlight or projector
- Index cards
- Hole puncher or pointed object (pencil)
- Modeling clay
- Wax paper

ENGAGE

a. Tell a child to stand behind a barrier or just outside the classroom so that she can be heard but not seen. Instruct the child to speak softly. Ask: *Can you hear her talking? Can you see her? Why can you hear someone talking when the person is out of sight?*

EXPLORE

b. Holding three or four index cards together, punch a 1/4 inch (7 mm) hole in the center of each card. Stand each card up in a lump of modeling clay. Instruct students to space the cards about 30 cm apart and to arrange them in such a way that light from a flashlight passes through the center hole in each of the cards.

EXPLAIN

c. Ask: *What must you do to the holes in the index cards if light is to pass through them? Do you think that light travels along a straight or curved pathway? What is your evidence, or why do you think so? Can light travel around an opaque object? Can sound travel around an opaque object? How can you test your inference about how sound travels?*

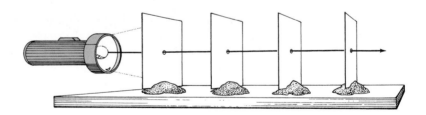

▶ *Science Background*

A pin-hole camera can be used to illustrate what happens in a regular camera. In a pin-hole camera, light passes through a small hole in the end of a box and forms an inverted image on a wax paper screen. In a real camera, light is focused by a lens and forms an inverted image on a strip of film.

2. HOW CAN YOU MAKE A PINHOLE CAMERA? (3–6)

Materials

For each student:

- Two plastic cups, opaque (16 oz) or two cardboard tubes
- Two rubber bands
- Scissors
- Recording sheets
  - Difference in image
  - Difference in number and arrangement of holes
  - Difference in size of hole

For each cooperative group:

- Aluminum foil
- Wax paper
- Masking tape
- Push pin
- Paper clip, large
- Nail
- Pencil

For whole class:

- Overhead projector
- Construction paper

DIFFERENCE IN IMAGE

Appearance of Arrow on Screen	Appearance of Arrow on Wax Paper in Pinhole Viewer
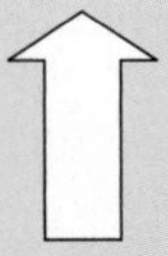 ⬆	
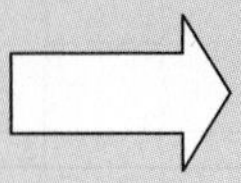 ➡	
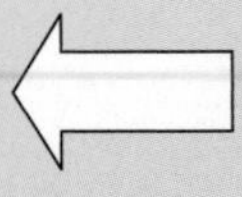 ⬅	
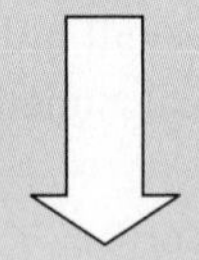 ⬇	

Describe how the image on the wax paper compares with the image on the screen.

What does the pinhole viewer seem to do to the image?

DIFFERENCE IN NUMBER AND ARRANGEMENT OF HOLES

Number of Holes	Appearance of Holes in Aluminum Foil	Prediction of Image on Wax Paper	Actual Image on Wax Paper
1			
2			
3			
4			

Describe how the number of holes in the aluminum foil affects the image produced.

Describe how the arrangement of holes in the aluminum foil
affects the image produced.

DIFFERENCE IN SIZE OF HOLE

Hole Size	Prediction of Image on Wax Paper	Actual Image on Wax Paper
• Pin Hole		
● Paperclip Hole		
⬤ Nail Hole		
⬤ Pencil Hole		

Describe how the size of the hole affects the image produced.

ENGAGE

a. Ask: *What are cameras used for?* (To create images of objects around us) Today each of you will build a pinhole camera, like this one. (Hold up a completed pinhole camera.) Then you will explore how changing the hole affects the image produced.

EXPLORE

b. Have students follow these directions to construct their pinhole cameras. It may be helpful to demonstrate pinhole camera construction for the class.
   1. Cut the bases off of both plastic cups.
   2. Cut a circle of wax paper and a circle of aluminum foil about 3 cm larger than the mouth of the cup.
   3. Place the circle of wax paper on the mouth of one of the cups. Use a rubberband and some tape to hold the wax paper in place.
   4. Hold the other cup so that the mouths of the two cups are together with the wax paper in between. Tape the cups together.
   5. Place the circle of aluminum foil over one of the open ends of one of the cups. Secure it in place with a rubber band and tape.
   6. Use the push pin to poke a small hole in the center of the aluminum foil.
c. Cut a large arrow from the center of the construction paper. Place the construction paper with the arrow-shaped hole on the overhead projector so that a large, bright arrow pointing upward appears on the screen or wall.
d. Encourage the students to hold their pinhole cameras with the aluminum foil end toward the bright arrow, then look into the open end. Ask: *What do you see on the wax paper screen in your pinhole camera? How does it compare to the bright arrow on the wall?*

Tell students to record their observations on the first row of the chart on the Difference in Image sheet by drawing what they see on the wax paper in the pinhole viewer.

e. Shift the orientation of the construction paper so the bright arrow on the screen or wall appears to point toward the right. Have students look into their pinhole viewers, then record the appearance of this arrow on the wax paper in the viewer. Reorient the construction paper two more times, first projecting a left-pointing arrow, then a downward-pointing arrow.

f. Have the students answer the questions at the bottom of the Difference in Image sheet: *Describe how the image on the wax paper compares with the image on the screen. What does the pin-hole viewer seem to do to the image?*

EXPLAIN

g. Encourage students to share and discuss their observations and the answers to their questions. The consensus should be that the arrow on the wax paper in the pinhole camera is smaller, not as bright, and the other way around, flipped, or backwards compared to the arrow on the wall.

h. Introduce the term *inverted* meaning "reversed in position."

i. Ask: *How does the image on the screen provide more evidence that light travels in straight lines?* Draw this figure below on the board. Ask: *Where does the ray of light from the top point of the arrow land on the wax paper, after it goes through the pinhole?* (On the bottom) *Where does the ray of light from the base of the arrow land on the wax paper, after it goes through the pinhole?* (On the top) Lead students to the conclusion that if the light travels in straight lines through the pinhole, then the image on the wax paper is inverted compared to the bright arrow on the wall. Remind students that there are rays coming from all lit parts of the arrow, not just the ends, and as they pass through the pinhole, the inverted image forms on the wax paper.

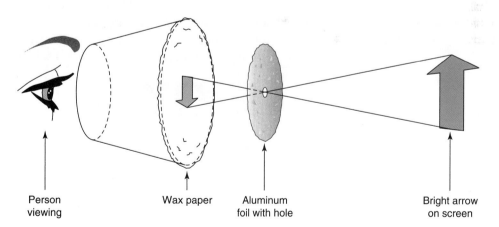

Person viewing   Wax paper   Aluminum foil with hole   Bright arrow on screen

ELABORATE

j. Ask: *What would happen to the image on the wax paper in the pinhole camera if the number or arrangement of the holes in the aluminum foil was changed?* Point out that the record sheet titled Difference in Number and Arrangement of Holes includes a chart on which they can record the appearance of the holes in the foil, their predictions of the image on wax paper, and their observations of the image on wax paper. Mention that the last three rows are left open for them to decide the number and arrangement of the holes. Tell the class that the bright arrow on the wall will stay in the pointing-upward position for all of their observations. Suggest that cooperation and sharing of pinhole viewers can reduce the replacement of aluminum foil, then allow them to investigate.

k. For an additional surprise, if students don't try rotating their pinhole cameras as they are observing with multiple holes, suggest that they try that.

l. Have students summarize their findings by responding to the two items at the bottom of the record sheet: *Describe how the number of holes in the aluminum foil affects the image produced. Describe how the arrangement of holes in the aluminum foil affects the image produced.*

m. Encourage groups to share their observations and summaries with the class. Ask: *Explain why you saw what you did on the wax paper during this investigation.*

n. Ask: *What would happen to the image on the wax paper in the pin-hole camera if the size of the hole in the aluminum foil was changed?* Point out that the record sheet titled Difference in Size of Hole includes a chart on which they can record the size of the hole in the foil, their predictions of the image on wax paper, and their observations of the image on wax paper. Mention that the last two rows are left open for them to try other sizes of holes. Provide groups with additional aluminum foil and suggest that one person make the hole shown on the first row, another make the hole for the second row, etc. Tell the class that the bright arrow on the wall will stay in the pointing-upward position for all of their observations, then encourage them to investigate.

o. Have students summarize their findings by responding to the item at the bottom of the record sheet: Describe how the size of the hole affects the image produced.

p. Encourage groups to share their observations and summary with the class. Ask: *Explain why you saw what you did on the wax paper during this investigation.*

EVALUATE

q. Ask students to respond to these items in their science notebooks.

1. You use your pinhole camera to look at a brightly lit EXIT sign. What will the image on the wax paper in the pinhole camera look like?

2. Explain why the appearance of the image on the wax paper in the pin-hole camera provides evidence that light travels in a straight line. You may use words and/or drawings.

C. LIGHT REFRACTION

▶ *Science Background*

Light ordinarily travels in straight lines, but it bends or refracts when it passes at an angle into a clear material, such as glass, plastic, or water. Lenses use the property of refraction to form images of objects. A magnifying lens bends the light coming from an object so that we see the object larger than it actually is. A lens can also be used to form an image of an object on a screen.

Objectives

1. Describe the refraction or bending of light rays passing through water, clear plastic, or glass.
2. Use knowledge of refraction to explain different light phenomena.
3. Define *magnifying power* and relate it to the curvature of a lens.
4. Define *image* and describe the image of an object formed on a screen.

1. WHAT IS REFRACTION? (3–6)

Materials

For the teacher:

* Glass
* Pencil

For each group:

* Flashlight
* Black rubber or plastic comb
* Two cylindrical jars of different diameters

ENGAGE

a. Place a pencil in a glass of water so that half of it is in water and half of it out of water. Ask: *What do you see? Why does the pencil seem distorted?*

EXPLORE

b. Provide each group with a flashlight, a comb, and two cylindrical jars of different diameters. Show them how to form rays of light by laying the flashlight on a white poster board and shining the flashlight through the comb. Instruct students to follow these directions:
   1. Fill a jar almost full of water, place it in the path of the rays, and observe what happens.
   2. Repeat the procedure with the other jar.
   3. Record your observations. Include any differences you observed.

EXPLAIN

c. In a large group, invite students to discuss their procedures and observations.
   Ask: *What did you observe? What differences did you observe in the effects of the two jars? Which jar, the larger or smaller diameter one, bent the light rays more and caused them to converge nearer to the jar?* Lead students to recognize that the smaller jar, which had the greater curvature of its surface, caused the most bending of the light rays.
   Explain that light rays are bent when they pass into and out of a clear material, such as water, plastic, or glass. The bending of light rays is called *refraction*.

Ask: *Why do you think the pencil appeared distorted in the glass of water?* Lead the students to understand that the water bent or refracted the light rays coming from the pencil, causing it to appear distorted.

2. WHAT IS A MAGNIFIER? HOW DOES IT WORK? (3–6)

Materials

For each group:

- Two or more cylindrical, glass jars or jugs of different diameters
- Magnifying lenses, including at least two lenses of different magnifying power
- Clear plastic sheets, such as transparency sheets (sandwich bags might be substituted)
- Dropper

ENGAGE

a. Obtain two cylindrical, glass jars of different diameters. Fill them with water within a few centimeters of the top. Allow students to look through each jar of water at some small writing. You can place the jars on a tray and carry them around the room for all students to see. Ask: *What do you see? Do you see the same thing through each jar? Which jar makes things appear larger? Why do you think the jars of water magnify? What other things will magnify?*

EXPLORE

b. Arrange students in small groups of three or four. Provide each group a clear plastic sheet, a dropper, and a small container of water. Tell students to place different-sized drops of water on the plastic sheet and to look through the drops at some very small writing. Ask: *What do you see through drops of different sizes? Do different-sized drops magnify differently?* (Note: Very small drops provide greater magnification.) Tell students to record their observations on a record sheet or in their science journals.

c. Provide at least two magnifiers of different magnifying power to each group. If necessary, show students how to use the magnifiers. Lead students to examine writing and different objects through each of the magnifying lenses. Lead students to compare the magnifying lenses. Ask: *How are your magnifying lenses different? What makes lenses have different magnifying power?*

EXPLAIN

d. Invite students to share their observations.

Explain that what your students see through a lens is called an *image*. Lenses fool our eyes; we think the light comes from the image, when it really comes from the object and only appears to come from the image. The lens bends or *refracts* the light, making it appear to come from the image.

Define the *magnifying power* of a lens as the number of times bigger it can make an object appear or how many times bigger the image is than the object. Ask: *Which jar had a greater magnifying power?* (The smaller one) *Which water drop had a greater magnifying power?* (The smaller one) *Why do you think this is so?* Guide students to understand that the smaller jar and smaller water drops have a greater curvature. Light is refracted or bent more when the surface at which refraction is occurring is curved more. The magnifying power of a magnifier depends on how much the surface of the magnifier is curved. The greater the curvature, the greater the magnifying power.

e. Ask: *Which magnifying lens had a greater magnifying power? Did that lens have a greater curvature?* If lenses are of the same diameter, the lens with greater curvature will be the one that is thicker in the middle.

ELABORATE

f. Challenge students to measure the magnifying power of each of their magnifying lenses. This might be done by examining a millimeter scale through a lens to determine the number of times bigger an image appears than the object.[3]

EVALUATE

g. To check students' understanding of the relationship between lens shape and magnification, have them answer the following question.
   1. Which of these lenses (viewed from the edge) would you expect to have the greatest magnifying power?

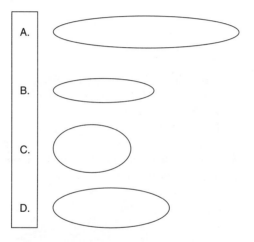

   2. Why did you select the lens that you did?

3. WHAT DO LENSES DO IN CAMERAS? (3–6)

Materials

For the class:

  * Lamp with 40 to 75 watt bulb

For each group:

  * At least two lenses of different magnifying power

ENGAGE

a. Ask: *Where have you seen lenses? What things have lenses in them?* List students' answers on the board. Students might suggest eyeglasses, contact lenses, the eye, microscopes, telescopes, projectors, binoculars, cameras, and other instruments.
   Ask: *What do lenses do in cameras? How do they work?*

---

[3]Adapted and modified from *More than Magnifiers*, one of more than 75 teacher's guides in the Great Explorations in Math and Science (GEMS) series, available from the Lawrence Hall of Science, University of California at Berkeley. For more information, visit the website at http://www.lhsgems.org.

EXPLORE

b. Arrange students in groups. Provide two lenses of different magnifying power to each group. Show students how to support a lens vertically by taping it to the bottom of a Styrofoam cup. Remove the shade from the lamp and place the lamp in the room so that all groups have an unobstructed view of it.

Provide these instructions to students:

1. Tape each of the two lenses to the bottom of cups. Label the cups and lenses A and B.
2. Place lens A, supported by a cup, on the table so that it faces the lamp.
3. Fold a white sheet of paper along two opposite edges so it will stand up.
4. Place the sheet of paper behind the lens and move it back and forth until you see an image of the lamp on the paper.

5. Measure and record the distance from the lens to the image on the paper.
6. Ask: *Is the image inverted or right side up?* (Inverted) *Is the image of the lamp larger or smaller than the lamp itself?* (Smaller) Record your answers on a record sheet or in your science journal.
7. Repeat the procedures for lens B. Is the image formed on the paper inverted or right side up? Is the image larger or smaller than the lamp?
8. Which lens, A or B, formed a larger image? For which lens, A or B, was the lens closer to the paper screen?

EXPLAIN

c. In a large group, invite students to discuss their procedures and observations.

Ask: *Why do you think the images formed of the lamp were inverted?* Draw the following diagram to show how light rays from the top of the lamp are bent or refracted by the lens and converge so that the lamp is upside down.

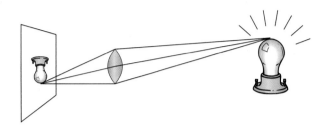

d. Ask: *How are lenses used in cameras? What do the lenses do? Do you think the images formed in cameras are right side up or upside down? Are they larger or smaller than the object forming the image?*

Draw on the board the illustration of a camera and lens showing an image formed on a film. Explain that some of the light coming from the bulb strikes the lens. The light is bent and converges on the film so that the image is small and upside down. The film is coated with a light-sensitive chemical. When the film is developed, the image of the bulb is clearly seen.[4]

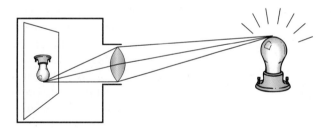

 D. LIGHT REFLECTION

▶ *Science Background*

Reflection, the bouncing of light rays, follows a pattern that can be discovered through investigations. Light reflects from a smooth, plane surface in such a way that the angle at which it strikes the surface is equal to the angle at which it reflects from the surface. Mirrors are excellent examples of reflecting surfaces. As a consequence of reflection, images can be seen in mirrors. In a flat, plane mirror, an image is symmetric with the object forming the image, but the image is reversed.

Objectives

1. Describe the reflection of light off reflecting surfaces.
2. Describe images in mirrors as symmetric with objects, but reversed.

---

[4]Adapted and modified from *More than Magnifiers*, one of more than 75 teacher's guides in the Great Explorations in Math and Science (GEMS) series, available from the Lawrence Hall of Science, University of California at Berkeley. For more information, visit the website at http://www.lhsgems.org.

1. WHAT ARE IMAGES IN MIRRORS LIKE? WHAT IS MEANT BY MIRROR SYMMETRY? (1–4)

Materials

For each cooperative group:

- Mirrors
- Set of pictures of butterflies, flowers, and other things that might show symmetry and of things that do not show symmetry (same set of pictures for each group)

ENGAGE

a. Ask: *When you look at something in a mirror, does it look exactly like the object when it is viewed directly? How could we find out?*

EXPLORE

b. Ask: *Do these pictures look the same in the mirror as when you view them directly?* Allow the students time to try it to find out. As you monitor their work, point out that the view in the mirror should be identical to the direct view, not upside down or switched around.

c. Challenge groups to sort the pictures into two groups: those that can look the same in the mirror as when viewed directly and those that cannot. Encourage them to look at the similarities of the pictures within each group. Ask: *What is special about the pictures in the group that can look the same in the mirror as when viewed directly?*

EXPLAIN

d. Ask: *What did you find out? Did all the pictures look the same in the mirror as when viewed directly?* (no) *How did they look in the mirror?* (upside down, backwards, switched, etc.) *Which pictures could look the same in the mirror and when viewed directly? Did you have to do anything to make them look the same?* (Put mirror in certain position; turn the picture a certain way) *How are the pictures in the group that look the same in the mirror and when viewed directly different from the pictures in the other group?* Lead students to realize that the image of an object is reversed in a mirror.

e. Introduce the term *symmetry* to describe a picture or shape that can look the same when viewed in a mirror as when viewed directly. Show how a symmetric picture can be completed.

f. Use one of the symmetric pictures from the students' collections and a mirror to introduce the term *axis of symmetry*.

   1. Find an axis (line) you think divides the picture in half so that if folded along that line, the two parts would match.
   2. Place a plane mirror along that axis.
   3. Look at the image of one-half of the picture in the mirror and compare it with the other half of the picture.

ELABORATE

g. Challenge groups to identify the axes of symmetry on the pictures they decided were symmetrical. Monitor their progress and clarify questions as you informally visit each group.

h. Provide students an activity sheet with all of the letters of the alphabet displayed in block lettering. Tell students to use a mirror to identify all of the axes of symmetry for each letter. For example, ask: *Does the letter* **A** *have an axis of symmetry? How many axes of symmetry can you find for an* **H**? Discuss with the students the axis or axes of symmetry of each letter of the alphabet.

Symmetry axis   Symmetry axis

EVALUATE

i. To assess student understanding of the concepts of mirror images and symmetry, have them complete the following items.

1. When you look in a mirror, do you see yourself as others see you when they are looking at you directly? Why or why not?

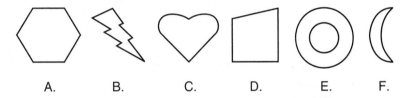

A.   B.   C.   D.   E.   F.

2. Which of the figures above could look the same in a mirror as when viewed directly. (A, C, E, F)
3. Which of the figures above are not symmetric? (B, D)
4. Which of the figures above have only one axis of symmetry? (C, F)

2. HOW DOES LIGHT REFLECT FROM A MIRROR? (3–6)

Materials

For each cooperative group:

- Light-ray source (flashlight, cardboard, scissors or knife, transparent tape)
- Mirror
- Rubber band
- Wood block
- Pencils or markers
- White poster board or large sheet of white paper

▶ *Preparation*

Make a light-ray source by obtaining a stiff cardboard shield about the diameter of a flashlight, cutting a slit in the shield, and attaching the shield over the lens of a strong flashlight with transparent tape. A light ray is formed when light from the flashlight passes through the slit.

ENGAGE

a. Ask: *When you look in a mirror, do you always see yourself?*

Hold a mirror facing the class. Adjust it so everyone might see themselves or another student's face. *Ask: Do you see yourself in the mirror?* (Only students directly in front of the mirror should say yes.) Ask a student who is looking into the mirror at an angle: *What or who do you see in the mirror?* (Someone or something on the other side of the classroom) After some discussion, ask: *What is the pattern of who sees what in the mirror?*

EXPLORE

b. In each cooperative group lay the light-ray source on a white poster board so you can see the light ray on the board. Attach a small, plane mirror to a block of wood with a rubber band. Put the mirror in the path of light. Tell children to mark a spot on the poster board and to orient the mirror so that the reflected ray hits the spot. Instruct the students to initially use trial and error to align the mirror so that the reflected light ray hits the desired spot. Gradually, the students should make and test predictions of how the mirror should be aligned to direct the reflected light ray to the spot.

EXPLAIN

c. Ask: *How does light reflect from a mirror? What pattern did you detect about how light reflects? How did you know how to align a mirror to make a reflected light ray hit a desired spot?* Lead students to understand that the angle formed between a reflected light ray and a mirror is the same as the angle between the incoming light ray and the mirror.

ELABORATE

d. Have students explore the rays and mirror positions again to check if the statement that "the angle between the reflected light ray and a mirror is the same as the angle between the incoming light ray and the mirror" is indeed true. Suggest that they place the edge of an index card against the reflective surface of the mirror. Then shine a light ray toward the mirror. Draw lines on the index card showing the incoming and reflected rays. By folding the index card at the point the light ray hit the mirror, students can check if the lines drawn on the card touch when folded. This would confirm that the angles with the edge were the same. If students know how to use a protractor, they can use it to compare the angles the rays made with the edge of the index card.

EVALUATE

e. To assess student understanding of the way a light beam would reflect from a plane mirror, have students respond to this item:

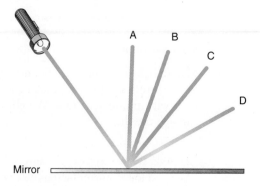

1. In this illustration, which line represents the reflected ray? How do you know?

E. LIGHT AND COLOR

▶ *Science Background*

Color is a response of the human eye to different frequencies of visible light. The visible color spectrum includes red, orange, yellow, green, blue, indigo, and violet. White light is a combination of all colors. An object appears black when all colors of visible light are absorbed by it. The color of an opaque object depends on the colors reflected by it. A red rubber ball, for instance, will appear red because it reflects mostly red and absorbs other colors of light. The color of a transparent or translucent object depends on the colors that are transmitted by it. For example, a green glass bottle on a sunny window sill will appear green because it transmits mostly green light and absorbs other colors of light.

1. WHAT IS WHITE LIGHT? (3–6)

Materials

- Prism
- Sheet of heavy, white cardboard
- Scissors
- Felt markers or crayons
- String
- Flashlights
- Colored filters (red, green, blue) for flashlights (these can be cut from colored clear plastic report covers)

ENGAGE

a. Obtain a prism. Place the prism in the path of a strong beam of light as indicated in the diagram.

Ask: *What do you see? What happened to the white light when it passed through the glass prism? What colors do you see?*

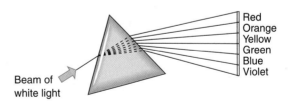

EXPLORE

b. This part of the activity can be done in small groups or as a whole group investigation.

Put a different colored filter on each of three flashlights. Darken the room for the best effect. Shine each of the flashlights on three different places on a white sheet of paper. Draw and color (or label) a picture to show how the paper looks.

c. Shine two of the flashlights so their beams overlap on the paper. Draw and color (or label) a picture to show how the paper looks.

Repeat this step with all possible pairs of colors (red-blue; blue-green; green-red).

d. Shine all three flashlights so their beams all overlap on the paper. Draw and color (or label) a picture to show how the paper looks.

EXPLAIN

e. Ask: *What did the prism do to the light?* (It separated white light into different colors.) *What does that tell you about the composition of white light?* (It is made up of different colors of light.)

f. Ask: *What happened when you mixed colored light beams from flashlights?* (A different color appeared.) Have students share what color was produced by each pair of overlapped colored light beams and what colors were produced when all three colored light beams were overlapped. Creating Venn diagrams based on student observations on the board might be helpful during this discussion. The class should agree that when these three colors of light were mixed, white light was produced. This supports the idea that white light is a combination of different colors of light.

ELABORATE

g. Introduce another way of mixing colors of light. Challenge students to construct spinning color wheels by following these directions:
   1. Cut out a circle about 10 cm in diameter from stiff cardboard.
   2. Divide the circle into three pie-shaped sections.
   3. Use red, green, and blue felt markers or crayons to color each section a different color.

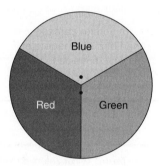

   4. Punch two small holes about a centimeter apart in the center of the cardboard circle.
   5. Pass a string about 60 cm long through the two holes; tie the free ends of the string forming a loop.
   6. Hold the loop by the ends and turn the cardboard color wheel many times, twisting the string as you go.
   7. Pull the two ends of the string suddenly and watch the color wheel spin. What do you see? What colors do you observe as the color wheel is spinning?

h. Encourage students to share their observations with the class. Expected comments include: *The wedges of color seem to disappear. The whole wheel looks white when it spins.* Ask: *What did the color wheel do to the light?* (It combined different colors to form a white color.) Ask: *Why do you think this happened?* Lead students to the idea that red, green, and blue light were reflecting from the wheel, and when it was spinning fast, our eyes couldn't see the sections separately so the reflected light mixed together so it looked white.

i. To further extend the lesson, let different groups color their color wheel sections differently. Have groups compare what they see with different color wheels.

j. Invite student groups to report on their procedures and findings related to their color wheels.

EVALUATE

k. To assess student understanding about the composition of white light have the class respond to the following question in their science notebook.

1. What evidence have you seen that white light is made up of many colors?

l. Use the following rubric to evaluate student responses to the question.

Exemplary:
- Clearly explains all three examples presented in the lesson.
  - White light separated into colors by a prism.
  - Colored beams mix to create white light.
  - Spinning color wheel.

Proficient:
- Clearly explains two of the examples presented in the lesson.

Developing:
- Clearly explains only one of the examples presented in the lesson.

Lacks Understanding:
- None of the examples presented in the lesson are suggested as evidence.

VI. MAGNETISM

▶ *Science Background*

The *National Science Education Standards* emphasize that, through the study of its history and nature, students should begin to understand science as a human endeavor. The study of magnetism is a good place for students to examine the long history of science and technology. As you guide students in learning about magnetism, provide them with interesting information about the history of the topic and make appropriate biographies and other books and resources available to them.

Four hundred years ago, William Gilbert, an English physician, wrote a book titled *On the Loadstone and Magnetic Bodies*. It was the first important work in physical science published in England. Gilbert's book provides the first written account of numerous experiments on magnetism, experiments that can be readily carried out in elementary and middle school science today. Gilbert argued for a new method of knowing, dedicating his book to those "ingenuous minds, who not only in books, but in things themselves look for knowledge."

 Science Standards

All students should develop an understanding of

- light, heat, electricity, and magnetism (K–4).

Concepts and Principles That Support the Standards

- Magnets attract each other and certain kinds of other materials (K–4).
- Magnets can be used to make things move without touching them (K–2).

A. MAGNETS AND MAGNETIC MATERIALS

Objectives

1. Identify materials that interact with magnets.
2. State that magnets come in many sizes and shapes.
3. Demonstrate that only some metal objects (those that contain iron) stick to magnets.
4. Demonstrate that magnetism will act through most materials.

1. HOW DOES A MAGNET INTERACT WITH DIFFERENT OBJECTS? (1–4)

Materials

For each group:

- Assortment of magnets, including bar magnets, U-shaped magnets, ring magnets, disc magnets, and other magnets
- Bag of assorted materials that are attracted to magnets (objects containing iron, such as paper clips and most screws and nails) and materials that are not attracted to magnets (such as wood, plastic, and paper objects, and non-iron metallic objects, such as aluminum nails, most soda cans, pennies, and brass fasteners)

Safety Precautions

- Keep computer disks, audio- and videocassettes, and credit cards away from magnets, as magnets can destroy information on them. Also, keep magnets away from computer and television screens and antique watches, as magnetism can damage them.
- Magnets must be treated with care so as not to destroy their magnetic effects. Magnets can be destroyed by dropping them, extreme heat, or storing two magnets of the same type together.

ENGAGE

a. Give each student a magnet. Without pointing out what it is or calling it a magnet, tell students to find out how the object interacts with the things within reach of their seats. Explain that when things interact, they do something to one another. Ask: *Did this object interact with anything you could reach from your seat? What?* Describe the interactions. Many possible interactions may be observed, but the key one is that some objects stick to a magnet.

EXPLORE

b. Ask: *What kinds of things will stick to this object?*

   Give each small group of students a bag of materials, some of which are attracted to magnets and some which are not. Instruct students to sort the objects into two piles, according to which objects they predict will stick to the object they were given earlier and which will not. When groups have made their predictions, have them use the magnets to test each object.

EXPLAIN

c. Ask: *How accurate were your predictions? Were you surprised by any objects you tested?* (Students might mention the aluminum nail or the brass fastener.) *Are there any metal objects in the things-that-don't-stick pile? What do you think is the difference between the metal objects in the "will stick" and "won't stick" piles?*

d. Ask: *Does anyone know the name of the object they have been using to test the objects in the bag?* (A magnet) *What have you discovered that magnets do? Are all magnets the same?* (No, they come in different shapes and sizes, but the same things stick to all of them.)

TEACHING BACKGROUND

Iron is the only common kind of metal that magnets attract. Magnets will not stick to such metals as aluminum, copper, and brass. Magnets stick to steel because steel is mostly iron.

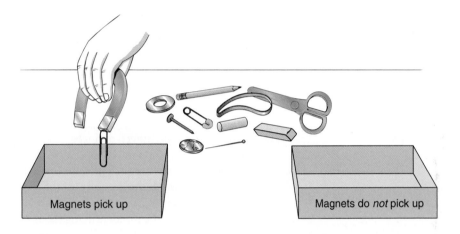

Magnets pick up | Magnets do *not* pick up

ELABORATE

e. Ask students to explore the room to determine which objects interact with magnets. Place "NO MAGNETS HERE!!" signs on computers, computer and television screens, computer disks, and audio- and videocassettes. Caution students not to bring magnets near these objects, because magnets can damage them.

EVALUATE

f. To check for understanding about which objects are attracted to magnets, ask students to answer the following questions in their science notebook:
　1. *Which objects in the room contain iron?*
　2. *What is your evidence?*
　3. *Did some objects, such as painted objects, turn out to contain iron when you thought they would not?*

2. CAN MAGNETS INTERACT WITH OBJECTS THROUGH DIFFERENT MATERIALS? (1–4)

Materials

- Magnets
- Paper clips

ENGAGE

a. Ask: *Will magnets work through paper and other materials? How do you know? How could you find out?*

EXPLORE

b. Ask students to investigate if a magnet will attract a paper clip through different materials. Students should try a sheet of paper, cardboard, plastic tumblers, glass jars, aluminum foil, a tin can, and a sheet of steel, such as the walls of a filing cabinet.

EXPLAIN   c. Ask: *What kinds of things did you find that magnetic forces act through?*

ELABORATE   d. Challenge students to investigate how many pages of a book magnets can act through. Ask: *Does it matter which magnet you are using?*

> ### TEACHING BACKGROUND
>
> Magnetic forces act through most materials, although the magnetic interaction decreases with the thickness of the materials.

B. MAGNETIC INTERACTIONS

Objectives
1. Define the terms *force*, *attract*, and *repel*, and apply them to the interactions between two magnets.
2. Demonstrate procedures for mapping magnetic fields.
3. State in their own words the meanings of the terms *pole*, *north-seeking* or *north pole* and *south-seeking* or *south pole*.
4. Demonstrate a procedure for identifying the north and south poles of magnets.
5. State and demonstrate that like poles of magnets repel and unlike poles attract.

1. WHAT HAPPENS WHEN TWO MAGNETS INTERACT? (2–4)

Materials   For each group:

- Three or four ring magnets
- A pencil

ENGAGE   a. Ask: *How do two magnets interact with each other?*

EXPLORE   b. Give each pair or small group of students three or four ring-shaped magnets. Ask the students to find out what happens when magnets interact. Suggest that they record their observations and new questions on an I Notice/I Wonder chart.

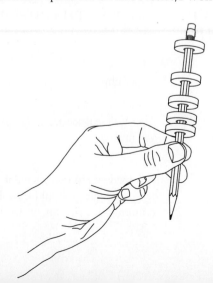

c. Allow time for exploration. If necessary, challenge students to try
  * using one magnet to move another magnet without the two magnets touching; and

  * placing several ring magnets over a pencil in different ways to see what happens.

EXPLAIN

d. Ask: *What did you do to test how the magnets interact? What did you find out about how the two magnets interact?* Building on the children's activities, use discussion and expository teaching to help them understand the terms *attract*, *repel*, and *force* to describe magnetic interactions.
  * When two magnets or a magnet and an object pull or stick together, we say they attract.

  * When two magnets push apart, we say they repel.

  * A force is a push or a pull. We can see some forces, such as when you push someone in a swing. Some forces, such as magnetic forces, are invisible and act without direct contact between objects.

  * Magnets can attract or repel each other. When two magnets come together, there is a force of attraction. When two magnets push apart, there is a force of repulsion.

  Ask: *What did you wonder about as you explored?* Collect the questions by writing them on the board or on chart paper.

ELABORATE

e. Tell students: In your group, select one of the questions you still wonder about. Design an investigation that will help you answer that question. Carry out your investigation. Then prepare a poster showing what you found out.

EVALUATE

f. Give each group a copy of the rubric so they have a clear idea of the expectations for their poster.

Rubric

Exemplary: Poster —
  * Includes all components of Proficient
  * Is very neat, easy to read, and well organized

Proficient: Poster includes —
  * Clear statement of the question being investigated
  * Clear statement of your procedure
  * Clear statement of what you found out
  * Correct use of the terms *attract*, *repel*, and *force*

Developing: Poster includes —
  * At least two of the components of Proficient

Needs Improvement: Poster includes —
  * Fewer than two of the components of Proficient

2. HOW DO THE ENDS (POLES) OF TWO BAR MAGNETS INTERACT WITH EACH OTHER? (2–6)

Materials
- Bar magnets
- Masking tape
- Red and blue crayons

ENGAGE

a. Ask: *How do bar magnets interact with each other? How could we find out?*

EXPLORE

b. Place masking tape over the ends of bar magnets so the N-pole and S-pole designations are obscured. Provide each group with three identical bar magnets with taped ends. Ask: *Can you find a way to determine which ends of the magnets are the same?* Give the class plenty of time to explore.

EXPLAIN

c. Ask: *What did you find out?* The students should arrive at the idea that if the ends of two magnets are the same, then they interact in the same way with the end of the third magnet. For example, if the ends of two magnets both attract one end of a third magnet, the ends of the first two magnets are the same. Tell children to use red and blue crayons to designate the like ends of the three magnets. (*Note:* Do not introduce the terms *magnetic pole* and *north* and *south magnetic poles* yet. They will be introduced through later investigations.)

d. Ask: *Now that you know which ends of the magnets are like and which are unlike, can you find a pattern or rule in how like and unlike ends of magnets interact?*

   Through exploration, discussion, and expository teaching of new concepts, make sure that students understand this rule:
   - When two magnets are brought together, like ends repel (push one another apart), while unlike ends attract (pull one another together).

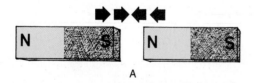

A

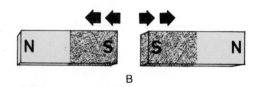

B

ELABORATE

e. Ask the students to try out their rule with other types of magnets, such as ring-shaped or horseshoe magnets.

EVALUATE

f. To check for student understanding about the interaction of the ends of magnets, have them answer the following items:

   Fill in the blanks, so that the following sentences are true.

   1. When like ends of magnets are brought close together, they _____.
   2. When unlike ends of magnets are brought close together, they _____.

3. WHAT ARE MAGNETIC FORCE LINES? (2–6)

Materials
- Magnets
- Iron filings
- Food storage bags

▶ *Preparation*

Sprinkle iron filings into a large, transparent, food storage bag so that a thin layer covers about three-fourths of the area of one side of each bag. Prepare a bag for each cooperative group of students.

ENGAGE

a. Ask: *How will a magnet interact with the material in this storage bag?*

EXPLORE

b. Ask students to explore what happens when a magnet touches or is brought near a bag containing iron filings. Give students these instructions:
   - Spread an iron filings bag out flat on your desk. Tap the bag lightly so that the iron filings are evenly distributed. Slide a bar magnet under the bag. Tap the bag again so that the iron filings move about. (See the diagram.)

   - Draw a diagram of the magnet's field as shown by the iron filings.

   - Investigate the field around two magnets placed end to end a few centimeters apart so that the magnets attract. Draw a diagram showing the reaction of the iron filings.

   - Investigate the field around two magnets placed end to end a few centimeters apart so that the magnets repel. Draw a diagram showing the reaction of the iron filings.

EXPLAIN

c. Ask: *What did you observe about the magnetic field around a single bar magnet? What did you observe about the magnetic field for attracting bar magnets? What did you observe about the magnetic field for repelling bar magnets?*

d. Explain that all magnets have two regions where the magnetic interaction with other magnets or magnetic materials is strongest. These regions are called *poles*. Point out that the concentration of iron filings is greatest at the poles of the magnets.

4. HOW DOES A MAGNET INTERACT WITH THE EARTH? WHAT ARE NORTH-SEEKING AND SOUTH-SEEKING POLES OF A MAGNET? (4–8)

Materials
- Ring magnets
- Bar magnets
- String
- Compasses

ENGAGE

a. Ask: *How can you use a magnet to tell directions?*

EXPLORE

b. Suspend a bar magnet by a string from a nonmagnetic support as in the diagram. Note the directions the ends of the bar magnet point. Compare the directions pointed to by the bar magnet and the directions indicated by a compass. How does the bar magnet interact with a second bar magnet? (See the following diagram.)

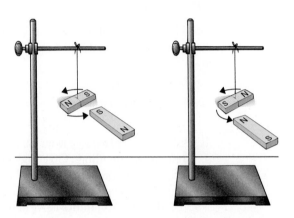

EXPLAIN

c. Ask: *What happens to the suspended bar magnet?* Lead students to compare the directions pointed to by the magnet and the directions indicated by the compass.

- One end of the magnet points toward the north (as indicated by the compass) and is called a north-seeking pole, or simply a north pole. The other pole of the magnet is a south-seeking pole or south pole.

- Our suspended magnet acts like a compass. The main part of a compass is a small permanent magnet attached to a pivot at the bottom of the compass.

- North and south are defined geographically by the rotational axis of the earth and astronomically by observations of the fixed North Star. The projection onto earth of a line drawn between us and our North Star, Polaris, will be within a degree of true, geographic north.

- The earth's magnetic poles are nearly a thousand miles from the geographic poles. Thus, a compass may point several degrees away from true north.

5. HOW CAN YOU MAKE A COMPASS? (4–8)

Materials

For each group:

- Steel needle
- Bar magnet
- Cork
- Plastic bowl of water

ENGAGE

a. Ask: *How can you make a compass?*

EXPLORE

b. Obtain a steel needle, a magnet, a cork (substitute a flat piece of Styrofoam), and a plastic bowl with a few centimeters of water in it. Holding the magnet in one hand and the needle in the other, stroke the needle about 25 times in one direction with the magnet.

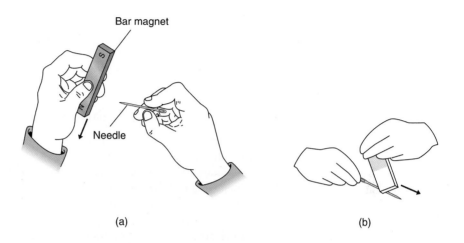

(a)   (b)

c. Float the cork in the water, and lay the needle on it.
    Ask: *What happens to the needle and the cork?* Rotate the needle and cork 90 degrees and then release it. *What happens to the needle-cork system when you release it?*

d. Bring the magnet near the needle on the cork. Ask: *What happens to the needle and cork now?*

EXPLAIN

e. Ask: *What is your evidence that stroking the needle magnetized it? What made the needle move when it was first placed on the cork? How is this like a compass? How can you make a compass? Which pole of the needle is the N-pole? What is your evidence?*

VII. ELECTRICITY

A. STATIC ELECTRICITY

▶ *Science Background*

More than 2,000 years ago, the Greeks were aware that when amber, a resinous substance, was rubbed with a cloth, the amber was able to attract small bits of straw. The Greek word for amber is *electron*, so the phenomenon came to be called *electricity*.

Benjamin Franklin, the American statesman and scientist, investigated electric phenomena in the 1700s. Franklin found that things could be not only attracted by electric forces but also repelled. Franklin proposed that the attracting and repelling forces of static electricity resulted from two kinds of electrical "fluids," which he called positive and negative fluids.

Static electricity is understood today in terms of these concepts and principles:

1. There are two kinds of electric charges in all materials: positive charges and negative charges.
2. In ordinary substances, positive charges and negative charges are balanced. These substances are electrically neutral.
3. When some materials are rubbed together, the friction causes the materials to acquire electrical charges.
4. Two electrically charged substances can interact.
5. An electrically charged substance can interact with a neutral substance by a process called *induction*.

NSES   Science Standards

All students should develop an understanding of:

- light, heat, electricity, and magnetism (K–4).

Concepts and Principles That Support the Standards

- The position or motion of an object can be changed by pushing or pulling (K–4).
- The size of the change is related to the strength of the push or pull (K–4).
- Without touching them, a material that has been electrically charged pulls on all other materials and may either push or pull other charged materials (*Benchmarks*, 3–5).

Objectives

1. Describe electrostatic investigations and identify materials that can interact electrostatically.
2. Describe ways electrostatic interactions are different from magnetic interactions.
3. Explain in their own words what is meant by electrical charge and how objects become electrically charged.

4. State and demonstrate evidence for the electrostatic force rule: Like charged bodies repel; unlike charged bodies attract.
5. Demonstrate and explain what is meant by electrostatic induction.
6. Apply the model of electrostatic interaction to explain evidence from electrostatic investigations.

1. HOW CAN YOU DEMONSTRATE STATIC ELECTRIC FORCES? (3–6)

Materials

- Plastic or acetate sheet
- Plastic rulers
- Hard rubber comb or resin rod
- Wool cloth
- Balloons
- Paper towels
- Paper clips
- Flour
- Salt
- Thread
- Bits of paper

ENGAGE

a. Have students rub a clear acetate sheet with a rough paper towel. (Coarse paper towels from restrooms work well.) Instruct them to bring the rubbed acetate near a pile of tiny bits of torn paper and observe what happens.

EXPLORE

b. Investigate to see what other materials interact with the acetate sheet. Try such materials as paper clips, bits of aluminum foil, flour, salt, cotton and nylon thread, and wood shavings from a pencil sharpener.
c. Rub a hard rubber comb or resin rod with a wool cloth. Try to pick up flour with the rubbed comb or rod.

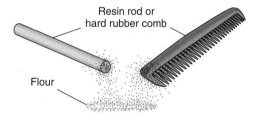

Resin rod or
hard rubber comb

Flour

d. Tie a 1 meter string around the mouth of an inflated balloon. Vigorously rub the inflated balloon with a piece of wool. Investigate to determine what materials interact with the balloon.

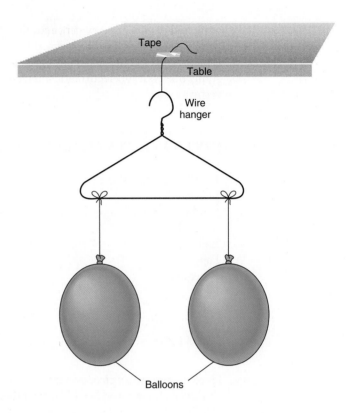

Tape

Table

Wire hanger

Balloons

e. Inflate a second balloon. Tie a 1 meter string around the mouth of the balloon. Vigorously rub the two balloons with wool. Suspend the two balloons by their strings from a support as in the diagram and investigate how they interact with each other.

EXPLAIN

f. Ask: *What happened when you rubbed the clear acetate sheet and moved it near the new materials? If the new materials moved, what must they have experienced?* (a force)

g. Ask: *What happened when you rubbed the comb or rod with a wool cloth and then moved it toward flour?*

h. Ask: *What did your rubbed balloon attract? Why do you think it happened? In what ways is this investigation similar to your previous investigation? Which materials did the ruler pick up? What materials did the balloon attract?*

i. Ask: *What happened when the two rubbed balloons were brought near one another? What kind of force did you observe, attraction or repulsion?*

j. Introduce the notions of positive and negative electric charges and electrical forces. Help the students relate each part of the explanation to some part of their investigation.

B. CURRENT ELECTRICITY

▶ *Science Background*

Current electricity refers to a movement of electrical charge along a conducting path. Electrical energy is produced in a battery and converted to heat, light, or motion in an electrical component such as a lightbulb or a motor. For energy to be transferred to an electrical component, there must be a complete conducting path—a complete circuit—from the battery along conducting wires through the electrical component and back to the battery along conducting wires.

If two or more electrical components are aligned so that current flows from one to the next, the circuit is a series circuit. If the components are arranged so that each is in an independent circuit, then the circuit is a parallel circuit. A switch is a device that breaks or opens a circuit so that it is not a continuous path and current cannot flow through it.

 Science Standards

All students should develop an understanding of

- light, heat, electricity, and magnetism (K–4).

Concepts and Principles That Support the Standards

- Electricity in circuits can produce light, heat, sound, and mechanical motion (K–4).
- Electrical circuits require a complete conducting loop through which an electric current can pass (K–4).
- Electrical circuits provide a means of transferring electrical energy to produce heat, light, sound, mechanical motion, and chemical changes (5–8).

Objectives

1. Demonstrate and explain through words and drawings how to make a bulb light in various ways, given one or two batteries, one or two bulbs, and one or two wires.
2. State, explain, and demonstrate the complete circuit rule:

   For a bulb to light,
   - the bulb must be touched on the side and the bottom;
   - the battery must be touched on both ends; and
   - there must be a complete circuit or continuous path along the wires and through the battery and bulb.
3. Explain in their own words what a conductor is and how to test a material to determine if it is an electrical conductor.
4. Identify and construct series circuits and use the complete circuit rule to explain why the other bulbs in a series circuit go out when one bulb is removed from its holder.
5. Identify and construct parallel circuits and use the complete circuit rule to explain why the other bulbs in a parallel circuit stay lit when one bulb is removed from its holder.
6. Demonstrate a switch and use the complete circuit rule to explain how it works.

1. HOW CAN YOU CONSTRUCT A CIRCUIT IN WHICH A BULB LIGHTS? (3–6)

Materials

For each student, at least:

- One flashlight bulb
- One battery (1.5 volt D-cell)
- One 15–25 cm wire

(Students initially need their own materials but will later combine materials with one or more other students.)

Safety Precautions   Discussing safe habits to use with electricity is a must.

- Caution children not to experiment with anything but 1.5 volt flashlight batteries (D-cells) and flashlight bulbs. There is no danger of electrical shock from these batteries.
- Children should wear safety goggles to protect their eyes from the sharp ends of the copper wires used in the activities.
- Tell children that if their wire gets hot, they should do something different with the connections of the wire(s).
- Children should never experiment with the electricity from wall sockets or from car batteries.
- Do not use electrical appliances near water; for example, do not use a hair dryer near a water-filled sink.
- When you pull an electrical cord out of a wall socket, grasp it by the plug and pull firmly.

ENGAGE   a. Tell a story about some hikers who lost their flashlight in a dark cave. One hiker had an extra battery, another had an extra bulb, and a third had a wire. *Can you help them light the bulb so they can get out of the cave?*

EXPLORE   b. Give each child a small flashlight bulb, a length of wire, and a 1.5 volt D-cell. (*Note:* A 1.5 volt D-cell is commonly referred to as a battery, although batteries actually have multiple cells.) Ask: *Can you make the bulb light?* Let the children work to light the bulb. Some children may take 20 minutes or longer to light the bulb. Resist the temptation to step in and "teach" them how to light the bulb. Encourage them to keep trying on their own. As they succeed, the children develop confidence in their own abilities to learn about electrical circuits.

As each child lights the bulb, ask: *Can you find another way to light the bulb?* Students may experiment by placing the bulb on its side or on the other end of the battery. If two or more children want to cooperate at this point, let them. More hands may be helpful. Be accepting and reinforcing of the children's efforts.

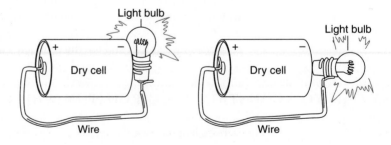

c. Ask children, individually, to draw pictures of what they did to light the bulb with one battery and one wire. Look at the children's drawings carefully to see if they have observed that the electrical path (circuit) is a continuous or complete one.

EXPLAIN

d. Ask the children to explain their drawings to you and to one another. Look at the drawings carefully to see if the wires touch the bulb on the bottom and the side.

Ask: *What two places must you touch a bulb for it to light? Where must the battery be touched?*

Referring to actual circuits and drawings, children should state, explain, and write the complete circuit rule:

For a bulb to light,

* the bulb must be touched on the side and the bottom;

* the battery must be touched on both ends; and

* there must be a continuous path through the battery, bulb, and wires.

ELABORATE

e. Give each pair of children a second wire. Ask: *Can you make the bulb light using two wires?* Children may simply twist the two wires together and make one wire of them. If so, ask: *Can you use two wires to light the bulb without the bulb touching the battery?* Also ask them to draw a picture of what they did to light the bulb using two wires, with the bulb not touching the battery.

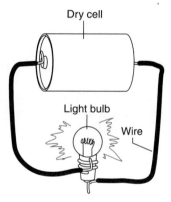

EVALUATE

f. As a self-evaluation of their understanding of how to light a bulb with just one battery and one wire, ask each child to do Prediction Sheet 1. For each frame the students should ask themselves: *Will the bulb light?* and then write *Yes* or *No* in the frame to record their prediction. After making predictions for all the frames, students should test their predictions by setting up a circuit like the one shown to try it and see. When all the children have completed the prediction sheet and checked it, go back over it with them. Ask: *Will this one light? Why won't it light? What could you do to get it to light?*

Prediction Sheet 1

Will the bulb light? If you are not sure, try it and see!

2. WHAT HAPPENS WHEN THERE IS MORE THAN ONE BULB OR BATTERY IN A CIRCUIT? (3–6)

Materials	
	• Batteries, bulbs, wires
	• Bulb holders
	• Battery holders

ENGAGE

a. Ask: *What happens when you try two bulbs? Try two batteries. Can you use three batteries and two bulbs? Does the orientation of the batteries matter? How could you find out?*

EXPLORE

b. Let children explore and discover. As they try different arrangements, have them complete an I Notice/I Wonder chart to record their observations and questions.

c. As the children try different arrangements, the need for "bulb holders" and "battery holders" arises. Give the children bulb holders and battery holders and demonstrate how to use them.

d. Children may discover that when batteries are placed end-to-end (in series), a positive terminal of one battery must be connected to the negative terminal of an adjacent battery.

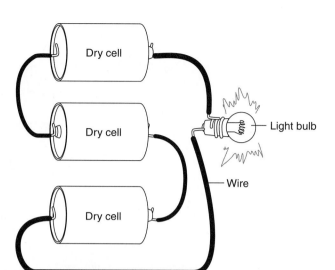

Dry cell

Dry cell

Dry cell

Light bulb

Wire

Safety Precautions   Do not allow children to experiment with more than three batteries. More batteries can result in burned-out bulbs. Remind students that if the wires become hot, the bulbs will not light, and they should immediately disconnect the wires from the batteries.

EXPLAIN

e. Encourage children to share and discuss the information on their I Notice/I Wonder charts with the class. If conversation lags, ask: *Who tried one battery and three bulbs? What did you notice? Did this make you wonder anything? What? Did everyone that tried this notice the same thing?*

f. Ask: *Can you trace the complete circuit path for each circuit you have built?* Help children see that the bulb holder is constructed so that one part of it is connected to the metal side of a bulb and another part is connected to the bottom base of the bulb. The terminals of the bulb holder are then connected to the battery. The bulb holder is doing the same thing the children were doing with their hands when they made the bulb light. The bulb holders provide a complete circuit path for the electricity.

3. WHAT IS A SERIES CIRCUIT? (3–6)

Materials

- Batteries, bulbs, wires
- Bulb holders

ENGAGE

a. Show the children the accompanying circuit illustration. Ask them to build the circuit using their materials.

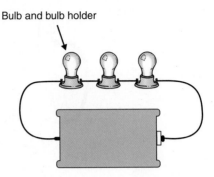

Bulb and bulb holder

EXPLORE

b. Ask: *What will happen to the other bulbs in a series circuit if one of the bulbs is removed from its holder? Try it and see.* (The other bulbs will go out.)

EXPLAIN

c. Ask: *What happened? Why did the other bulbs go out?* The children should tell you that the continuous path was broken when the bulb was removed.

Tell the children that electricians, scientists, and engineers call this circuit a *series circuit* because the bulbs are lined up in a series and electricity flows from bulb to bulb.

4. WHAT IS A PARALLEL CIRCUIT? (3–6)

ENGAGE

a. Show the children the accompanying circuit illustration and ask them to build it.

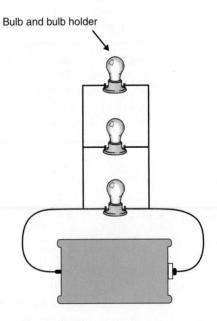

Bulb and bulb holder

EXPLORE

    b.   Ask: *What will happen to the other bulbs if one of the bulbs is removed from its bulb holder? Try it and see.* (The other bulbs remain lit.)

EXPLAIN

    c.   Ask: *What happened to the other bulbs when you removed one? Why did it happen?* The students should observe and explain that the other bulbs stay lit because it is still part of a continuous path with the battery.

       This circuit is called a *parallel circuit* because there are parallel paths through the bulbs for the electricity. Each bulb is part of an independent circuit with the battery.

    d.   Ask: *How are the electrical circuits in the classroom wired, series or parallel? If one light burns out, will the others light?* Through discussion, lead children to understand that electrical circuits in the classroom are wired in parallel. If the lights in the room are off, the TV or computers will still work. If one light bulb (or bank of lights) is out, the others still work.

       You might discuss strings of Christmas tree or holiday lights at this point. Most strings of lights sold today are wired in parallel. If one bulb burns out, the others still light. If the bulbs were in series, if one bulb burned out, none of the others would light. You would have to test each one of them to determine which one needed to be replaced.

5. WHAT ARE CONDUCTORS AND NONCONDUCTORS? (3–6)

Materials

- Batteries
- Bulbs
- Wires
- Bulb holders
- Battery holders
- Diverse array of conducting and nonconducting materials made from paper, cloth, wood, plastic, and metals of different kinds

ENGAGE

    a.   Hold up a battery, a bulb, and a wire. Then put down the wire. Ask: *If I didn't have a wire, could I complete this circuit so the bulb would light?*

EXPLORE

    b.   Make available to each cooperative group a diverse array of conducting and nonconducting materials. Instruct students to use the test circuit illustrated to find out which materials could be substituted for the wire and which materials could not. Place the test object (made of metal, cloth, wood, plastic, etc.) between the bare ends of the two pieces of wire. If the bulb lights, then electricity flows easily through that material, so it could be substituted for a wire. If the bulb does not light, then electricity does not flow easily through the material, so it would not be a good substitute for a wire.

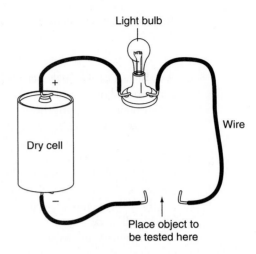

Light bulb

Wire

Dry cell

+

−

Place object to
be tested here

c. Design and use a data table in which to record your findings.

EXPLAIN

d. Ask students to share their findings with the rest of the class. They will probably report that the bulb lit when they tested some of the materials and did not light when they tested other materials. As students describe their findings, summarize the class data on the board using a T-chart with the headings *Bulb Lights* and *Bulb Does Not Light*.

e. Through discussion lead children to understand that some materials will conduct electricity. Others will not. Materials that conduct electricity well are called *conductors*. If conductors are substituted for wires, the circuit would be complete and the bulb would light. Materials that do not conduct electricity well are called *insulators* or *nonconductors*. If insulators or nonconductors are substituted for wires, the circuit would not be complete and the bulb would not light.

f. Ask: *What types of materials are good conductors of electricity?* (Metals) *How do you know?* (The bulb lights when metals are tested.) *Can you tell which of the metals you tested is the best conductor? How? What types of materials are good insulators of electricity?* (nonmetals) *How do you know?* (The bulb does not light when nonmetals are tested.)

EVALUATE

g. To assess student understanding about conductors and insulators of electricity, have students respond to the following items:
   1. How can you determine if a material is a good conductor or a good insulator of electricity?
   2. Predict which of these items is a good conductor of electricity. (Display or give each student a new collection of conductors and insulators to consider. Do not give students the testing device. They are only to make predictions.)
   3. What evidence from this investigation supports your prediction?

6. WHAT IS A SWITCH AND HOW DOES IT WORK? (3–6)

Materials
- Heavy cardboard
- Brass paper fasteners
- Paper clips

ENGAGE

a. Ask: *What does a switch do? How does a switch work? How can you make a switch?*

EXPLORE

b. Ask your students to make an electrical "switch" using a 10 cm by 10 cm piece of corrugated cardboard, two brass paper fasteners, and a paper clip, as in the illustration. Tell them to connect the switch into an electric circuit as shown.

EXPLAIN

c. Ask: *What happens when the switch is open (with the paper clip not touching the second fastener)? What happens when the switch is closed (with the paper clip touching the second fastener)?*

    The children should note that when the switch is closed, a complete circuit is formed and the bulb lights. When the switch is open, the circuit is broken and the bulb does not light. Take time for children to identify and talk about the electrical switches in the classroom.

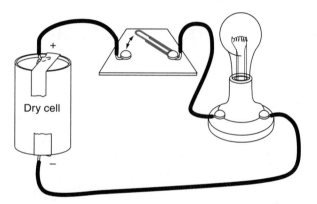

Dry cell

C. ELECTROMAGNETS

▶ *Science Background*

All magnetism is the result of moving electrical charges. When current flows in a wire, a magnetic field is set up. If the wire is placed over a compass, the magnetic field of the wire interacts with the magnetic field of the compass needle, causing it to deflect. Since the earth's magnetic field also affects the compass needle strongly, the needle may deflect only a small amount. More coils of wire increase the magnetic effects of the current. When the current is less, which occurs when a bulb is wired into the circuit, the resulting magnetic field produced will also be less.

NSES   Science Standards

All students should develop an understanding of

• light, heat, electricity, and magnetism (K–4).

Concepts and Principles That Support the Standards

• Electricity in circuits can produce heat, light, sound, and magnetic effects (K–4).
• Electric currents and magnets can exert a force on each other (*Benchmarks*, 6–8).

Objectives

1. Describe interactions between compass needles and current-carrying wires.
2. Construct an electromagnet.
3. Design and conduct an experiment to determine the effects of variables such as the type of core, number of loops of wire, and amount of current on the strength of an electromagnet.
4. Explain the cause of electromagnetic effects.

Materials

- Batteries
- Bulbs
- Wires (various materials and gauges)
- Iron nails or rivets
- Other rods to use as a core (wood dowel, plastic rod, pencil, etc.)
- Switches
- Paper clips

....

1. HOW DO COMPASS NEEDLES INTERACT WITH CURRENT-CARRYING WIRES? (4–6)

ENGAGE

a. *How does a current-carrying wire interact with a magnetic compass?*

EXPLORE

b. Instruct students to take a 50 cm length of wire and stretch it out on a table. Lay a compass over the wire as in the diagram. Orient the wire so the compass needle is perpendicular to the wire. Connect one end of the wire to one of the terminals of a D-cell. Quickly touch the other end of the wire to the other terminal of the D-cell and then disconnect it. Observe what happens to the compass needle. Move the wire so it points in different directions. Quickly connect and disconnect the wire to the D-cell.

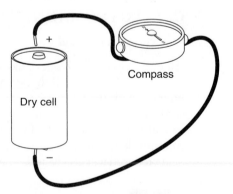

Compass

Dry cell

Safety Precautions

Since there is no light bulb or other resisting component in the circuit in this investigation, it is a "short" circuit. You must connect and disconnect the short circuit quickly so that the wire does not get too hot and the D-cell is not drained of electrical energy.

EXPLAIN

c. Ask: *What did you observe in this investigation?* (The compass needle moved.) *Why do you think this happened? What is your evidence that the electric current in the wire produced some magnetism?*

ELABORATE

d. Tell students to obtain a wire about 50 cm long and to wrap five loops of the wire around a compass as in the diagram. Leave the ends of the wire long enough to connect to a D-cell. Quickly connect and disconnect the wire to a single D-cell. Ask: *What did you observe?* (The compass needle deflected more than before.)

e. *Why do you think this happened? What evidence can you state that a magnetic interaction took place? Was the effect stronger or weaker than in the first investigation? What is your evidence that the electric current in the loops of wire produced some magnetism?*

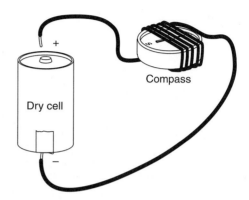

Compass

Dry cell

+

−

2. WHAT IS AN ELECTROMAGNET, AND HOW CAN YOU MAKE ONE? (3–6)

ENGAGE

a. Show children an electromagnet. Demonstrate how it can attract small objects like paper clips. Ask: *How can we make an electromagnet?*

EXPLORE

b. Give students these directions:
   1. Obtain a D-cell, a large iron nail or rivet, a 50 cm length of insulated (enameled) copper wire, some iron filings in a plastic bag, and some paper clips.
   2. Wrap the nail around the wire about 15 times as shown in the diagram.
   3. Place the nail on the bag of iron filings.
   4. Scrape the insulation off the two ends of the wire. Connect one end of the wire to one of the terminals of the D-cell.
   5. Holding the other end of the wire along the insulated portion, touch the bare end of the wire to the other terminal of the D-cell for only a few seconds. Move the nail around on the plastic bag and observe how it interacts with the iron filings.
   6. Repeat the activities using paper clips rather than iron filings to observe electromagnetic effects.

Safety Precautions

Do not let the wire and terminal remain in contact for more than a few seconds because

* intense heat builds up, and you could get a burn through the insulation; and
* the electrical energy in the battery will be used up quickly.

EXPLAIN

c. Ask: *What happens to the iron filings and the paper clip when the circuit is completed (or when the wire is touched to the battery)? What happens to the iron filings and the paper clip when the circuit is broken (or when the wire is removed from the battery)? What is the evidence that the nail became a magnet temporarily?*

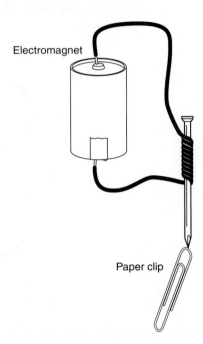

Electromagnet

Paper clip

d. Explain that when a loop of wire is placed around an iron object and current runs through the wire, the system becomes an electromagnet. The electromagnetic effect is suddenly reduced when current no longer runs through the wire.

3. HOW CAN YOU INCREASE THE STRENGTH OF AN ELECTROMAGNET? (3–6)

ENGAGE

a. Hold up the electromagnet from the previous activity. Ask: *How could you measure the strength of an electromagnet?* (By seeing how much mass it can pick up) *How could you change the strength of an electromagnet?* (Change or vary a component of the system.) *What are the possible variables in an electromagnet?* (Number of coils of wire, the way in which the coils are wrapped, core material, diameter of core, length of core, number of batteries, etc.)

Safety Precautions

Remember to only leave the wires from the electromagnet connected to the battery for a short time, as they will become hot. Do not use more than three batteries to power your electromagnet, because the increased voltage will cause the wires to get very hot very quickly.

EXPLORE

b. Tell students to design and conduct a controlled experiment to determine how the number of coils of wire around the core affects the strength of the electromagnet. State the question you are investigating, and state a hypothesis. Measure the strength of the electromagnet by how long a chain of paper clips it can pick up. Create a data table on which to record your findings. Instruct students to display their data in a graph like the one shown here.

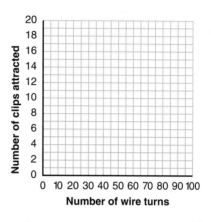

EXPLAIN

c. Ask: *What is the responding variable in this experiment?* (Number of paper clips lifted) *What is the manipulated variable in the experiment?* (Number of coils of wire around the core) *What variables have you controlled in this experiment?* (Type of wire, number of batteries, length of wire, core material, length of core, diameter of coil)

d. Have each group report their results to the class and post their graphs. Ask: *What similarities do you notice in the data?* (Slope of the line on the graph) *What relationship did you find between the number of coils and the strength of the electromagnet?* (The greater the number of coils, the greater the strength of the electromagnet.)

ELABORATE

e. Ask: *Do you think other variables might affect the strength of an electromagnet?* Have each group select another variable that they think might affect the strength of an electromagnet. Encourage each group to select a different variable to investigate. Have each group: develop a research question; state a hypothesis; design and conduct a controlled experiment to test the hypothesis; record data and graph it as before; and write a conclusion that describes the relationship between the manipulated and responding variables.

f. Have each group present its research question, hypothesis, procedure, results, and conclusion. Encourage discussion and questions. Lead the class to identify which of the variables studied affected the strength of the electromagnet. Have them give evidence from their data that supports their selection.

EVALUATE

g. To assess student understanding about the variables in this experiment, have students answer the following questions:
  1. What was the manipulated variable in your last experiment?
  2. What was the responding variable in your last experiment?
  3. What variables were controlled in your last experiment?

h. To assess student understanding about the variables that affect the strength of an electromagnet, have students answer the following questions:

    4. Based on the data collected by you and your classmates, which variable has the most effect on the strength of an electromagnet?

    5. Did any other variables have an effect on the strength of an electromagnet? If so, list them in order of the amount of the effect each variable has, from greatest effect to least effect.

    6. What evidence did you use to answer question 5?

    7. Describe how you would build the strongest possible electromagnet?

NOTES:

Information, recipes, and activities related to oobleck are excerpted from the GEMS teacher's guide, *Oobleck: What Do Scientists Do?* by Cary L. Sneider (Lawrence Hall of Science, University of California at Berkeley).

William Gilbert's book on magnetism is readily available as part of Volume 28 of the Great Books Series published by the Encyclopedia Britannica and found in many libraries.

Some of the concepts and activities in this section are adapted from a FOSS (Full Option Science System) grade 3–4 unit on Magnetism and Electricity.

Moisture in the air can interfere with electrostatic effects. Thus, electrostatic investigations are best done on a cool, dry day.

SECTION III
Life Science Activities

Life is a complex, exciting, and mysterious subject for inquiry. Students should have the opportunity to develop a deep and personal appreciation for the variety and wonder of life. Children are naturally curious about the diversity of life around them. Studying characteristics of plants and animals and of their habitats provides a good context for students to develop inquiry skills. Investigations in life science might involve:

1. asking different kinds of questions that suggest different kinds of scientific investigations;
2. observing and describing plants and animals;
3. classifying plants and animals (insects, fish, birds, mammals) according to their properties;
4. investigating plant and animal life cycles;
5. planning and carrying out investigations that show the function of different parts/structures of plants and animals;
6. investigating how different habitats or environments enable the needs of plants and animals to be met; and
7. investigating how the activities of people bring about changes in the environment.

As students learn more and more about plants, animals, and the environment, they become better prepared to assume responsibility for the well-being of living things on our planet.

Investigation Journals. Life science activities provide an excellent context for students to learn how to keep good records of investigations. Records may be kept in student observation journals, or you may want students to keep their records on pages you prepare.

Here is a sample prepared form for student investigation journals and examples of a child's journal entries from a seed germination experiment.

My Investigation Journal	
1. Key Question	• *Is moisture needed for seeds to sprout?*
2. My Investigation	• *We put a sponge in a bowl of water and sprinkled grass seeds on it. We put grass seeds on a dry sponge. We watched the seeds for several days.*
3. My Prediction	• *I think the dry seeds won't grow but the moist ones will.*
4. What Happened	

Day	What I Observed on the Wet Sponge	What I Observed on the Dry Sponge
1	• *Nothing is happening.*	• *Nothing is happening.*
2	• *Nothing.*	• *Nothing.*
3	• *Some sprouts are coming up on the moist sponge.*	• *Nothing.*
6	• *There was lots of grass on the moist sponge but nothing growing on the dry one.*	• *Nothing.*

5. What I Concluded	• *Seeds need moisture to sprout.*

I. CHARACTERISTICS OF ORGANISMS

Children can begin to appreciate the astounding variety of living things on our planet as they investigate seeds, plants, insects, and birds.

A. SEEDS

▶ *Science Background*

Amazingly, seeds contain the ingredients of life. A living seed may lie dormant for years until it is awakened by just the right conditions. To begin the **germination** or sprouting process, seeds need moisture, air, and moderate temperatures.

Seeds typically have very hard **seed coats** that keep water from penetrating them. Thus, they will germinate more quickly after being soaked or scarified to allow water inside the seeds. Within every viable seed lives a tiny **embryo plant**, complete with leaf, stem, and root parts. When the seed begins to germinate, a temporary food supply, stored within the **cotyledons** of the seeds, nourishes the growing embryo. Eventually, as the leaves develop, the plant obtains its energy for growth and survival from sunlight through the process of **photosynthesis**.

NSES Science Standards

All students should develop an understanding of

- characteristics of organisms (K–4).
- structure and function in living systems (5–8).
- life cycles of organisms (K–4).
- organisms and their environments (K–4).

> ### NSES
> **Concepts and Principles That Support the Standards**
>
> - Some animals and plants are alike in the way they look and the things they do, and others are very different from one another (K–2).
> - A great variety of living things can be sorted into groups in many ways using various features to decide which living things belong to which group (3–5).
> - Features used for grouping depend on the purpose of the grouping (3–5).
> - Organisms have basic needs. Plants require air, water, nutrients, and light (K–4).
> - Organisms can survive only in environments in which their basic needs are met (K–4).
> - Each plant or animal has different structures that serve different functions in growth, survival, and reproduction (K–4).
> - Plants and animals have life cycles that include being born, developing into adults, reproducing, and eventually dying. The details of this life cycle are different for different organisms (K–4).
> - All animals depend on plants (K–4).
> - Some animals eat plants for food (K–4).

Objectives

1. Recognize the wide variation in seeds.
2. Name the part of a plant where seeds are found.
3. Identify and describe different parts/structures of seeds (seed coats, cotyledons, embryo plants) and describe the functions of each.
4. Define *germination* and describe the sequence of events in the germination of a seed.
5. Ask questions about seeds that can be answered through investigations.
6. Design and carry out descriptive, classificatory, and experimental investigations to gather information for answering questions about seeds.
7. Use simple equipment and tools to gather data and extend the senses.
8. Through investigations, identify basic conditions for seed germination: air, water, and moderate temperature.
9. Use evidence from investigations and science knowledge to answer questions about seeds, construct explanations, and make predictions.

1. WHAT IS INSIDE A BEAN POD? (K–4)

Materials

- Bean pods
- Plastic knives
- Paper plates
- Paper
- Crayons, markers, or colored pencils
- Pea pods

ENGAGE

a. Distribute two bean pods to each small group. Ask: *What are these? What are their properties? What do you predict will be inside of them?*

EXPLORE

b. Encourage students to use all of their senses, except taste, to observe the outside of their objects. They should observe color, texture, size, shape, and other features. Ask students to record their findings using drawings and words.

c. Distribute a plastic knife to each group. Provide instructions on safe use of the plastic knife. Challenge students to use the knives to open their objects.

d. Encourage students to use all of their senses, except taste, to observe the inside of their objects. They should observe color, texture, size, shape, and other features. Ask students to record their findings using drawings and words.

EXPLAIN

e. Ask: *What observations did you make? What did you find inside? What are the properties of what is inside? Were both of your objects the same? Why or why not?* List the students' observations on the board. Encourage discussion about their findings. If the students don't use the terms *pod* and *seed*, introduce them. Tell students that the pod is the part of the bean plant that holds the seeds. Have them label the pod and seeds on their drawings.

f. Explain that although in everyday language we call bean pods *vegetables*, in scientific terms they are *fruits*. Scientifically, a plant part that contains seeds is called a *fruit*. The special name of the fruit of a bean or pea plant is pod. Tell students that they will study more about fruits in future lessons.

ELABORATE

g. Distribute two pea pods to each small group. Just as they did with the bean pods, students should observe and record about the outside of the pods.

h. Then students should open the pods. Ask them to observe and record about the inside of the pods. Tell them to label the pod and the seeds on their new drawing.

i. Lead a discussion of their findings. Ask: *What did you observe about the outside and inside of the pea pods?*

j. Ask: *How are the pea pods like the bean pods? How are they different?* Draw a Venn diagram (two partially overlapping circles) on the board on which to record student ideas. Label one circle *Bean Pods*. Label the other circle *Pea Pods*. As ideas are suggested, if there are ways the pods are alike, write them in the intersection of the circles. If suggestions are ways one type of pod is different from the other, write the idea in the nonoverlapped part of the appropriately labeled circle.

k. When all ideas have been added, review how the Venn diagram is a good way to record ideas when you find ways things are alike and different.

EVALUATE

l. Formatively evaluate students' observation and recording skills during the explore and elaborate phases of the lesson. The following checklists may be helpful to guide and organize the data you collect about your students' skills.

Observation Skills
☐ Takes time to carefully examine objects.
☐ Makes use of several senses in exploring objects.
☐ Identifies obvious ways objects are alike and different.
☐ Identifies detailed ways objects are alike and different.

Recording Skills
☐ Uses words.
☐ Uses phrases.
☐ Uses complete sentences.
☐ Uses drawings.
☐ Uses words and drawings together (labeled drawings or drawings with related descriptions).
☐ Drawings bear a resemblance to the objects that were observed.

☐ Realistic color is used in drawings.
☐ Size of drawing is similar to size of the real thing.
☐ Drawings are either an enlarged or reduced version of the objects, and they enable relative size comparison of objects observed.
☐ Drawings include much detail.

2. WHERE ARE SEEDS FOUND? HOW ARE SEEDS ALIKE AND DIFFERENT? (K–2)

Materials
- Paper plates
- Plastic knives
- Variety of fresh fruits (Children might be encouraged to bring a fruit from home. Tomatoes, apples, corn on the cob, apples, cherries, cantaloupes, bean and pea pods, and bell peppers make interesting fruits for children to observe.)

ENGAGE

a. Ask: *Are there seeds in each of these fruits? How many seeds are in each of the fruits? How can we find out?*

EXPLORE

b. Distribute paper plates and several fruits to each group. Tell children to use their plastic knives to cut their fruits open. They should find and observe the seeds in each one.

EXPLAIN

c. Ask: *Did you find seeds in your fruit? How many seeds did you find? What are the properties of the seeds? How are they alike? How are they different?*

ELABORATE

d. Tell the students to take turns sorting the seeds on the paper plates. Ask: *How have you sorted the seeds?* Allow groups to describe and explain how they sorted the seeds. Lead students to compare and contrast the different ways they have sorted the seeds and to discuss the best ways to sort them.

EVALUATE

e. To check for understanding about where seeds are found and how they are alike and different, have students respond to these questions.
   1. Draw pictures to show where the seeds were in two of the fruits you observed.
   2. How are seeds alike?
   3. How are seeds different?

3. HOW DO SEED PODS VARY? (3–6)

Materials
- Large number of pea pods
- Paper plates

ENGAGE

a. Ask: *Do all pea pods have the same number of peas?*

EXPLORE

b. Give two pea pods to each pair of students. Tell students to open the pods, count the number of peas in each pod, and put the peas and pods on their paper plates.

EXPLAIN

c. Ask: *Who found the most peas in their pods?* Record this number on the chalkboard. Also ask: *Who found the least number of peas in their pods?* Record this number on the board. Let each group report the number of peas they found in their pods.

d. Construct a histogram showing the numbers of peas in the different pods. Have one student from each pair come to the chalkboard and place an *x* above the numbers that correspond to the number of peas in each of their two pods. Ask: *What does the graph (histogram) show? What does it tell about peas and pods? If you open another pea pod, what might be the most likely number of peas in the pod? Why do you think so?* Discuss the notion of predictions and how predictions are based on collected evidence.

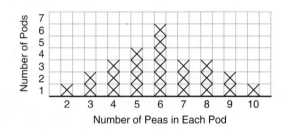

e. Give each pair another pea pod, and tell them to make predictions about the number of peas in each pod. Tell them to open the pea pods to test their predictions. Ask: *How accurate were your predictions? Why were your predictions so accurate (or so inaccurate)?*

ELABORATE

f. Ask: *Do you think there is a relationship between the number of peas in a pod and the length of the pod? How would you investigate to find out?* Carry out an investigation to see if the number of peas in a pod is related to the length (in centimeters) of the pod. Display class data in a line graph (number of peas in a pod on the y-axis; length of the pod in centimeters on the x-axis). Use the graph to make predictions about the number of peas in pods of different lengths.

Nature of Scientific Inquiry

g. Discuss how scientists use mathematics and how science can enable students to put mathematical skills, such as graphing, to work. Discuss the use of graphs to display data from investigations and to make predictions.

EVALUATE

h. To check students' ability to construct and analyze graphs, have them complete the following activity.

Another class collected data about bean pods. Their data table follows:

Bean Pod	Number of Seeds	Length of Pod (cm)
1	6	9
2	7	11
3	6	11
4	7	10
5	6	7
6	7	12
7	5	9
8	7	10
9	7	11
10	6	11
11	6	9
12	7	10
13	5	9

1. Construct a histogram showing the number of beans in different pods.
2. What does your histogram tell you about the beans and pods?
3. If the students opened another bean pod, what is the most likely number of beans it would contain? Why?
4. Construct a line graph (length of pod in centimeters on the x-axis; number of seeds in pod on the y-axis). Be sure to title your graph and label your axes.
5. Is there a relationship between the length of the pod and the number of beans in it? If so, describe the relationship.

4. WHAT ARE THE PROPERTIES OF SEEDS? (K–4)

Materials
- Assortment of seeds, perhaps from old seed packets
- Magnifying lens

ENGAGE

a. Give each group an assortment of 10 to 15 seeds. Ask: *How are the seeds alike? How are they different? How many different kinds of seeds do you have? What are the properties of each seed?*

EXPLORE

b. Students should be encouraged to notice and talk about the color, shape, size, and texture of each kind of seed. Provide magnifying lenses to each group to better observe details.

For very young children, include other small objects with the seed assortments, such as marbles, small pebbles (gravel), jelly beans, and other small pieces of candy. As children observe and talk about their collection, discuss what is living and what is not living. Caution children not to place small objects in their mouths, noses, or ears.

c. Invite students within small groups to play "I'm thinking of . . ." with their assortment of seeds. One child describes a particular seed or a type of seed and the other children try to figure out which one is being described.

EXPLAIN

d. Ask: *What characteristics do seeds seem to have in common? What makes a seed a seed? How can you tell a seed from a nonseed?*

5. WHAT DOES THE INSIDE OF A SEED LOOK LIKE? (K–4)

Materials
- Lima bean seeds
- Magnifying lenses

ENGAGE

a. Ask: *What do you think the inside of a seed looks like?* Discuss possibilities.

EXPLORE

b. Give each pair or group of students four lima bean seeds, one-half cup of water, and a magnifying lens. Have them place two seeds in the water for 24 hours and observe them regularly. After 24 hours, ask: *How have the seeds in the water changed? How are the soaked seeds different from the unsoaked seeds?* (They are larger.) *Why are the soaked seeds larger?* (They have soaked up water.)

c. Ask: *What do you think was happening inside the seed?* Have students carefully peel the outer coat from one of the seeds and examine it with the magnifying lens. Show students how to pull the coatless seed in half with a fingernail. Ask: *What does the inside of the seed look like? What are the distinctive parts of a seed?* Tell students to draw a picture of the inside of the seed.

EXPLAIN

d. Ask students to compare their drawings with the illustration.

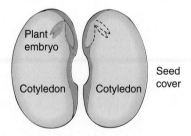

e. Provide names for the main parts of the bean seed: *seed coat* or cover; *cotyledon* or the meaty, pulpy part of the seed; and the *embryo*, with its embryo leaves, stem, and root.

6. HOW MUCH WATER CAN A BEAN SEED SOAK UP? (2–6)

Materials

- Unsoaked lima bean seeds
- Lima bean seeds that have been soaked overnight
- Balances
- 1 g weights
- Plastic containers

ENGAGE

a. Ask: *If the seeds are soaking up water, how can we find out how much water they are holding?* Through discussion, arrive at the possibility of weighing the seeds before and after they have been soaked to gather data on how much water seeds can soak up.

EXPLORE

b. Provide each group 10 unsoaked bean seeds and a plastic container. Tell students to use a balance to find the mass of their 10 bean seeds and to record their measurements in the data table:

DATA TABLE

Mass of 10 soaked bean seeds _____
Mass of 10 unsoaked bean seeds _____
How much water did the bean seeds soak up? _____

c. Instruct students to add water to the container to a level of about 1 cm above the bean seeds. Set the bean seeds aside for 24–48 hours to soak up water. Allow students to add water to their containers if necessary during this time. After the bean seeds have soaked, students should pour off the excess water and use a balance to determine the mass of the soaked seeds and to record this measurement in the data table.

EXPLAIN

d. Ask: *How much water did the bean seeds absorb?* Lead students to subtract the before-soaking measurement from the after-soaking measurement to determine how much water the seeds soaked up. Enter the difference in the data table.

e. Ask: *How does the amount of water soaked up compare to the initial mass of the bean seeds? Is it larger, much larger, smaller, much smaller, or about the same? Why do you think water is important in the sprouting of the dry seeds?*

Nature of Scientific Inquiry

f. Explain that scientists use mathematics in all aspects of scientific inquiry. Ask: *How did we use mathematics in this activity?* (Measuring, putting data in a table, subtracting, comparing) Discuss that one value of mathematics is using it to answer questions in science. *Mathematics is the language of science.*

7. WHAT HAPPENS TO SEEDS WHEN THEY GERMINATE? (K–4)

Materials
- A quart size plastic storage bag for each child
- Paper towels
- Stapler
- Lima bean seeds
- Ruler

ENGAGE

a. Ask: *What are some things we do with seeds?* When students suggest that we plant them, ask: *What happens to seeds when they are planted?* Explain that if we plant the seeds in the soil, we cannot see what happens to them underground. Tell them we will place the seeds in a plastic bag and observe what happens for a few days.

EXPLORE

b. Give each child a quart size plastic storage bag. Show students how to line the inside of the bag with a paper towel. Place eight or nine staples along the bottom portion of the bag about 4 to 5 cm from the bottom. Place five lima bean seeds above the staples inside the bag, as in the illustration. Gently pour water into the bag, being careful not to dislodge the seeds (the water should bulge slightly at the bottom of the bag to about a finger's thickness). There should be enough water to keep the seeds moist, but the seeds should not rest in water. Some of the seeds will germinate within 24–48 hours. Others may take longer.

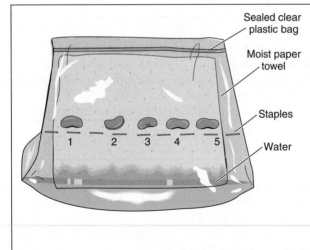

Sealed clear plastic bag

Moist paper towel

Staples

1 2 3 4 5

Water

- Line a quart size sealable, trans-parent storage bag with a moist paper towel.
- Place nine staples across the bag about 4 to 5 cm from the bottom, as shown in the diagram.
- Position five seeds to be germinated above the staples.
- The seeds may be presoaked for about 24 hours.
- Gently pour water from a small container into the bag, being careful not to dislodge the seeds (the water should bulge slightly at the bottom of the bag to about a finger's thickness).

The water will soak the paper towel and keep the seeds moist. The staples keep the seeds from lying in the water at the bottom of the bag. The transparent bag allows the seeds and roots to be observed.

c. Children should observe their germinating seeds and developing plants regularly for 2 weeks or more, recording daily in their investigation journals or on a prepared chart any changes in color, length, shape, texture, special features, and so on. To make the growth sequence clear, ask students to make drawings of changes they observe for one of their germinating bean seeds.

d. This investigation is a good one to promote careful measurement. Tell students to use a ruler to measure the length of the stem and root each day and to record the measurements in a chart. The chart should show length in centimeters for each day observed. The measurement data can then be displayed in a graph, which provides a picture of growth.

At lower grade levels, rather than measuring with a ruler, students can cut a green strip of paper to the length of the stem and a brown strip of paper to the length of the root. If the strips of paper are attached to a time line, such as a calendar, with the green strip above the line and the brown strip below, a visual display of growth over 2 or 3 weeks can be seen.

   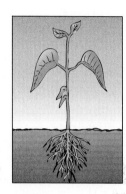

EXPLAIN

e. From their observational data, you want children to discover the sequence of growth changes for the beans from day to day—to learn that the root appears first and grows downward, that the stem is connected to the root and grows upward carrying the cotyledon with it, and that leaves grow on the stems.

f. In addition to observing the sequence of growth, students should also learn to recognize the seed coat, cotyledons, and embryo plant of seeds, and the root, stems, and leaves of the developing plants. Provide the names of these seed and plant parts.

ELABORATE

g. Have students add labels for seed and plant parts to the sequential drawings they have recorded.

EVALUATE

h. A good opportunity for peer assessment is available at the end of the elaborate phase. Students can exchange their recorded data with a peer and check for such things as correct placement of labels; neat, detailed drawings; and meaningful comments. A class discussion to select the criteria to assess creates focus for the analysis of each other's work. Students could write comments about their partner's work or just talk to their partner about his or her work.

i. To evaluate student awareness of the changes that occur during the germination process, have them write a description of how their seed changed into a seedling over time.

8. WHAT IS THE FUNCTION OF EACH SEED PART IN THE GROWTH OF THE SEEDLING? (3–6)

Materials
- Transparent storage bags
- Paper towels
- Soaked bean seeds

ENGAGE

a. Ask: *What are the parts of a seed? How do different parts of a seed change during germination? Which part of the seed do you think grows into a plant? How could we investigate to find out?* Lead children to observe that a lima bean seed has two cotyledons (it is a dicot), with the embryo embedded in one of them. Lead them to consider trying to germinate a cotyledon by itself, an embryo plant and cotyledon, an embryo plant by itself, and a whole lima bean, and to observe what happens.

EXPLORE

b. Assist children to set up a germination bag (as in Activity 7) containing
   1. one cotyledon by itself;
   2. one cotyledon with an embedded embryo plant;
   3. an embryo plant by itself; and
   4. a whole lima bean.
   Allow the students to observe their germination bags for several days, keeping records on their observations. *Note:* Open the bags daily for 15 minutes to prevent mold formation. Add just enough water to keep the paper towel slightly moist.

EXPLAIN

c. Ask: *Which of the seed parts, if any, started to grow? Why do you think that is so? Which parts did not grow at all? What do you conclude from your investigation about what seed parts are necessary for seed germination and growth into a plant?* (Only the whole seed and the one cotyledon and embryo produced growth.) *What do you think the role of the embryo was in sprouting? What do you think the role of the cotyledon was? Why do seeds not germinate (sprout) if the embryo is removed? Why do seeds not germinate if the cotyledon is removed?*

9. WHAT CONDITIONS ARE NEEDED FOR SEEDS TO GERMINATE OR SPROUT? (3–6)

Materials

- Lima bean seeds
- Radish seeds
- Transparent storage bags
- Paper towels
- Stapler

ENGAGE

a. Ask: *What do seeds need to germinate?*

EXPLORE

b. Ask: *How could we find out?* Lead children to suggest an investigation to determine if light is needed for seed germination. In the investigation, the same kinds of seeds are placed in two germination bags. One bag is placed in a well-lit place; the other in a very dark place. Ask: *What is the manipulated variable?* (The amount of light) *What is the responding variable?* (The germination of the seeds) *What variables should be controlled?* Emphasize that to be a controlled investigation, the moisture in each bag and its temperature have to be the same.

c. Let groups of children set up the investigation and observe the seeds for about 2 weeks, being careful not to expose the dark seeds to light. Tell students to keep their observational records in a chart like the one illustrated.

Seed name and amount	Date planted	Germination date		Germination conditions	Number of seeds germinated
		Predicted	Actual		

EXPLAIN

d. Ask: *What did you observe? What do you conclude?* (Light is not necessary for seed germination. After all, seeds germinate underground in the dark.)

ELABORATE

e. Ask: *Are there other factors that affect the germination of seeds? How could we determine the range of temperatures that seeds can tolerate and still sprout?* Lead the students to plan a controlled investigation using two germination bags, with one bag placed in the refrigerator and one in a warm, dark place. Discuss the responding variable (growth), the manipulated variable (temperature), and the variables to be controlled (amount of light, kinds of seeds, amount of water, etc.). Ask: *If one bag is placed in a refrigerator, why would the other one need to be in a "dark" place?*

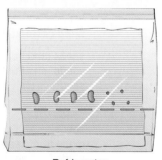

Refrigerator

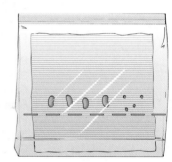

Dark cabinet

f. Tell students to place four lima bean seeds and four radish seeds in two separate plastic germination bags. Have students carry out the controlled investigation they planned. Put one bag in a cool, dark place (e.g., inside a refrigerator) and one bag in a warm, dark place (e.g., inside a cabinet). Make sure the two bags have the same amount of moisture and light.

g. Instruct students to observe the two bags regularly for about 2 weeks and to record their observations in their chart (like the one in the previous illustration). *Note:* Open the bags daily for about 15 minutes to prevent the formation of mold. Also, keep the paper towels just slightly moist.

EVALUATE

h. Ask students to respond in writing to the following questions at the end of the observation period, as an assessment of their understanding of their experiment, its results, and the conclusions that can be drawn from it.
   1. What question were you investigating?
   2. How were the conditions for the two bags different?

3. How do the seeds in the two bags compare?
4. What do you think is the effect of temperature on germination (sprouting)? Why do you think so? What is your evidence?

10. WHAT SEEDS DO WE EAT? (K–4)

ENGAGE

a. Ask: *What seeds or seed products do we eat?*

EXPLORE

b. Hold a classroom "seed feast." Provide a variety of seeds for children to eat. Consider some of the seeds and seed products in the accompanying chart for the seed feast.

Safety Precautions

Make sure children are not allergic to any food you provide for them to eat, such as peanuts.

EXPLAIN

c. Using the chart, conduct a discussion of the various seeds and seed products we eat. Emphasize that rather than the cotyledons providing food for the seeds to germinate and begin growth, they are providing food energy for our survival and growth.

SEEDS AND SEED PRODUCTS WE EAT

Food	Seed or Seed Product
Peas	seeds (and fruit)
Beans	seeds (and fruit)
Corn	seeds
Rice	seeds
Peanuts	seeds
Sunflower seeds	seeds
Chocolate	made from seeds of cacao plant
Coffee	made from seeds of coffee plant
Vanilla	made from seeds of orchid
Cumin (spice)	made from cumin seeds
Flour	made from wheat, barley, or other grass seeds
Pretzels	made from flour
Bread	made from flour
Tortillas	made from flour or corn
Breakfast cereals	made from the seeds of grasses including wheat, rye, oats, and barley

Source: Adapted from National Gardening Association, 1990. *GrowLab.* National Gardening Association, Burlington, VT.

ELABORATE

d. As a take-home activity, have the students keep a mini-journal about the seeds they eat for a week. Have a discussion with the class to identify the kinds of information that should be included in their journal. Draft a letter to parents describing the project.

EVALUATE

e. Create a checklist, to be included with the parent letter, that students can use to self-evaluate their work. Use the same checklist to assist in your evaluation of the final products.

f. Post the mini-journals so students can view and have discussions about the different kinds of seeds their classmates eat. This is a form of informal peer assessment.

B. PLANTS

▶ *Science Background*

Biologists classify organisms on the basis of their structures and behaviors. Most easily observed organisms can be classified as plants or animals. Each type of plant or animal has different structures that serve different functions in growth, survival, and reproduction. All organisms have basic needs. Plants need light, air, water, and nutrients. Animals need air, water, and nutrients. Plants and animals can survive only in environments in which their needs are met. Roots absorb water and nutrients through small root hairs. Water and nutrients are carried from the roots to the leaves through small tubes, called *capillaries*, that are inside the stem. Plants get their energy for survival and growth directly from sunlight through a process called *photosynthesis*. Animals live by consuming the energy-rich foods initially synthesized by plants.[1]

 NSES Science Standards

All students should develop an understanding of

- characteristics of organisms (K–4).
- structure and function in living systems (5–8).
- life cycles of organisms (K–4).
- organisms and their environments (K–4).

Concepts and Principles That Support the Standards

- Some animals and plants are alike in the way they look and the things they do, and others are very different from one another (K–2).
- A great variety of living things can be sorted into groups in many ways using various features to decide which things belong to which group (3–5).
- Features used for grouping depend on the purpose of the grouping (3–5).
- Each plant or animal has different structures that serve different functions in growth, survival, and reproduction (K–4).

Objectives

1. Recognize and discuss the wide variation in plant life.
2. Identify and describe different parts/structures of plants (roots, stems, leaves) and describe the functions of each.
3. Observe and describe the life cycles of plants.
4. Ask questions about plants that can be answered through investigations.
5. Design and carry out descriptive, classificatory, and explanatory investigations to gather information for answering questions about plants.
6. Use simple equipment and tools to gather data and extend the senses.
7. Through investigations, identify basic needs of plants: air, water, nutrients, and light.
8. Use evidence from investigations and science knowledge to answer questions about plant life, construct explanations, and make predictions.

---

[1]Adapted from National Research Council, 1996. *National Science Education Standards.*

1. WHAT IS A TREE LIKE? (K–2)

Materials

- Paper
- Crayons or markers
- String
- Scissors
- Glue or tape

ENGAGE

a. Have students draw a picture of a tree. Give them between 5 and 10 minutes to complete their drawing. Post all of the drawings so the class can see them. Ask: *How are the drawings of trees different? How are they alike?*

EXPLORE

b. Assign groups to trees in or near the school yard. Have students feel the surface of their assigned tree and describe how it feels. Have them make a rubbing of the bark using the same color as the bark. Have them use string to measure the trunk. Encourage students to smell the bark.

EXPLAIN

c. Ask: *What was your group's tree like? What did it look like? How did it smell? How did it differ from other trees?* Compare rubbings. Ask: *What do the rubbings show? Why do some rubbings look different? Why do some rubbings look the same?* Compare the lengths of the strings that were used to measure the trunks of the groups' trees. Ask: *Which group studied the tree with the widest trunk? Narrowest trunk? How do you know?* Discuss children's findings with them.

ELABORATE

d. Have each student create a poster about the tree he or she studied during the explore stage of the lesson. The poster should include a drawing of the tree, the rubbing of its bark, the distance around the tree, and a brief description of the tree. Posters can be placed beside their initial tree drawing to show how much students have learned.

EVALUATE

e. Informal assessment of the change in students conceptual understanding of trees is possible by comparing students' initial drawing with their posters.

2. HOW DO THE CHARACTERISTICS OF LEAVES VARY? (K–2)

Materials

- Assortment of leaves
- Magazines
- Newspapers
- Colored paper
- Paintbrushes
- Poster paint

ENGAGE

a. Ask: *What are leaves like? What are the similarities in leaves from different trees? What are the differences in the leaves from different trees?*

b. Invite students to collect a variety of fallen leaves and bring them to class.

Safety Precautions Stress collecting fallen leaves only. Do not allow students to pick from living trees and plants.

EXPLORE c. Instruct students to spread the leaves out and compare them. Ask: *How are the leaves alike? How are they different? How do the leaves differ in shape? size? color? number of points? arrangement of veins? How do they differ in other ways? Why do you think the leaves vary so much from one another?*

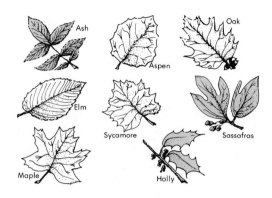

d. Tell the students to place the leaves in groups according to color, shape, size, or some other characteristic.

EXPLAIN e. Ask: *How many groups did you form?* Then tell them to rearrange the leaves according to other characteristics. Ask: *How many groups did you form?*

3. HOW CAN SOME PLANTS GROW WITHOUT SEEDS? (K–2)

Materials
- Small tumblers (preferably clear plastic)
- Small sweet potatoes, white potatoes, and carrot tops (with some leaves)
- Toothpicks
- Cuttings from coleus, philodendron, ivy, and other houseplants

ENGAGE a. Ask: *What is needed for new plants to grow? How can we get new plants to grow without planting them in soil?*

EXPLORE b. Put three toothpicks each in a sweet potato, white potato, and carrot, as shown in the diagram. Place them in small tumblers of water. Take cuttings of houseplants and place them in small tumblers of water. Put all the tumblers in a well-lit place and make sure the water levels are maintained so that the water always touches the plants. Have students observe, measure, and record the changes in the plants, such as root development, height, and number of leaves.

Coleus and philodendron   Sweet potato   White potato   Carrot

EXPLAIN

c. Ask: *Do new plants come only from seeds? What is your evidence?*

d. Ask: *What do plants need to grow?* Explain to students that plants require air, water, nutrients, and light. Plants can survive only in environments in which these basic needs are met. Ask: *How do you think these basic needs of plants are met when they are growing in water?*

4. WHAT ARE ROOTS LIKE? (K–5)

Materials

- Lima bean plants and radish plants growing in a germination bag
- Magnifying lenses
- Small, healthy coleus, geranium, or petunia plants
- Potting soil
- Planting containers (such as clean, empty milk cartons)

ENGAGE

a. Ask: *What do the roots of a young plant look like? What could you do to find out?*

EXPLORE

b. Lead students to answer this question through their observations of the roots of bean plants and radish plants growing in a germination bag. Instruct students to use a magnifying lens and to record their observations, including drawings, of the structure of roots.

c. Continue the observation of the roots of plants for several days. Require students to make daily records of their observations in their journals.

EXPLAIN

d. After several days of observation, ask: *What do you notice about the roots? How are the roots of the bean plant and radish plant similar? How are they different? What are the small, fuzzlike projections coming from the roots?* (Root hairs)

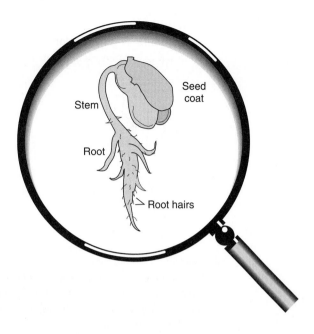

ELABORATE

e. Permit students to grow other seeds in order to compare and contrast roots from other types of young plants. Allow time for students to discuss their findings about their new roots and relate their discoveries to the bean and radish roots they examined previously.

EVALUATE

f. Challenge students to use a Venn diagram or some other graphic organizer to summarize the similarities and differences among the roots of the three young plants they observed. The detail they include should provide evidence of their observation and comparison skills.

5. WHAT IS THE FUNCTION OF ROOTS? (K–5)

ENGAGE

a. Ask: *What do you think is the function of the roots and the root hairs? What could you do to investigate to find out?* Lead students to suggest that functions of roots may be to absorb water and nutrients for plant growth and to provide support for plants. Ask: *How might you investigate these hypotheses?*

EXPLORE

b. Obtain two similar coleus, petunia, or geranium plants and remove all the roots from one plant. Fill the bottom half of two milk cartons or other planting containers with soil. Place the plant without roots down on top of the soil. Release the plant and observe what happens. Ask: *How might roots have helped this plant?* Explain that one function of the roots is to provide support for plants.

c. Push the bottom part of the stem of the plant without roots to a depth of about 5 cm into the soil. Water the plant daily. Observe the plant for 4 or 5 days. As a control, plant the other plant with roots in a container of soil.

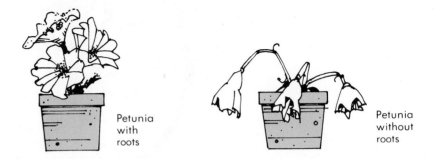

Petunia
with
roots

Petunia
without
roots

EXPLAIN

d. Ask: *What did you observe about the two plants? Why do you think this happens?* Explain that one function of the root hairs is to absorb water and nutrients for the plant. Because the root hairs are critical to the life of the plant, it is important that they not be damaged when a plant is pulled up or transplanted.

Gently pull the plant without roots from the soil. If this plant has developed new roots, discuss the function of the newly developed roots.

ELABORATE

e. Ask: *Why do you think some roots grow comparatively shallow and others grow deep? What are some ways people use the roots of plants?* Permit students to use library and Internet resources to find information to help them answer these questions.

EVALUATE

f. To assess student understanding about the function of roots, have each student complete this chart based on this investigation.

Function of Root	Evidence

6. DO PLANTS GET WATER THROUGH ROOTS OR LEAVES? (K–5)

ENGAGE

a. Ask: *Do plants get water through their roots or leaves? What could we do to find out?*

EXPLORE

b. To gather evidence to answer this key question, lead children to set up a controlled investigation like the one illustrated. This investigation involves two plants. Water is added to the soil of one plant so that it can reach the roots. Water is sprinkled on the leaves of the second plant, with a plastic bib keeping the water from reaching the soil and roots. All other conditions are controlled.

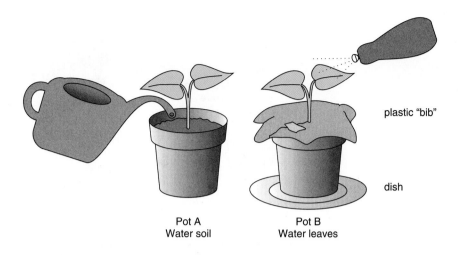

Pot A
Water soil

Pot B
Water leaves

plastic "bib"

dish

c. Tell the children to keep daily records of their observations.

EXPLAIN

d. After about 2 weeks, lead a discussion of the children's findings. Ask: *What did you do in the investigation? What did you observe? How did your findings compare with your predictions? What can you infer about the role of leaves in taking in water? Did you actually see roots taking in water? What makes you confident in your inference that water is taken in by roots? What factors might have affected the results of your investigation?* (For example, watering might have damaged the leaves.)[2]

7. WHAT IS THE FUNCTION OF A STEM? (K–5)

Materials

- Carnations
- Geranium or celery stem
- Red and blue food coloring
- Drinking glass or clear plastic cup
- Paper towel

Preparation

Place the stem of a white carnation in a cup containing water with blue food coloring. Leave the carnation in the water until it has turned blue.

ENGAGE

a. Ask: *Why is this carnation blue? Aren't carnations usually white? Do you think I planted a blue carnation seed? How does water get from the roots of a plant to the leaves? How do you think a florist produces blue carnations? If you wanted to change a white carnation into a blue carnation, what would you do? How could you find out if your idea was correct?*

[2]Adapted from National Gardening Association, 1990. *GrowLab: Activities for Growing Minds*. National Gardening Association, 180 Flynn Avenue, Burlington, Vermont 05401.

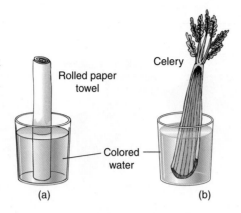

(a)   (b)   (c)

EXPLORE

b. Fill a cup with water, tint with food coloring, and add a rolled paper towel, as in diagram (a).

Ask: *What do you see happening to the paper towel? Why do you think this happens? How could this work in plants?*

c. Tell children to put some water in the drinking glass and add the food coloring. Cut a small slice off the bottom of the celery stem. Set the stem into the glass of colored water as in diagram (b). Allow it to sit in a sunny area for 2 hours. At the end of this period, cut open the stem. See diagram (c).

EXPLAIN

d. Ask: *What has happened to the celery stem? What parts of the stem appear to contain the colored water? How do you know? What can you conclude about the function of a stem?*

ELABORATE

e. Ask: *What do you think might happen if you put half of a split stem in one color of water and the other half in another color of water? Try it and see.*

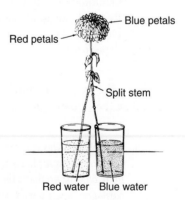

f. Ask: *What do you think might happen to the upward movement of water in a stem when the plant is in the dark or out of sunlight? How could you find out?*

EVALUATE

g. Use the following multiple-choice item to check student knowledge of the function of stems.

Stems:

    A. Hold the entire plant in place.
    B. Get water from the soil.
    C. Transport water to the upper parts of a plant.
    D. Determine the color of the flower.

8. HOW MUCH WATER IS ENOUGH FOR HEALTHY PLANT GROWTH? (3–6)

Materials

- Young bean or radish plants
- Milk cartons or plastic cups
- Graduated cylinder or measuring cup

ENGAGE

a. Ask: *How much water do you need each day? How much water do you think a plant needs to grow in a healthy way? How could you find out?*

EXPLORE

b. Guide students to design an investigation to determine how much water a plant needs to grow. Tell them each group will have three similar plants to test and we will decide together how to make our experiment a "fair test." Ask: *What should be different for each of your three pots?* (how much we water it) *What should be kept the same for each of your three pots?* (Size of pot, where we put it, kind of soil, etc.) *What should be observed?* (The way the plant looks, color of leaves, number of leaves, height, etc.) *When should we observe? How long will the experiment last?* Based on class consensus, develop a procedure for all groups to follow. For example, students might decide to label each group's cups A, B, C. Then water daily as follows: cup A—0 ml water; cup B—20 ml water; cup C—40 ml water. All other variables will be controlled.

EXPLAIN

c. At the end of the observation period defined by the class, ask: *How do the conditions of the plants differ? Which one seems healthiest? What are the indications of health?*

9. HOW MUCH FERTILIZER IS ENOUGH FOR HEALTHY PLANT GROWTH? (3–6)

Materials

- Young bean or radish plants
- Milk cartons or plastic cups
- Fertilizer
- Graduated cylinder or measuring cup

ENGAGE

a. Ask: *How much fertilizer do plants need?*

EXPLORE

b. Guide children to plan and set up an investigation similar to that in the illustration to determine how much fertilizer is enough for plants.

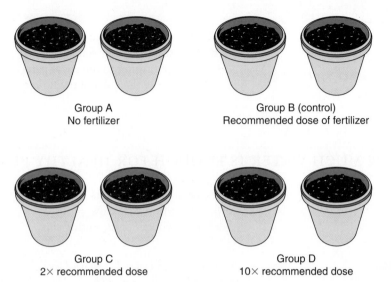

Group A
No fertilizer

Group B (control)
Recommended dose of fertilizer

Group C
2× recommended dose

Group D
10× recommended dose

c. Lead students to observe the plants and make records in their observation journals. They might observe, measure, and compare the height of each plant, leaf color, number of leaves, and leaf size.

EXPLAIN

d. Ask: *How do the conditions of the plants differ? Which one seems healthiest? What do you conclude about the amount of fertilizer a plant needs? What does fertilizer supply for plants?*

▶ *Teaching Background*
Plants require **mineral nutrients** for growth, repair, and proper functioning. Mineral nutrients are formed by the breakdown of rocks and found in soil. Mineral nutrients can also be supplied by fertilizers applied by humans. Humans ordinarily obtain minerals by eating plants or animals. Nutrients can also be obtained from supplements.[3]

10. WHAT IS THE EFFECT OF LIGHT ON PLANT GROWTH? (3–6)

Materials

- Germinated bean seeds
- Sunny window or light source
- Ruler
- Potting soil
- Clean milk carton
- Shoe box with cover

ENGAGE

a. Ask: *What effect does light have on the way a plant grows? What do you think might happen to a plant if the amount of light from a light source is very limited? What do you think might happen if a plant is placed near a window? What could you do to find out?*

---

[3]Adapted from National Gardening Association, 1990. *GrowLab: Activities for Growing Minds.* National Gardening Association, 180 Flynn Avenue, Burlington, Vermont 05401.

EXPLORE

b. Plant four bean plants 2 cm deep in moist soil in a clean milk carton.

c. Place the milk carton in a shoe box that has only a single, 2 cm hole cut in the middle of one end. Cover the box and turn the opening toward bright sunlight or a strong lamp, as shown in the diagram.

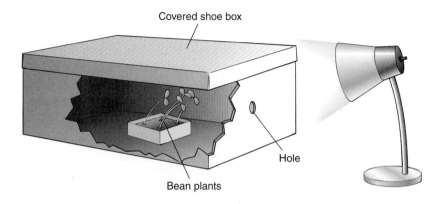

Covered shoe box

Hole

Bean plants

d. Lift the cover every 2 days and see how the bean plants are growing. Record observations. Add water as needed.

EXPLAIN

e. Ask: *What is happening to the stems and leaves? Why do you think they are growing as they are? What do you think might happen if you turned the milk carton with the plants completely around in the shoe box?*

f. Try it and observe what happens in 2 days.

▶ *Teaching Background*

Students should see that the beans grow toward the opening in the shoe box. When turned around, they reverse their direction of growth toward the opening again. The stems and leaves of plants turn toward the light because of phototropism. This adaptation causes the cells on the dark side of stems to grow more rapidly than the cells on the lit side. This causes the leaves to turn to the light, allowing the plant to produce more food by photosynthesis than it would if the leaves were not turned to the light.

11. HOW DOES LIGHT AFFECT PLANTS? (K–2)

Materials

- Two similar healthy plants growing in separate similar pots.
- Water
- Crayons or markers

ENGAGE

a. Show students two similar healthy plants growing in separate similar pots. Ask: *Do these two plants appear to be the same? How do you know? Do plants need light in order to grow and stay healthy? How could we use these two plants to find out?*

EXPLORE

b. Lead students to suggest that one plant should be put in a dark place, and the other plant should be put in a place that it gets sunlight. Point out that the plants are about the same now and that their pots are the same, too. Ask: *Is there anything else that should be kept the same to make this experiment a fair test?* If students don't suggest that they each be watered the same amount, lead them to that idea.

c. Have students record their first observation of the plants in their investigation journal or on a chart that you provide. Tell students that they will observe the plants each week for the next 3 weeks. Each time they will draw and write about how the plants look.

EXPLAIN

d. After each weekly observation, ask: *What do you see? Why do you think this happened?*

e. In addition, after the last observation, ask: *Do you think plants need light to grow and stay healthy? How do you know?*

12. DO LEAVES GIVE OFF MOISTURE? (3–5)

Materials

- Two clear plastic bags
- Two small, identical geranium plants
- Plastic ties
- Magnifying lenses

ENGAGE

a. Ask: *Do leaves contain moisture?*

EXPLORE

b. Instruct students to do this activity:

1. Place a clear plastic bag over one geranium and tie the bag around the stem, just above the soil level.
2. Wave a second plastic bag through the air and tie it as well, as illustrated in the diagram.
3. Put both plastic bags in direct sunlight for at least 3 hours.
4. After at least 3 hours, observe both plastic bags. Notice any differences.

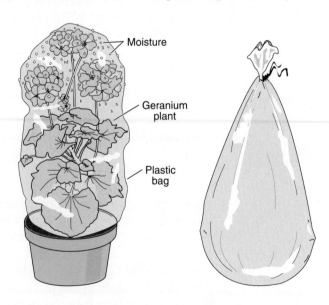

EXPLAIN

c. Ask:

* *What do you see forming near the top of the plant in the plastic bag? Where do you think the moisture came from?* (From the leaves of the plant)

* *What is your evidence that the moisture came from the leaves and not the soil?* (The plastic bag was tied off above the soil line.)

* *How is the plastic bag without the plant different after 3 hours? Why do you think this happened? Why do you think the empty plastic bag was used in this activity?*

* *What makes this investigation a controlled experiment?* (Two identical bags containing air are used, one with a plant and one without a plant. The condition varied—the manipulated variable—is whether or not a bag has a plant. The outcome or responding variable is the production of moisture.)

▶ *Teaching Background*

Moisture is formed in the plastic bag with the plant because leaves give off water in a process called *transpiration*. The purpose of tying off the bag at the stem was to prevent moisture evaporating from the soil from entering the bag. The "empty" clear plastic bag is the control.

13. WHAT IS THE EFFECT OF GRAVITY ON THE GROWTH OF ROOTS AND STEMS? (5–8)

Materials

* Young, growing bean plants
* Paper towels
* Two pieces of glass or thick plastic to place growing plants between
* Craft sticks or tongue depressors
* Small pebbles
* Tape

ENGAGE

a. Ask: *What do you think might happen to roots of a plant if they were planted facing up or sideways rather than facing down? What do you think might happen to roots if something were in their way? What could we do to find out? What do you think would happen to the stems of plants that are planted upside down or sideways?*

EXPLORE

b. Lead students to design an investigation in which the plant is planted upside down so that the growth of roots and stems can be observed.

   This investigation might be done as a class demonstration. Place four young bean plants between two moist paper towels. Put the paper towels with the seedlings between two pieces of glass or rigid, clear plastic. Put small pebbles under each root. Place the applicator sticks or tongue depressors between the pieces of glass or clear plastic, and tape as shown in the diagram.

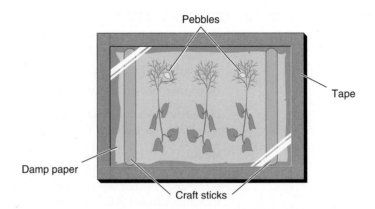

Pebbles

Tape

Damp paper

Craft sticks

c. Stand the glass so the roots point up and the stems point down. Instruct the students to observe the plant growth for several days and record their observations.

EXPLAIN

d. Ask: *What did you observe about the roots? What did you observe about the stems? Why do you think this happened?* Through discussion, lead students to conclude that roots grow downward under the influence of gravity and that they grow around objects in the soil. Stems grow upward.

▶ *Teaching Background*

The roots will grow down (toward the earth), and the stems will grow up (away from the earth). The plant responses that cause this are called **tropisms. Geotropism** forces roots down as auxins (plant hormones) are concentrated by gravity along the bottom cells of stems and root tips. The bottom cells in the stem are stimulated by the hormones to grow faster than cells higher up; they get longer and curl upward. Root cells are more sensitive to these hormones than are stem cells, so the root cells inhibit cell growth. Root top cells elongate faster, and root tips curve downward.

C. INSECTS

▶ *Science Background*

Insects are the most successful group of animals on earth. Insects dominate the planet in terms of number of individuals and species. There are more kinds of insects than all other kinds of animals put together. All insects have six legs and three body parts: the head, thorax, and abdomen. Insects that may be familiar to children include dragonflies, crickets, lice, beetles, butterflies, flies, fleas, and ants.

Insects change in form through a process called *metamorphosis* as they grow and mature. Some insects progress from egg, to larva, to a pupal stage, and then to adults. Other insects look pretty much like adults when they hatch from eggs.[4]

[4]Adapted from FOSS (Full Option Science System), 1995. *Insects.* Lawrence Hall of Science, Berkeley, CA. (Published by Delta Education, Nashua, NH.)

Science Standards

All students should develop an understanding of
- characteristics of organisms (K–4).
- structure and function in living systems (5–8).
- life cycles of organisms (K–4).
- organisms and their environments (K–4).

Concepts and Principles That Support the Standards

- Plants and animals have life cycles that include being born, developing into adults, reproducing, and eventually dying. The details of this life cycle are different for different organisms (K–4).
- Organisms have basic needs. Animals need air, water, and food (K–4).
- Organisms can survive only in environments in which their basic needs are met (K–4).
- Each plant or animal has different structures that serve different functions in growth, survival, and reproduction (K–4).

Objectives

1. Recognize the wide variation in insects.
2. Identify and describe different parts/structures of insects.
3. Define *metamorphosis* and name the stages in the metamorphosis of a mealworm.
4. Describe the sequence of stages in the development of a mealworm.
5. Ask questions about ants that can be answered through investigations.
6. Design and carry out descriptive investigations to gather information and answer questions about ants.

1. WHAT STAGES DO MEALWORMS GO THROUGH? (K–5)

Materials

- Jars with covers (clear plastic, if possible)
- Mealworms (from pet shop)
- Branmeal, or other cereal flakes
- Magnifying lenses
- Spoons
- Pictures or drawings of mealworms at different times during their life cycle (These can be made during the explore phase of the lesson.)
- Tape or glue

ENGAGE

a. Ask: *What are the stages people go through as they grow and change? Do insects, like mealworms, go through stages too? How could we find out?*

EXPLORE

b. Obtain some mealworms from a pet store or commercial supplier (see Appendix C). Introduce the mealworms and challenge students to predict how the mealworms will change over time. Using spoons, you or the students can transfer several mealworms and some bran or cereal flakes into a jar or other container with a lid. Provide a container for each student or group of two or three students. Punch several small holes in the lids for air.

c. Have students observe the mealworms several times a week and record on a chart or log any observed changes in appearance (color, length, stage, etc.) or behavior.

EXPLAIN

d. Using their charts or logs as a reference, students should discuss how the mealworms have changed over time. Ask: *What happened to the mealworms? Did they all change in the same way? Did they all change at the same time? Which stage do you think is the adult? Why do you think that?*

e. Introduce the term *metamorphosis* for this type of change during an organism's life cycle. Using pictures of mealworms at different stages of growth, discuss how these living things grow. Point out that when people grow, they change but not in such extreme ways as a metamorphosing insect. Human children, teenagers, and adults look a lot like each other, while mealworm larvae, pupae, and adults don't look much alike at all. Help students make a table comparing the stages of mealworms' lives with humans', like the one shown.

Stages	
People	*Mealworms*
Child	Larva
Teenager	Pupa
Adult	Adult

f. In addition, guide students to make a diagram, similar to the one shown, and include photos or drawings to visualize the stages of mealworm metamorphosis.

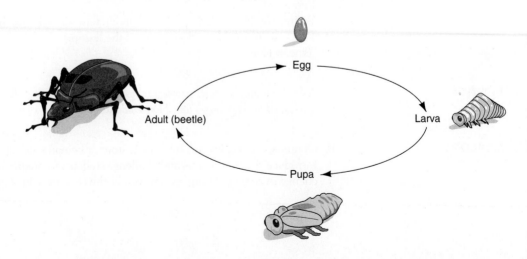

ELABORATE

g. Have students use print and online resources to learn about the life cycles of other insects. Students should report back to their class about their findings. Ask: *Are all insect life cycles just like the mealworm's life cycle? If not, how are they different?*

EVALUATE

h. To assess student knowledge about the series of changes that occur during mealworm metamorphosis, prepare cards with drawings or photographs of mealworms during their life cycle. (You could take these pictures with a digital microscope or camera during the explore phase of the investigation.) Give each child a set of cards. Have them put them in order to represent the mealworm's life cycle. Ask them to label parts of the mealworm life cycle using terms they learned during this lesson. Finally, ask them to explain why they arranged the cards in the way they did.

2. HOW DO ANTS LIVE? (K–2)

Materials

- Widemouthed glass jar (commercial mayonnaise or pickle jar) with screw top punctured with very small holes
- Empty washed soup can
- Soil to fill the jar two-thirds full
- Small sponge
- Pan large enough to hold the widemouthed glass jar
- Sheet of black construction paper
- Crumbs and bits of food such as bread, cake, sugar, and seeds
- Colony of ants (from pet shop or science materials supplier)

Safety Precautions

- Caution children not to handle the ants. As a defense, ants bite and sting. Sometimes after biting an enemy, ants will spray a chemical into the open wound.
- Use ants from a pet store or science materials supplier, so that you don't disrupt a natural colony and to avoid accidentally bringing fire ants or other dangerous types of ants into the classroom.

ENGAGE

a. Ask: *What do ants look like? Are all ants alike, or are there different kinds of ants? Where do ants make their homes?* Lead children to draw pictures of ants and to describe and explain their pictures.

EXPLORE

b. Set up an ant colony following these directions:
   1. Place the soup can in the center of the widemouthed glass jar as in the diagram.
   2. Fill the jar two-thirds full of soil.
   3. Punch several airholes in the screw cover.
   4. Place a sheet of black construction paper around the outside of the jar.
   5. Add a small sponge with water. Add crumbs and bits of food (bread, cake, sugar, and seeds).
   6. Add ants.
   7. Place a cloth over the top of the jar and screw the jar lid in place.
   8. Place the jar in a pan of water.

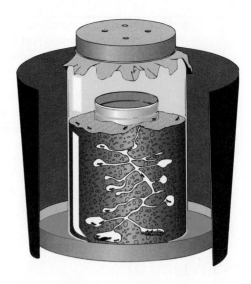

EXPLAIN

c. Ask: *What effect will a sheet of black paper placed around the jar have on the ants?* (This simulates the dark underground so ants will tunnel close to the sides of the glass jar.) *Why place the soup can in the center of the jar with soil around it?* (So ants will not burrow into the center but will tunnel out to the jar's sides and be more visible.) *What is the purpose of placing the jar in a pan of water?* (So the ants cannot escape.)

ELABORATE

d. Guide children to observe ants, including observing with magnifying lenses. Instruct students to make records, including drawings, of what ants look like and what the ants do. Students should observe body characteristics such as are shown in the diagram.[5]

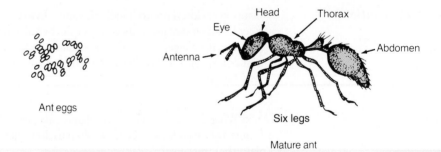

e. Your class should also keep an I Notice–I Wonder chart about the ants and their colony. Over time, children can confirm or find evidence against the things others noticed and can design investigations to address the *I Wonder* questions generated by the class.

---

[5] Adapted and modified from *Ant Homes Under the Ground*, one of more than 75 teacher's guides in the Great Explorations in Math and Science (GEMS) series, available from the Lawrence Hall of Science, Berkeley, CA. (For more information, visit the website at http://www.lhsgems.org.)

EVALUATE

f. Formatively assess students' curiosity as they investigate the ant colony over time. Use the following indicators, which become more sophisticated as you move down the list, as a checklist to record your observations about your students.[6]

Students:

☐ Give some attention to new things happening in the ant colony, but are easily distracted and ask few questions.

☐ Show interest in new things happening in the ant colony by asking "what" questions.

☐ Explore the ant colony and ask questions about it in response to invitations to do so.

☐ Examine the ant colony carefully and ask "how" and "why" questions as well as "what" questions.

☐ Explore and investigate things about the ant colony to answer their own questions.

☐ Spontaneously seek information about ants and their colonies from books or other sources to satisfy their own curiosity.

D. BIRDS

▶ *Science Background*

Birds are familiar animals in the child's environment. Birds differ in a variety of ways. Children can observe many different characteristics of birds, such as colors and sizes. Birds sing different songs, eat different kinds of food, and make different kinds of nests where they care for their young. The male bird may have a more colorful plumage than the female. Some birds change color with the season. Some birds migrate. Birds need trees and shrubs for protection from their predators, including small mammals, humans, and even other birds.

NSES **Science Standards**

All students should develop an understanding of

- characteristics of organisms (K–4).
- structure and function in living systems (5–8).
- organisms and their environments (K–4).

Concepts and Principles That Support the Standards

- Some animals and plants are alike in the way they look and the things they do, and others are very different from one another (K–2).
- A great variety of living things can be sorted into groups in many ways using various features to decide which things belong to which group (3–5).
- Organisms have basic needs. Animals need air, water, and food (K–4).
- Organisms can survive only in environments in which their basic needs are met (K–4).

---

[6]Adapted from Harlen, W. (2000). *Teaching, learning and assessing science 5-12* (3rd ed.). Thousand Oaks, CA: Sage Publications.

Objectives

1. Recognize the wide variation in birds.
2. Identify and describe different characteristics of birds.
3. Ask questions about birds that can be answered through investigations.
4. Design and carry out descriptive and classificatory investigations to gather information for answering questions about birds.

1. WHAT DO YOU KNOW ABOUT THE BIRDS AROUND YOU? (K–6)

Materials

- Bird book (showing local birds)
- Pictures of birds
- Bird feeders (commercial or made in class)

ENGAGE

a. Lead children in a discussion of what they know about birds.
   Ask:
   How are all birds alike? How do birds differ from each other?
   Where do some birds go during the winter?
   What kinds of homes do birds live in?
   What do birds do that is different from what other animals do?
   What kinds of foods do birds eat?
   What are the names of some local birds?
   What do these birds look like?

EXPLORE

b. If the natural environment lends itself to observing birds, have students observe birds on the way to and from school, or take a class field trip to a local area, park, or zoo. In a city, you will probably see sparrows or pigeons, jays in picnic areas, ducks in ponds, geese on golf courses, and seagulls at the seashore. In addition, you may want to provide pictures of different birds, nests, and eggs for students to handle, observe, and discuss.

EXPLAIN

c. Ask: *What birds did you see? How did you know which birds you saw? How were the types of birds different from each other? In what ways were all the birds you observed the same?*
d. Record students' responses to this question on the board: *How could we attract birds to our school grounds?* Ask: *Where could we make a good bird observing area?* (Tree and shrub shelter that is free from predators and visible from the classroom)

ELABORATE

e. Set up a bird observing area.
   1. With your students, survey your school grounds and pick the best spot for a bird feeding and observing area.
   2. Find out what kinds of birds are common in your area, what their food preferences are, how they eat (on the ground or from feeders), and any other information that will enhance observations. Discuss and provide information to children about common birds in your area, what they prefer to eat, and how they eat. Encourage them to find and use additional resources in the library or online.
   3. Develop investigatable questions that observational data from your bird feeding and observing areas could help to answer. Let small groups of students select a question for investigation, then carry it out.

EVALUATE

f. Allow children to present their findings from their investigation. Their oral report should address:

* the question they were investigating,
* their hypothesis,
* their observational procedures,
* their data, presented in a way that is easy to understand (table and/or graph), and
* their conclusions.

The group should also be prepared to answer questions from their classmates and their teacher.

2. HOW DO BIRD BONES DIFFER FROM MAMMAL BONES? (3–6)

Materials

* Beef and chicken bones (one of each for every two students). If possible, these should be cut in half so the inside of the bone is visible.
* Wing bones of chickens (or any other bird)

Safety Precautions

Be sure that students wash hands thoroughly after handling the bones.

ENGAGE

a. Ask: *In what ways do birds behave differently than mammals? How would you expect bird bones to differ from the bones of mammals?*

EXPLORE

b. Allow students to help furnish beef and chicken bones.
   1. Obtain a cut chicken bone, a cut beef bone, and a wing bone of a chicken.
   2. Ask: *How did you know which bone was from a chicken and which was from a cow?*
   3. Examine the centers of the two bones and record how the structure of the beef bone differs from that of the chicken bone.
   4. Look at the chicken wing bone. Ask: *How does its structure compare with the arm bones of a person?*

EXPLAIN

c. Ask: *What advantages do you think bones of birds and mammals have for them? What are some other structural differences between birds and mammals?*

II. ORGANISMS AND THEIR ENVIRONMENTS

Organisms have basic needs. Animals need air, water, and food. Plants require air, water, nutrients, and light. Organisms can survive only in environments in which their basic needs are met.

A. AQUARIUM HABITATS

▶ *Science Background*

An aquarium is a wonderful context for studying aquatic life. Many environmental factors are important to life in aquarium habitats, including temperature, water transparency, nutrients, and concentrations of dissolved gases (oxygen and carbon dioxide).

Both plants and animals use oxygen and give off carbon dioxide through respiration. Plants also use carbon dioxide and give off oxygen in the process of photosynthesis. During daylight hours, aquatic plants produce more oxygen than plants and animals consume in respiration. At night, both plants and animals use accumulated oxygen.

When carbon dioxide dissolves in water, it makes the water acidic. Bromothymol blue (BTB) is a chemical indicator that can be used to monitor acid concentration in aquariums. BTB changes color, depending on the acidity of the water. A few drops of BTB in a container of water that is neutral produces a pale blue. If the water is acidic, its color shifts to green or yellow when BTB is added. If the water is basic, the color turns to deep blue.

NSES Science Standards

All students should develop an understanding of

- organisms and their environments (K–4).

Concepts and Principles That Support the Standards

- Organisms have basic needs. Animals need air, water, and food. Plants require air, water, nutrients, and light. Organisms can survive only in environments in which their basic needs are met (K–4).
- An organism's patterns of behavior are related to the nature of that organism's environment, including the kinds and numbers of other organisms present, the availability of food and resources, and the physical characteristics of the environment (K–4).
- When the environment changes, some plants and animals survive and reproduce, and others die or move to new locations (K–4).

Objectives

1. Define *habitat* and *ecosystem*.
2. Identify and describe the parts of an aquarium habitat and describe how the parts of this system interact.
3. Construct an aquarium habitat.
4. Ask questions and design and carry out investigations about components and interactions within ecosystems.

1. HOW CAN WE CONSTRUCT AN AQUARIUM HABITAT? (1–5)

Materials

- A 6 liter, clear plastic basin (used as the aquarium)
- Five small aquatic plants (approximately 10 cm in height)
- Freshwater fantailed guppy
- Two water snails

Prepare

a. Ask: *What is an aquarium? What lives in an aquarium? What are some of the things fish, plants, and other organisms need in order to survive in an aquarium? How must an aquarium be constructed and maintained to support living things?*

Construct

b. It is preferable for each group of students to have their own aquarium. Teachers should guide and work with students to construct and maintain a freshwater aquarium, following these instructions:

1. *Container.* Obtain a 4 to 6 liter (1 to 1.5 gallons), rectangular clear plastic container with strong walls. The container should have a large surface area to allow gas exchange with the atmosphere, but should not be too shallow. Wash the container well with water, but not soap.

2. *Sand.* Obtain a supply of coarse white sand. Rinse the sand in a bucket to remove debris. Add white sand to a depth of about 4 cm to the bottom of the aquarium container.

3. *Water.* Age tap water in an open container for 24 to 48 hours to allow chlorine in the water to escape. You may choose to use bottled spring water (but not distilled water). Gently pour the water into the container, perhaps over clean paper to prevent disturbing the sand.

4. *Plants.* Obtain water plants from a pond or purchase them from a science supply company or a local pet shop (see Appendix B). Root about two sprigs of waterweed (elodea) and two sprigs of eelgrass in the sand. Add some duckweed as a floating plant. Overplanting is better for your aquarium than underplanting. Allow 1 to 2 weeks for the plants to become acclimated to the water before adding animals.

5. *Fish.* Purchase small fish from a pet store or obtain some free from an aquarium hobbyist. Obtain male and female guppies or goldfish. Place the plastic bag containing the fish in your aquarium water for a few hours for the water temperatures in the bag and the aquarium to become equal. Use a dip net to add three to four fish to the aquarium. A rule of thumb is not to have more than 1 cm of fish (excluding tail) per liter of water. Dispose of the plastic container and water the fish came in.

6. *Snails.* Add several small pond snails to your aquarium.

7. *Care.* Add a plastic lid to your aquarium. Lift the corners of the lid to allow exchange of gases between the water and the atmosphere. Thus, you will not need a pump for aeration. Keep a supply of aged tap water available to replace evaporated water as necessary, keeping the water in the aquarium at a predetermined level.

8. *Temperature.* Place your aquarium in the room so that it can get light, but not direct sunlight. Too much light will promote the growth of algae (which can, if you desire, be observed and studied by students). The aquarium should be maintained at room temperature (70° to 78°F or 21° to 25°C). A gooseneck lamp with a 60 to 75 watt bulb can be used to warm the water if necessary. Adjust the lamp so the bulb is a few centimeters above the water, until the temperature is maintained at the desired level. Check with your principal about school regulations concerning leaving the lamp on over the weekend.

9. *Food.* Feed the fish a small amount (a pinch) of commercial fish food every other day (or as instructed on the package). Do not overfeed. Uneaten food will decay, polluting the water. Fish can go as long as 2 weeks without food. Fish may supplement their diet by eating from the water plants. Snails do not require any special food. They eat water plants or the debris that collects on the bottom of the aquarium.

c. Two alternative containers for aquariums are shown in the following illustrations.

Food jar
aquarium

Soda bottle
aquarium

2. WHAT CAN WE OBSERVE IN AN AQUARIUM? (1–3)

Materials
- Aquarium
- Plants
- Fish
- Snails
- Magnifying lenses

ENGAGE

a. Ask: *What happens to the living things within an aquarium? How can we find out?*

EXPLORE

b. Let the children assist you in preparing one aquarium for each group of four students, following the instructions in Activity 1. Tell each group to observe their aquarium closely. Provide magnifying lenses to assist the students in their observations. Encourage them to talk freely about what they see. While the students are observing, move from group to group and listen to their discourse and questions. Do not answer their questions yet, but use them to help you plan class discussion.

c. Instruct the children to make records in their investigation journals of what they observe. Students might write about what they see and make labeled drawings with crayons, markers, pens, and pencils. Let children use their own terminology in their journals at first, gradually introducing (inventing) technical terms to supplement descriptions.

EXPLAIN

d. Take time on a regular basis to discuss with students what they are observing, changes they have noted, and questions they may have raised. Gather the students in a large group and ask such questions as: *What did you observe? Did anyone observe anything else? What is on the bottom of the aquarium?* (Sand)

e. Explain that a **habitat** is a place where an animal or plant naturally lives or grows. A habitat provides the food, shelter, moisture, light, air, and protection the plants or animals need to survive. Ask: *Think of the aquarium as a habitat for fish; what components of the aquarium habitat support the fish and snails that live there?*

ELABORATE

f. Ask: *What do you wonder about fish and snails?* Lead the children to ask questions that can be answered through further observations or investigations. Children might ask such questions as: *What do the fish and snails eat? How much do they eat? Do the snails have mouths? What are those feelers on the snails?* (Tentacles) *What do they do?* (They contain the snails' eyes.) *What do the snails eat?* (Algae) *Do the fish and snails sleep? Can they see me? What makes the water green? Will the fish have babies? Which is the mother fish and which is the daddy fish?* (The male guppies are more brightly colored than the females, and the females give birth to the baby guppies.) *What is the black stuff on the bottom of the aquarium?* (Detritus; waste products from fish)

g. Do not answer the children's questions yet. Post their questions in the room for them to see, think about, and answer through further observation and investigation. Encourage them to observe carefully to try to answer the questions they have posed. Students should add to their journals and drawings regularly.

▶ *Teaching Background*

Encourage children to look for changes in their aquariums. Point out that they will need their records to help them determine what is new in their aquariums.

- Children might observe clumps of transparent spheres on plants and the aquarium sides. These are eggs laid by the snails. Baby snails will hatch from the eggs. Mark the location of snail eggs on the outside of the aquarium with a marking pen. Ask students to observe the clumps regularly. Eventually, a small, black spot will appear in each sphere, becoming larger each day. After a week or two a small snail will hatch.

- If you are keeping guppies in your aquariums, children might also observe the birth of baby guppies. Female guppies carry their eggs in their bodies and deliver their young live. Children might note, with much amazement, that the baby guppies are eaten by the adults. To keep the young from being devoured, use a fish net to transfer the adults to another aquarium.

EVALUATE

h. Use concept maps as a formative evaluation tool throughout the year. Have students construct a concept map about their aquarium shortly after it is set up. Then periodically, have them add new learning to their concept map throughout the year. If you want to be able to see what they add at different times during the year, provide transparencies or tracing paper so that new additions will be on separate sheets.

i. Alternatively, develop a rubric for their aquarium work in their investigation journals. Share the rubric with the students so they know your expectations for their work. Better yet, involve the students in the development of the rubric. Then use the rubric periodically to formatively assess learning and to guide feedback to the students on their work.

B. TERRARIUM HABITATS

▶ *Science Background*

A terrarium is a habitat for plants and small animals, such as earthworms, pill bugs, and frogs. Terrariums must include everything a plant or animal needs to survive.

> **NSES**   Science Standards
>
> All students should develop an understanding of
>
> - organisms and their environments (K–4).
>
> **Concepts and Principles That Support the Standards**
>
> - Organisms have basic needs. Animals need air, water, and food. Plants require air, water, nutrients, and light. Organisms can survive only in environments in which their basic needs are met (K–4).
> - An organism's patterns of behavior are related to the nature of that organism's environment, including the kinds and numbers of other organisms present, the availability of food and resources, and the physical characteristics of the environment (K–4).
> - When the environment changes, some plants and animals survive and reproduce, and others die or move to new locations (K–4).

Objectives

1. Define habitat and ecosystem.
2. Identify and describe the parts of a terrarium habitat and describe how the parts in each system interact.
3. Construct a terrarium habitat.
4. Ask questions and design and carry out investigations about components and interactions within ecosystems.

1. WHAT IS IN SOIL? (K–5)

Materials
- Soil
- Magnifying lenses
- Plastic spoons

ENGAGE

a. Show the class some soil. Ask: What is this? *Where do you find soil? What do you think is in soil?*

EXPLORE

b. Instruct materials managers to pick up materials. Tell students to use the spoon to spread out their soil on a piece of white paper. Ask: *What do you observe about the soil?* Challenge students to use all of their senses, except taste, and a magnifier to observe the soil and to record at least three observations using each sense. To enhance the smell of soil, tell students to spray a bit of moisture on it.

EXPLAIN

c. Ask: *What did you observe? What was in your soil sample? With which senses was it easier to make observations?*

ELABORATE

d. Challenge each group to sort their soil into components (different sizes of particles, pieces of living things, etc.). They can then estimate what part of the soil is composed of each of the components they have identified. Then each group should construct a pie chart or a bar graph to show the relative amounts or weights of the components in their soil sample.

EVALUATE

e. To check student understanding about the composition of soil, have students complete the following writing prompt:
   1. Soil is made up of. . .
      Apply the following rubric to assess students' written responses.
   Exemplary—Response includes:
   * ideas from Proficient response and mentions evidence for including these ideas.
   Proficient—Response includes:
   * Soil is a mixture of different sized particles.
   * Some particles are small pieces of rock.
   * Some particles came from living things.
   Developing—Response includes:
   * Only two of the points from Proficient
   Lacks Concept—Response includes:
   * Only one or none of the points from Proficient

2. WHAT IS AN EARTHWORM LIKE? (K–5)

Materials

* Earthworms
* Magnifying lenses

ENGAGE

a. Ask: *What are earthworms like? How do they move? Where do they live? What do they eat? How could we find the answers to these questions?*

EXPLORE

b. Distribute an earthworm in a clear plastic cup to each group. Ask: *What do you observe about the earthworm?* Encourage students to use magnifying lenses to see details of the earthworms. If students wish, allow them to gently feel the earthworms or to hold them in their hands. Use the spoons to gently move the earthworms and see how they respond. Tell students to draw pictures of the earthworms in their investigation journals.

EXPLAIN

c. Ask: *What did you observe about the earthworm? What were its characteristics? Did your earthworm have eyes and ears? How do you think it senses things, finds food, and finds its way around? What did your earthworm tend to eat? What did it do?*

▶ *Teaching Background*

Worms are segmented and have bristles on each segment. Worms have no eyes or ears, but their pointed head and round body is sensitive to vibrations and chemicals. Earthworms absorb water and oxygen through their skin. Remind students to keep an earthworm moist at all times when observing or it can dry out and die.

Earthworms prefer to eat dried leaves and other organic matter, but will eat soil and extract the decomposing nutrients if nothing else is available. A worm's waste or casings contain nutrients that enrich the soil and provide the necessary nutrients for plant growth. An earthworm's tunneling mixes and aerates the soil.[7]

3. HOW CAN WE BUILD A TERRARIUM ENVIRONMENT FOR EARTHWORMS? (1–3)

Materials

- Container for the terrarium (e.g., glass or plastic tanks, storage boxes, deli salad containers, fish bowls, plastic bottles, or jars)
- Soil
- Sand
- Small plants
- Birdseed or grass seeds
- Spray bottle for water
- Litter (twigs, bark, and leaves)
- Earthworms (obtained from digging in moist soil, from bait shop, or from commercial supplier—see Appendix C)

Safety Precautions

Collect soil from clean areas so that it is free from contaminants; wash your hands and have students wash their hands thoroughly after handling soil.

Prepare

a. Show the class a terrarium or a picture of one. Ask: *Do you think earthworms could survive in a container like this? Why?*

b. Explain that a **terrarium** is any enclosed container that has been set up to house plants and small animals. Terrariums must contain all the components the plants and animals need to survive.

Construct

c. Assist your students to construct a terrarium for each cooperative group in your classroom. To build a terrarium, follow these instructions:
   1. Obtain a container for your terrarium.
   2. Clean the container with water and rinse it well.
   3. Mix three parts soil with one part sand and fill the terrarium container one-third full of the mixture.
   4. Make small holes in the soil and plant two or three small plants in the holes. Cover the roots with soil and firmly press soil on all sides of the stems. Sprinkle some seeds over the soil.
   5. Add litter—twigs, bark, and leaves.
   6. Add moisture with a spray bottle. Limit the amount of moisture in a terrarium to about four squirts of water. *Caution:* Do not overwater the terrarium during this investigation.
   7. Carefully place an earthworm and a dry leaf for the earthworm to eat in the terrarium.

---

[7]Adapted from GEMS (Great Explorations in Math and Science), 1994. *Terrarium Habitats*. Lawrence Hall of Science, Berkeley, CA.

8. Place a lid on the terrarium and put it in a cool place where it can get natural light, but no direct sunlight.

9. Your terrarium should need no more than about two squirts of water per week.[8]

4. WHAT CAN WE OBSERVE IN A TERRARIUM FOR EARTHWORMS? (1–3)

Materials
- Terrarium for earthworms (constructed in previous activity)
- Magnifying lenses
- Spray bottle for water
- Investigation journals

ENGAGE

a. Ask: *What happens to the living and nonliving things within a terrarium for earthworms over time? How can we find out?*

EXPLORE

b. Allow small groups of students to observe and discuss their terrariums regularly for several weeks. Provide magnifying lenses to assist students in making detailed observations. While the students are observing, move from group to group and listen to their discourse and questions. Do not answer their questions. Instead, challenge them to think of ways they could find answers on their own. If groups seem stuck, ask a focusing question to restart their observations, such as: *What are the earthworms doing? How have the plants in your terrarium changed? Is there any moisture in your terrarium? How do you know?*

c. Remind students to use their investigation journals to document their work. Students might use I Notice / I Wonder charts, write about what they observe, and/or make labeled drawings. Let children use their own terminology in their journals during the explore phase. Technical terms will be introduced later.

EXPLAIN

d. In a whole-class setting, ask: *What changes have taken place in your terrarium? What do the earthworms do? What evidence do you have about what earthworms eat? What happened to the plants? What happened to the seeds? Was there moisture in your terrarium? What evidence supports your answer?*

e. Ask: *What is a habitat?* Explain that a **habitat** is a place where an animal or plant naturally lives or grows. A habitat provides the food, shelter, moisture, light, air, and protection that the plants or animals need to survive. Your terrarium is a habitat for plants and earthworms. Ask: *How are the needs of earthworms met by the terrarium habitat? What other habitats do you observe regularly? What is the habitat for birds? fish? deer? humans?*

ELABORATE

f. Encourage groups to select several new questions they have about what's happening in their terrariums. Challenge them to collect data through observation that would provide evidence leading to answers to their questions.

---

[8]Adapted from GEMS (Great Explorations in Math and Science), 1994. *Terrarium Habitats.* Lawrence Hall of Science, Berkeley, CA.

g. Allow small groups to continue to monitor changes and collect data about their terrarium. Encourage groups to share findings with the class, throughout the school year.

EVALUATE

h. Have students draw a concept map to represent their knowledge about the components of their terrarium and the interactions among them. Examining the number of components identified, the details included, and the interrelationships shown by links provides data about the students' understanding of the concepts.

5. HOW CAN WE BUILD A DESERT TERRARIUM? (3–5)

Materials

- Terrarium container
- Cactus plant
- Twig
- Bottle cap
- Desert animal, such as a lizard or horned toad

Prepare

a. Ask: *What is a desert terrarium? What animals and plants might live there? How can we build desert terrariums?*

Construct

b. A desert terrarium can be built out of a large mayonnaise jar, soda bottle, or other container, as in the illustrations.
   1. Select and clean a container for the terrarium.
   2. Place about 2 cups of sand onto the bottom of the jar or bottle.
   3. Place a small cactus plant, a twig, and a small bottle cap filled with water in the terrarium.
   4. Place a small desert animal, such as a lizard or horned toad, in the desert terrarium habitat.
   5. Place the terrarium so that it receives sunlight every day.
   6. Feed the animals live mealworms. These can be obtained from a local pet shop.
   7. Keep the bottle cap filled with water.
   8. Spray one or two squirts of water into the terrarium every 2 weeks, only if the terrarium is dry.

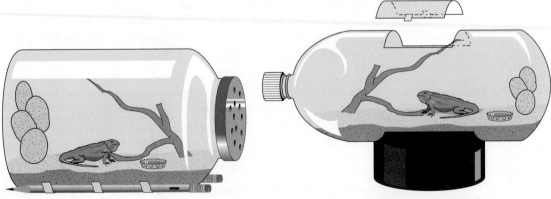

Food jar terrarium   Soda bottle desert terrarium

6. WHAT CAN WE OBSERVE IN A DESERT TERRARIUM? (3–5)

Materials

- Desert terrarium (constructed in previous activity)
- Magnifiying lenses
- Investigation journals

ENGAGE

a. Ask: *What happens to the living and nonliving things within a desert terrarium over time? How can we find out?*

EXPLORE

b. Over several weeks, allow small groups of students to regularly observe and discuss how the desert animals interact with their terrarium habitat. Provide magnifying lenses to assist students in making detailed observations. During observation times, move from group to group and listen to their discourse and questions. Do not answer their questions. Instead, challenge them to think of ways they could find answers on their own. If groups seem stuck, ask a focusing question to restart their observations, such as: *How are the living things interacting with each other? with the nonliving things in the terrarium?*

c. Remind students to use their investigation journals to document their work. Students might use I Notice/I Wonder charts, write about what they observe, and/or make labeled drawings. Let students use their own terminology in their journals during the explore phase. Technical terms will be introduced later.

EXPLAIN

d. Ask: *What natural habitat is this terrarium modeling? How do the living things in the terrarium have their needs met? What interactions have you observed between the organisms in the terrarium and the nonliving things in their environment?*

ELABORATE

e. Provide time for students to do library or Internet research about other organisms that live in a desert habitat.

EVALUATE

f. Have each student produce an educational poster about the organism they have researched. Posters should include: the name of the organism; a picture or drawing of the organism; a concise description of the organism; a description of the organism's habitat; the organism's range (where it can be found on the earth); and its interrelationship to other organisms in its environment (what it eats, what eats it, etc.).

g. Assess the posters based on the presence of all of the required components, the quality of information in the components, and how well others can learn from it. You might want to involve the class in the development of a rubric for this product.

7. HOW CAN WE BUILD A WETLAND TERRARIUM? (3–5)

Materials

- Terrarium container with lid
- Gravel
- Ferns, mosses, lichens, and liverworts
- Small water turtle or frog

Prepare

a. Ask: *What is a wetland terrarium? What animals and plants might live there? How can we build wetland terrariums?*

Construct

b. A wetland terrarium can be built in a large mayonnaise jar or other container, as in the illustration.
1. Select and clean a container for the terrarium.
2. Spread gravel out on the bottom of the jar so it will be concentrated toward the back of the jar, as shown in the diagram.
3. Place ferns, mosses, lichens, and liverworts over the gravel.
4. Pour some water in the jar. (Do not put in so much that it covers the back portion of the arrangement.)
5. Place a dried twig in the jar.
6. Place a small water turtle or frog in the jar.
7. Cover the jar with the punctured lid.
8. Feed the turtle or frog insects or turtle food every other day.
9. Place the terrarium in an area where light is weak.

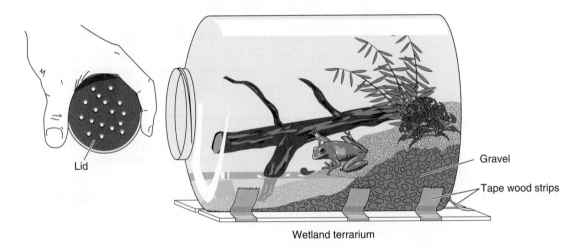

Lid

Gravel

Tape wood strips

Wetland terrarium

8. WHAT CAN WE OBSERVE IN A WETLAND TERRARIUM? (3–5)

Materials
- Wetland terrarium (constructed in previous activity)
- Magnifiying lenses
- Investigation journals

ENGAGE

a. Ask: *What happens to the living and nonliving things within a wetland terrarium over time? How can we find out?*

EXPLORE

b. Allow students time to regularly observe and keep records on how the wetland animal interacts with its terrarium habitat over several weeks.

EXPLAIN

c. Ask: *What natural habitat is this terrarium modeling? How do the living things in the terrarium have their needs met? What interactions have you observed between the organisms in the terrarium and the nonliving things in their environment?*

ELABORATE

d. The questions generated by your students' wonderings and those that follow can drive focused observational investigations related to the wetland terrariums or lead to library and/or Internet research.

Ask:
What kinds of conditions does the turtle, frog, or lizard need to survive in its particular habitat?
What kinds of conditions do the wetland plants require to grow well?
What kinds of food does the turtle, frog, or lizard eat?
What do you think would happen to the turtle if you left it in the desert habitat or to the lizard if you put it in the wetland habitat?
What other kinds of environments or habitats could you make?
What does the environment have to do with the kinds of organisms found in it?
What might happen to a fern plant if it were transplanted to a desert region?
What might happen to a penguin if it were taken to live in a desert?
What would humans need to survive in an arctic region?

EVALUATE

e. Have students complete the following chart for the wetland terrarium habitats they constructed and observed, describing the food, water, shelter, and other conditions you provided for the organisms living there.

NAME OF HABITAT:	
Habitat Living Conditions	Description
Food	
Shelter	
Air	
Temperature	
Climate	
Water	
Others	

f. If the class has constructed other terrariums or aquariums modeling other habitats, students could complete charts for all of them, then write a brief report comparing and contrasting those habitats.

III. STRUCTURES AND FUNCTIONS OF HUMAN SYSTEMS

Each plant or animal has different structures that serve different functions in growth, survival, and reproduction. For example, animals, including humans, have body structures for respiration, protection from disease, and digestion of food. Warm-blooded animals have structures for regulating temperature. Humans have distinct body structures for walking, holding, seeing, and talking.

A. THE HUMAN SYSTEM FOR RESPIRATION

▶ *Science Background*

Humans, like other animals, need oxygen to survive. Oxygen is taken in through breathing. Breathing is controlled by movement of the diaphragm. When the diaphragm moves down, air is forced into the lungs. When the diaphragm moves up in the rib cage, air is forced out of the lungs. Gases and water vapor are exhaled from the lungs. When a person exercises, breathing rate increases. Breathing increases because more carbon dioxide is produced. Carbon dioxide causes the diaphragm to involuntarily work more rapidly. Lung capacity varies from person to person and can be increased by aerobic training.

NSES   Science Standards

All students should develop an understanding of

- characteristics of organisms (K–4).
- structure and function in living systems (5–8).

Concepts and Principles That Support the Standarads

- Living systems at all levels of organization demonstrate the complementary nature of structure and function (5–8).
- The human organism has systems for digestion, respiration, reproduction, circulation, excretion, movement, control and coordination, and protection from disease. These systems interact with one another (5–8).

Objectives

1. Define *system* and apply the term to human systems.
2. Ask questions and design and carry out investigations to answer questions about structure and function in the human respiratory system.
3. Describe the form and function of the human system for respiration.

1. IS THE AIR WE BREATHE IN THE SAME AS THE AIR WE BREATHE OUT? (5–8)

Materials

- Three plastic cups
- Turkey baster or large syringe
- Plastic drinking straws
- Calcium hydroxide tablets (limewater tablets; obtain from a drugstore or science materials supplier)

ENGAGE

a. Ask: *Is there a difference in the composition of the air around us and the air we exhale? How could we find out?*

EXPLORE

b. This investigation can be done as a teacher demonstration or by students in cooperative groups:
    1. Obtain two clear plastic cups, a turkey baster, a straw, and 100 cc of limewater made by dissolving a calcium hydroxide tablet in a large container of water. Mix half the limewater with regular water in each cup. Let the water settle.
    2. Put a straw in one cup and a turkey baster or large syringe in the other. Describe how the limewater in the cups looks.

(a) Breathe in limewater

(b) Baster in limewater

    3. One student should blow through a straw into one cup of limewater while the other pumps the bulb of the turkey baster into the other cup of limewater.

EXPLAIN

c. Ask:
    What happens to the limewater as you blow (exhale) through the straw into the water?
    Why does the water get "cloudy"?
    What happens to the limewater when you squeeze the turkey baster into it?
    Why do you think the limewater did not change?
    Why is this a controlled experiment? What condition is varied?
    What is the responding variable? What do you think is controlled?

d. Tell the class that limewater is an indicator for carbon dioxide. When carbon dioxide is bubbled through limewater, it turns milky. Ask: *Based on this information, is there more carbon dioxide in the air you breathe in (inhale) or in the air you breathe out (exhale)? What is your evidence?*

▶ *Teaching Background*

This investigation compares breathed air that is blown through a straw with regular air that is pumped from a turkey baster. The test results suggest that breathed air contains a significant amount of carbon dioxide gas. When carbon dioxide is added to limewater, the water changes to a milky color because the carbon dioxide combines with calcium hydroxide to form a white precipitate. You can see the white powder precipitate on the bottom of the cup. You can test the white powder that falls to the bottom by adding some vinegar; vinegar will cause calcium or carbonate to foam. Regular air may also contain carbon dioxide, but not enough to detect by this procedure.

2. WHAT MAKES YOU BREATHE FASTER? (3–8)

Materials
- Stopwatch
- Mirror

ENGAGE

a. Ask: *How many times a minute do you breathe? How do you know? How would you go about finding out?*

EXPLORE

b. This activity should be done in groups of three: one student does the activity, the second student counts the number of breaths, and the third student is the timekeeper. At the completion of each activity, the students should rotate in their tasks until all have completed the activity. Explain that students should count the number of exhaled breaths in a time interval. Students may use a mirror to see the exhaled breaths.
   1. Student 1 should breathe normally. Student 2 should count the number of exhaled breaths in 15 seconds. Student 3 should use a stopwatch to start the count at an inhale phase and stop the count after 15 seconds.
   2. Have the student being tested run in place for 1 minute and then repeat step 1.
   3. Use this table for recording your data.

	Breaths/15 seconds			
	Student 1	Student 2	Student 3	Average
At rest				
After running in place for 1 minute				

4. When "At rest" and "After running in place for 1 minute" data have been collected for each student in the group. Calculate the group average for each experimental condition.

5. Graph your group's average data using the axes shown here.

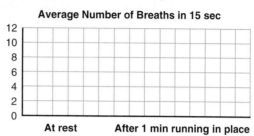

EXPLAIN

c. Have groups present and post their graphs so the entire class can compare their findings. Ask: *What is the average number of times per minute a person in this class breathes at rest? . . . after running in place for 1 minute? How could we find out?* (Average the group results for each experimental condition.) *Why do you think exercise makes a person breathe faster?*

3. HOW CAN WE MAKE A MODEL OF LUNGS? (3–8)

Materials

For each group:

- Plastic cup
- Drinking straw
- Small plastic bag
- Small balloon
- Rubber band
- Scissors

ENGAGE

a. Ask: *How do your lungs work to inhale and exhale gases?*

Construct

b. Guide students to conduct this activity. You may wish to punch a hole in the plastic cups (see step 3) before students begin the activity. The heated tip of an ice pick will pierce the plastic easily.

1. Obtain a plastic drinking straw, a small plastic bag, two rubber bands, a clear plastic cup, a small balloon, and scissors.
2. Cut the straw in half.
3. In the bottom of the cup, punch a hole the same width as the straw.

4. Stretch and blow up the balloon a few times.
5. Using a tightly wound rubber band, attach the balloon to the straw. Be sure the balloon does not come off when you blow into the straw and the rubber band does not crush the straw.
6. Push the free end of the straw through the cup's hole and pull until the balloon is in the middle of the cup. Seal the area around the hole and straw with modeling clay.
7. Place the open end of the cup into the small plastic bag and fold the bag around the cup, securing it tightly with a rubber band or masking tape. The plastic bag should be loose, not stretched taut, across the cup's opening.

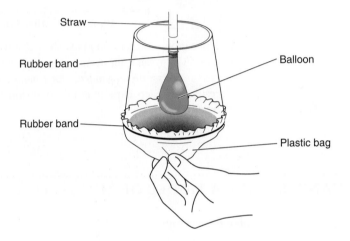

EXPLORE

8. Ask: *What do you think might happen to the balloon if you pull down on the plastic bag at the bottom of the cup?*
9. Pull down on the plastic bag. Record your observation. Ask: *What do you think might happen if you push up on the plastic bag?*
10. Push up on the plastic bag. Record your observation.

EXPLAIN

c. Ask: *What changes did you observe in the system? Why do these changes happen? Where in your body do you have something that works like this?*

Referring to a model or illustration of the chest cavity, guide students to identify the parts of the body used in breathing and describe how they function. Ask: *How is this physical model like the lungs?*

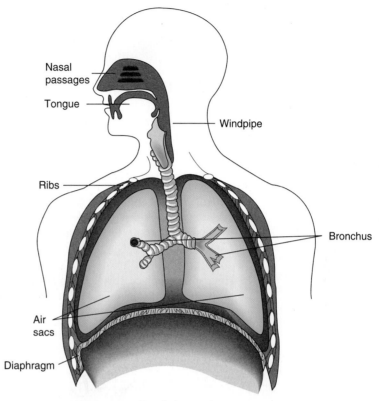

Respiratory system

 B. THE HUMAN SYSTEM FOR REGULATING TEMPERATURE

▶ *Science Background*

Normal body temperature is 98.6°F. To maintain this temperature, the body converts food energy to heat energy. When the environment is very warm or through exercise, the temperature of the body may exceed the normal level. The body then cools itself through perspiring. When perspiration evaporates from the body, the body is cooled.

NSES **Science Standards**

All students should develop an understanding of

- structure and function in living systems (5–8).

Concepts and Principles That Support the Standards

- All organisms must be able to obtain and use resources, grow, reproduce, and maintain stable internal conditions while living in a constantly changing external environment (5–8).
- Regulation of an organism's internal environment involves sensing the internal environment and changing physiological activities to keep conditions within the range required to survive (5–8).

Objectives

1. Describe and explain how the evaporation of perspiration cools the body.

1. HOW DOES YOUR BODY COOL ITSELF? (K–5)

Materials

- Two old socks (wool or cotton are best) for each student
- Electric fan

ENGAGE

a. Using a medicine dropper, place a few drops of water on the back of the hand of each student. Tell the students to gently blow across the water drop. Ask: *What happened to the water drop?* (It disappeared—evaporated.) *How did your hand feel?* (It got cooler.) Ask: *How does your body use evaporation to cool itself?*

EXPLORE

b. Have students place a dry sock on one hand and a wet sock on the other hand. To improve the cooling effect, use a fan to blow air over the students' hands.

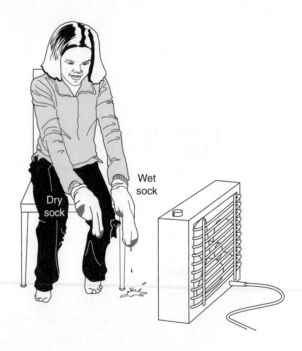

EXPLAIN

c. Invite students to share their findings from the explore phase. Ask: *Which hand felt cooler, the one with the wet sock or the one with the dry sock? Why?* Explain that evaporation is a cooling process. When water evaporates, the surface from which it evaporated gets cooler.

Ask: *What is the role of the moisture in cooling? What do you think happens when perspiration evaporates? Why does a fan cool us even on a hot day? Why do you feel cool on a hot summer day when you come out of the water after swimming?*

ELABORATE

    d. Encourage students to develop a question that can be investigated related to evaporative cooling, then plan and carry out an experiment to help answer that question. If temperature probes and CBL software are available, familiarize students with their use as they may provide more accurate temperature data than simple laboratory thermometers. In addition, temperature probes enable students to look at real-time graphs showing cooling trends rather than first collecting data and then graphing it manually.

EVALUATE

    e. To assess student understanding of why the human body perspires, administer this multiple choice item:

        1. When we are hot, our body perspires because:
          A. when liquids evaporate, they cause cooling.
          B. heat causes the pores in our skin open.
          C. we need to stay hydrated (drink lots of water) in hot weather.
          D. cells in our body are melting due to the heat.

 ## C. FOOD AND THE HUMAN SYSTEM FOR DIGESTION

▶ *Science Background*

Food provides energy and nutrients for growth, development, and normal functioning. Good nutrition is essential for good health. Foods contain starches, sugars, fats, and proteins the body needs. During digestion, our body breaks down starches into glucose, a type of sugar, and the glucose then supplies energy for our muscles. Rice, corn, and potatoes are major sources of starch. Glucose itself is another major source of energy. Grapes, raisins, and bananas are natural sources of glucose. Soft drinks are another source of glucose. Fatty foods, such as fried foods, candy bars, cookies, and chips, can supply a great deal of energy per gram, but if the energy is not used, it is stored as fat within the body. During digestion, proteins are broken down into amino acids, substances our bodies need to build and repair tissues.

    Specific chemical and physical tests can be conducted to determine which nutrients are in foods. Iodine can be used to test for starches. Tes-Tape can be used to test for glucose. Brown paper can be used to test for fats. Protein test papers (Coomassie blue test papers), purchased from a scientific supply company, can be used to test for proteins.

NSES

      Science Standards

All students should develop an understanding of

- structure and function in living systems (5–8).
- regulation and behavior (5–8).

Concepts and Principles That Support the Standards

- The human organism has systems for digestion, respiration, reproduction, circulation, excretion, movement, control and coordination, and protection from disease (5–8).
- Behavior is one kind of response an organism can make to an internal or environmental stimulus (5–8).
- Behavioral response is a set of actions determined in part by heredity and in part from experience (5–8).

....

1. HOW MUCH WATER IS IN OUR FOODS? (5–8)

Materials

- Blunt plastic knives
- Scale for weighing
- Lettuce, tomatoes, apples, oranges
- Hand juicer
- Paper plates
- Small paper cups
- Thick white bread
- Bread toaster

ENGAGE

a. Display a collection of foods. Ask: *How much water is in our foods? How could we find out?*

EXPLORE

b. As a class or in cooperative groups, guide students to carry out these activities:
   1. Weigh each of the foods individually on a scale and record their weights in the "before" column of the chart.

WATER CONTENT CHART

Weight of Food in Grams or Paper Clips			
Food	Before	After	Weight of Water in Food
Lettuce			
Tomato			
Orange			
Apple			
Bread			

   2. Using a hand juicer, squeeze out all of the juice from the tomato. Weigh the tomato pulp (without the juice) and record the weight in the after column.
   3. Spread the lettuce leaves out on paper plates to dry overnight. The next day, weigh the lettuce leaves and record their weight in the after column.
   4. Repeat the previous step for the apple and the orange.
   5. Toast the bread in the toaster, weigh the bread, and record the number in the after column.
   6. Calculate the fractions of water in each food by dividing the weight of water in the food by the original weight of the food.

EXPLAIN

c. Ask: *What changes did you note in the foods? Why do you think the weight of each food changed? Which food initially had the highest fraction of water? Which food had the lowest fraction of water?*

ELABORATE

d. Ask: *What foods can you think of that are eaten in both fresh and dried form?* (grapes/raisins, plums/prunes, and so on) *What would you do to investigate what happens to raisins or prunes when they are soaked in water?* (Try it and see.)

▶ *Teaching Background*

Although water is not one of the basic nutrients, we must have it every day. We could not live without it. Besides drinking liquids, here are some common foods and the percentages of water by weight we get when we eat them. Students' test results may not agree with these. Even after students treat the various foods, they still will likely contain some water.

Lettuce	95%	Carrot	90%
Yogurt	90%	Apple	85%
Pizza	50%	Bread	35%

EVALUATE

e. To assess if your students have grasped the general concept that our foods contain a lot of water, have them respond to the following:

1. Which of the following statements about water in food do you agree with most?
   A. Most of the foods we eat contain very little water.
   B. Most of the foods we eat are more than 25% water by weight.
   C. Most of the foods we eat are made only of water.

2. Give evidence that supports your choice.

2. WHAT IS STARCH, AND HOW CAN WE TEST FOR IT? (5–8)

Materials

- Paper plates
- Dropper
- Thin slices of banana, apple, potato, white bread, cheese, egg white, butter
- Cracker
- Cornstarch
- Iodine solution
- Granulated sugar

ENGAGE

a. Ask: *Which of these foods contains starch? How might we find out?*

Safety Precautions

Iodine solution is poisonous, may cause burns if it is too strong, and can stain clothing. It must not be eaten. Because iodine is poisonous, do *not* eat any of the tested foods or give them to pets. Dispose of them properly.

EXPLORE

b. Assist cooperative groups to carry out this investigation.
1. On a paper plate, arrange and label each food sample as shown in the illustration.

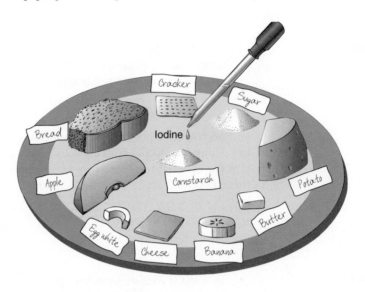

2. Look at the colors of each food and record them on a chart.
3. Place a drop of iodine solution on each sample of food.
4. Look at the color of each food where the iodine drop touched it.

EXPLAIN

c. Ask: *How have some of the food colors changed? Which foods have something in common after getting an iodine drop?*

Explain that the chemical iodine can be used to test foods for starches. When iodine is placed on a starchy food, the food turns varying shades of purple-black in relation to the amount of starch present in it.

Ask: *If starch turns purple-black in iodine, which of your sample foods would you say contain starch? Which do not have starch?*

As you've seen, some foods contain starch. Starch is a nutrient that provides energy for cells to use.

▶ *Teaching Background*

Starch provides energy for cells to use. Major sources of starch are rice, corn, and potatoes. Like most starchy foods, these foods also contain vitamins and minerals. During digestion, the body breaks down starch into glucose, and the glucose provides energy for cells.

Some starchy foods are also high in fiber, indigestible material that helps move matter through the digestive tract. Fruits, vegetables, and whole grains are some sources of fiber.

Because they contain large amounts of starch, rice and flour turn purple-black when iodine is added. Certain vegetables and fruits contain little starch and may turn only a very faint purple-black during an iodine test.[9]

---

[9]Adapted from Science and Technology for Children (STC), 1994. *Food Chemistry*. Carolina Biological Supply Co., Burlington, NC.

3. WHAT ARE FATS, AND HOW DO WE TEST FOR THEM? (5–8)

Materials

- Paper plates
- Water
- Butter
- Vegetable oil
- Samples of common snack foods: peanuts, bread, margarine, celery, carrots, mayonnaise, lettuce, bacon, corn or potato chips, pretzels, cheese, cookies, cake, apple, whole milk, yogurt, chocolate
- Brown paper bags or brown paper towels cut into 5 cm squares (enough so that there is one square for each food sample)
- Source of light: sunlight or lamp
- Dropper

ENGAGE

a. Ask: *Do some foods contain fats? Which ones? How could we test to see if foods contain fat?*

EXPLORE

b. Assist students to carry out this test in cooperative groups:
   1. Put several drops of water on one square of brown paper, as in diagram (a). On a second square, put drops of oil as in diagram (b).

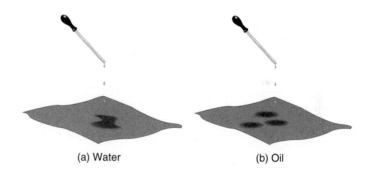

(a) Water   (b) Oil

   2. Fats feel slippery when rubbed between the fingers.
      Ask: *How does the water stain feel? How does the oil stain feel?*
   3. Ask: *How do the two stains look? What do you think will happen to the two stains after 10 minutes?*
   4. After 10 minutes, check the two squares of paper.

EXPLAIN

c. Ask: *What happened to each stain? Where did the water stain go? How do the oil stains look?*
   Explain that the water evaporated, but the oil stains remained shiny. This is the spot test for fats. Explain that fats leave greasy spots on brown paper. Tell students that like starches, fats are a nutrient that supply energy for the body.

ELABORATE

d. Have groups of students conduct their own spot tests using the samples of snack foods.
   1. Get a paper plate containing samples of snack foods, squares of brown paper, and a copy of the lab sheet shown in the diagram.

FAT SPOT TEST LAB SHEET		
Food Samples	Predicted Fat	Contains Fat
Peanuts		
Bread		
Margarine		
Celery		
Carrots		
Mayonnaise		
Lettuce		
Bacon		
Corn/Potato chips		
Pretzels		
Cheese		
Cookies		
Cake		
Apple		
Whole milk		
Yogurt		
Chocolate		

2. Mark an **X** in the "predicted fat" column for foods you think contain fat.
3. Firmly rub each food sample 10 times on a separate square of brown paper, and label the paper with the food's name.
4. After 10 minutes, hold each paper square up to a source of light as in the illustration.

Safety Precautions   It is all right to use illumination from a window as a source of light, but caution children not to look directly into the sun.

5. Mark an **X** in the "contains fat" column of your chart for each food that left a greasy spot.

e. Ask: *How did your predictions compare with your findings? How would you summarize your test findings as to which foods contained fat?*

f. Discuss with students the importance of reading food labels for ingredients. Also discuss how they might select foods with less fat.

Ask: *Why might it be healthier to eat such foods as skim milk, low-fat cottage cheese, and nonfat ice cream? How could we have a party, serving good-tasting foods, and still cut down on the amount of fat we eat?*

▶ *Teaching Background*

Some foods have a lot of fat, and others have little or no fat. Fats that are thick (solid) at room temperature usually come from animals like cows, pigs, and sheep. These fats are called **saturated fats**. Fats that are soft (semisolid) at room temperature usually are made from animals (e.g., lard and butter) or are manufactured (e.g., margarine). Fats that are liquid at room temperature usually come from plants (e.g., peanut oil, olive oil, corn oil).

EVALUATE

g. To check student understanding about the presence of fat in food, have them respond to the following writing prompt:

1. You have been given a sample of food that you do not recognize. Before you eat it, you want to know if it contains fat. *What would you do to find out?*

4. WHAT IS GLUCOSE, AND HOW DO WE TEST FOR IT? (5–8)

Materials

- Tes-Tape (get in drugstore)
- Bananas (fairly ripe)
- Milk
- Different kinds of apples (McIntosh, Delicious, Rome)
- Granular sugar, moistened with water
- Oranges
- Maple syrup
- Honey
- Paper plates
- Small paper cups

Preparation

For efficiency in distribution, the teacher or designated students should prepare the following beforehand for each group of two to four students: paper plate containing cut samples of foods and small cups with very small samples of honey, milk, and maple syrup; 1 inch Tes-Tape strip for each food to be tested; data collection sheet.

ENGAGE

a. Ask: *What is glucose? How can we test foods for glucose?*

EXPLORE

b. Guide cooperative groups of students to conduct this investigation:
   1. Get a paper plate that contains food samples, Tes-Tape strips, and a data collection sheet.
   2. Assign one group member to each of the following tasks: tester, observer, and recorder.
   3. The tester should number each food, then write the numerals 1 through 10 on separate Tes-Tape strips.
   4. Using the appropriately numbered strip that corresponds to the food being tested, the tester should touch a 1 inch strip of the Tes-Tape to each food separately, until the strip is wet, and hand the Tes-Tape to the observer.

   5. The observer should look at the wet end of the Tes-Tape to see what color it is.
   6. The observer gives the following information to the recorder:
      a. Number of the sample Tes-Tape strip
      b. Name of the food sample
      c. Color of the wet end of the Tes-Tape strip
   7. The students should repeat the preceding procedures with all of the food samples.
   8. As each food is tested, the recorder notes on the Tes-Tape data collection sheet the data that the observer provides. The recorder attaches each Tes-Tape strip in the appropriate place on the data table.

TES-TAPE SUGAR TEST DATA COLLECTION SHEET		
Food Samples	Tape Color After Test	Tape Strip
Orange		
Banana, ripe		
Banana, green		
Maple syrup		
Milk		
Honey		
McIntosh apple		
Yellow Delicious apple		
Rome apple		
Granulated sugar		

EXPLAIN

c. Explain that glucose is one kind of sugar. Many foods contain glucose. Glucose is a major source of energy for our bodies. Explain to students that they used Tes-Tape to test different foods for glucose. Tes-Tape is a special chemically treated paper designed for use by people who have diabetes.

d. Ask:

From the data collected, which foods contain glucose? What evidence do you have to support this?

From the changes in the Tes-Tape color, which foods appear to have the most glucose? the least?

Which foods, if any, did not change the color of the Tes-Tape? Why do you think this happened?

ELABORATE

e. Have students bring in labels from food packages, read the ingredients list, and list all the forms of sugar each food contains, such as honey, brown sugar syrup, sweeteners, corn sugar, corn sweeteners, molasses, invert sugar, sucrose, fructose, dextrose, maltose, lactose, and so on.

Find out the amounts of sugar (both labeled and "hidden") in the common foods you eat. For example, soft drinks can contain about 8 teaspoons per 12 ounces, and many breakfast cereals contain about 2½ teaspoons (10 g) of sugar plus 3 teaspoons (13 g) of other carbohydrates for a total of 5½ teaspoons (23 g) per 1 ounce serving.

Ask:

What do you think might happen if you tested artificial sweeteners (saccharin, aspartame, etc.) with Tes-Tape?

Why would it be healthier to eat fresh fruit as a snack rather than cakes, candy, and soft drinks, even though all of these contain sugar?

▶ *Teaching Background*

There are several types of sugars, including sucrose, lactose, fructose, and glucose. Glucose is a major source of energy for the body. Starches consist of long linked chains of glucose. Much of the glucose the body needs comes from the breakdown of starches. Natural sources of glucose include apples, grapes, raisins, and bananas. Soft drinks are another source of glucose. Sweets ordinarily contain other types of sugars.[10]

EVALUATE

f. To check student understanding about the presence of glucose in food, have them respond to the following writing prompt:
   1. You have been given a sample of food that you do not recognize. Before you eat it, you want to know if it contains glucose. What would you do to find out?

5. HOW CAN YOU DETERMINE WHICH SODA HAS MORE SUGAR? (5–8)

Materials

- Three pairs of 12 ounce cans of soft drinks, unopened, assorted flavors and brands (each pair should contain one diet and one regular of same flavor and brand)
- Aquarium or large transparent tub filled with water
- Scale for weighing

ENGAGE

a. Ask: *What would happen if we placed a can of diet cola and regular cola in a container of water?*

EXPLORE

b. Place a can of regular cola and a can of diet cola in an aquarium filled with water. Ask: *What did you observe?* (The regular can of cola sinks, but, surprisingly, the can of diet cola floats.)

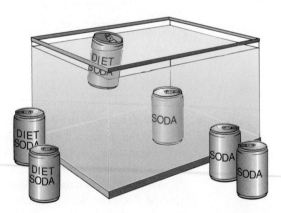

EXPLAIN

c. Ask: *What happened? Why do you think the can of diet cola floated while the can of regular cola sank?*

When students suggest that the can of diet cola was lighter, ask: *How could we test this hypothesis?*

---

[10]Adapted from Science and Technology for Children (STC), 1994. *Food Chemistry*. Carolina Biological Supply Co., Burlington, NC.

ELABORATE

    d. Instruct students to
1. weigh each of the six cans of diet and regular soft drinks;
2. record the weights in a table like the one illustrated;
3. test each of the six cans to determine if it floats or sinks; and
4. record their observations about floating or sinking in the table.

SUGAR CONTENT OF DIET AND REGULAR SOFT DRINKS

Pair	Brand	Diet Weight	Regular Weight	Float or Sink?
1				Diet
				Regular
2				Diet
				Regular
3				Diet
				Regular

    e. Ask: *What did you determine in your tests? Did your data support the hypothesis that the cans of regular soft drinks were heavier than the cans of diet soft drinks?*

    f. Ask: *Why do you think a can of diet cola is lighter than a can of regular cola of the same brand and flavor?* When students suggest that the cans of regular soft drink contain more liquid than the cans of diet soft drink, lead them to examine labels to compare the volumes of liquid in the regular and diet soft drink cans. Students might also open the cans and measure the volume using a graduated cylinder.

        If students do not suggest it, also ask them to compare the ingredients of the regular and diet soft drinks. The weight of a diet soft drink is usually about 10 to 15 g less than the weight of a regular soft drink. The difference is usually sugar or corn syrup.

6. WHAT ARE PROTEINS, AND HOW DO WE TEST FOR THEM? (5–8)

Materials

For each group:

- Six Coomassie blue protein test strips in a clean envelope
- Test tray
- Forceps
- Petri dish
- Toothpicks
- Paper towels

(Protein test strips and other materials are available from Carolina Biological Supply—see Appendix C for address.)

For the class:

- Half liter (1 pint) white vinegar
- Half liter (1 pint) rubbing alcohol

- 1 liter plastic bottle to mix and store developing solution
- Medicine droppers
- Plastic spoons
- One carton skim milk, 237 ml (one-half pint)
- Unshelled peanuts
- Rice grains

Preparation

To test for proteins, students immerse a Coomassie blue test strip in a liquid or food, and then place the test strip in a developing solution for several minutes. To prepare the developing solution, mix together half a liter of white vinegar and half a liter of rubbing alcohol in a 1 liter plastic mixing bottle. Close the bottle and store the developing solution.

ENGAGE

a. Ask: *What nutrients have we tested for so far?* [Starch, fat, and glucose (sugar)] *What do you know about proteins? What foods contain proteins? How can we test liquids and foods for proteins?*

EXPLORE

b. Hold up a strip of protein test paper. Handle the test strip only with forceps so as not to contaminate it with your hands. Explain to students that the strip contains a special chemical—Coomassie blue—that reacts to proteins. During testing, the paper must be developed in a special solution. When developed, the color of the paper will stay deep blue if the protein content of the food being tested is high; the blue color will fade if there is a medium amount of protein in the food; and the blue color will disappear if the food contains little or no protein.

c. To test liquids or foods for proteins, have students follow these directions:
1. Put three drops of milk in section 1 of the test tray.
2. Put three drops of water in section 2 of the test tray.
3. Using a spoon, put a few grains of rice in section 3 of the test tray. Put two or three drops of tap water on the rice and stir for about a minute with a toothpick.
4. Shell a peanut (without touching the nut itself) and place it in section 4 of the test tray. Use a plastic spoon to crush the peanut. Add two or three drops of water and stir with a new toothpick.
5. Using a spoon, put a small amount of crushed granola bar in section 5 of the test tray. Add two or three drops of water and stir with a new toothpick.
6. Obtain six test strips and number them 1 to 6 on the white end of the strips. Be careful not to touch the test strips. Holding a test strip by its white end with forceps, immerse the blue end in the liquid or food just long enough to wet the strip—test strip 1 in the milk, test strip 2 in water, test strip 3 in the moistened rice, test strip 4 in the moistened peanut, and test strip 5 in the moistened granola bar. Place test strip 6 in the empty section 6 of the test tray as a control. Use clean toothpicks to make sure each food is in contact with the test paper. Be sure the white end of each test strip is not in contact with the liquid or food being tested.

7. Leave the test strips in the tray sections just long enough to wet the strips. Using forceps, remove each of the numbered test strips from the tray sections and place them on a paper towel. Use clean toothpicks to clean any food particles from them and use a paper towel to blot off any excess liquid.

8. Ask your teacher to pour a little developing solution in the bottom of your petri dish. Using forceps, transfer each of the test strips to the developing solution. Make sure the blue tip of the test strip is immersed.

9. Leave the test strips in the developing solution for about 5 minutes. Keep stirring the solution with a toothpick.

10. After 5 minutes, remove the protein test papers from the developing solution and place them on a paper towel.

11. Note and record the color of each test strip in the following chart. Based on the color observed, determine the protein content of each food—high, medium, or low.

PROTEIN TEST RESULTS

Liquid or Food	Color of Protein Test Strip	Protein Content (High, Medium, or Low)
1. Milk		
2. Tap water		
3. Rice		
4. Peanut		
5. Granola bar		
6. Control		

EXPLAIN

d. In a class-sized group, invite students to discuss their procedures and share their results.

Ask: *What happened to the protein test strips in each liquid or food? Which food or liquids were high in proteins? Which had a medium protein content? Which foods had a low amount or no proteins?* Share the following master chart of protein test results with students.

PROTEIN TEST RESULTS

Liquid or Food	Color of Protein Test Strip	Protein Content (High, Medium, or Low)
1. Milk	Remains blue	High
2. Tap water	Blue disappears	Low
3. Rice	Blue disappears	Low
4. Peanut	Remains blue	High
5. Granola bar	Blue almost disappears	Medium
6. Control	Blue disappears	Low or none

▶ *Teaching Background*

Protein is one group of food nutrients that the body uses for building tissues and repairing broken-down cells. Proteins are vital for children's proper physical and mental growth and development. Because protein cannot be made by or stored in the body, it must be eaten regularly to promote the repair of used body cells. Eggs, cheese, meat, fish, and legumes are some foods that contain large proportions of protein.

In a protein test, the chemical Coomassie blue actually binds to protein. Because of this chemical reaction, the protein and Coomassie blue will remain on the test paper after it has been in the developing solution. In the absence of protein, the Coomassie blue will dissolve in the developing solution.[11]

---

[11]Activities on proteins adapted from Science and Technology for Children (STC), 1994. *Food Chemistry.* Carolina Biological Supply Co., Burlington, NC. (Reprinted with permission from the National Science Resources Center, Washington, DC.)

7. WHAT IS VITAMIN C, AND HOW DO WE TEST FOR IT? (5–8)

Materials

To make vitamin C indicator liquid for the class:

- Teaspoon
- Cornstarch
- Measuring cup
- Water
- Pan
- Hot plate
- Empty plastic gallon jug
- Iodine

For each group:

- Ruler
- Six clean baby food jars
- Variety of at least six different juices that are canned, frozen, or fresh (e.g., orange, apple, grape, pineapple, etc.)
- Six droppers
- Six wooden stirrers

Preparation

A simple vitamin C indicator liquid can be made ahead of time and will keep for several days. You will know when it is time to dispose of it, because it will lighten from its optimum color of royal blue to a very pale blue. To make 1 gallon of vitamin C indicator:

1. Boil 1½ teaspoons (6 ml) of cornstarch in 1 cup (250 ml) of water for 2 minutes.
2. Put 10 full droppers of the cornstarch mixture into a gallon jug of water, use a clean dropper to add 1 dropper full of iodine, cover the jug, and shake it until you have a uniform blue color.

ENGAGE

a. Ask: *What do you know about vitamin C? How can we test foods for vitamin C?*

EXPLORE

b. Instruct students to follow these directions to test foods for vitamin C:
   1. Using your ruler to measure, pour 1 cm of vitamin C indicator liquid into each of six clean baby food jars. Label each jar with the name of the juice you will test for vitamin C.
   2. Using a clean dropper for each juice, add one kind of juice to each jar of indicator liquid, one drop at a time, and count the number of drops. (See the diagram.) Stir the liquid indicator with a clean wooden stirrer as you add drops.
   3. When the indicator is no longer blue, the test is finished.
   4. Record the number of drops of each juice needed to clear up the blue vitamin C indicator liquid.

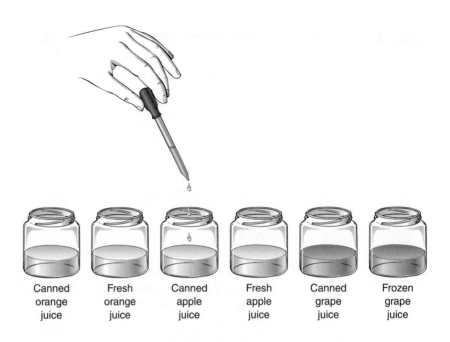

Canned orange juice Fresh orange juice Canned apple juice Fresh apple juice Canned grape juice Frozen grape juice

EXPLAIN

c. Invite students to discuss their procedures and results.

Ask: *Which juice(s) caused the blue color to disappear with the least number of drops? Which juice(s) caused the blue color to disappear with the most drops?*

d. Tell students that we tested for vitamin C by testing how it reacts with a special mixture of cornstarch, iodine, and water. Explain that the fewer drops of juice needed to make the blue color disappear, the more vitamin C that juice contains.

Explain that scientists have discovered more than 26 vitamins our bodies need. The lack of one vitamin could result in a vitamin deficiency disease. Vitamin C is probably the best known vitamin. It is found in citrus fruits, tomatoes, raw cabbage, strawberries, and cantaloupe.

Ask: *From these tests, which juice(s) had the most vitamin C? the least vitamin C? How do you know?*

ELABORATE

e. Ask: *How do you think the following conditions could affect the vitamin C content of foods: heat, sunlight, air, age of food, and so on? How could you design experiments to test these variables?* If time permits, allow student groups to carry out their experiments and report their findings to the class.

EVALUATE

f. You could use these investigations to formatively assess students' ability to plan and conduct investigations through observations of their work. The following indicators, based on Wynne Harlen's work on process skill indicators,[12] are listed in order of sophistication and can be used to judge students' performance level for these process skills.

---

[12]Adapted from Harlen, W. (2000). *Teaching, learning and assessing science 5-12* (3rd ed.). Thousand Oaks, CA: Sage Publications.

Indicators for Planning and Conducting Investigations

Students:

☐ Start with a useful general approach even if details are lacking or need further thought.

☐ Have some ideas of which variable should be changed, or what things should be compared.

☐ Do not change those variables that must be kept constant to have a fair test.

☐ Have some idea before they start the investigation of what they must look for to get results.

☐ Choose a realistic way to measure or compare things to get results.

☐ Take steps to ensure that their results are as accurate as possible.

8. HOW MUCH OF EACH NUTRIENT DOES YOUR BODY NEED, AND HOW CAN YOU FIND OUT WHAT IS IN EACH FOOD? (5–8)

Materials

• Food labels from a large variety of packaged foods. Collect food labels yourself, and ask students to collect and bring in empty food packages or labels from the packages. You will need at least one food label for each pair of students.

ENGAGE

a. Ask: *Can you think of another way, besides testing, to determine the nutritional content of foods?* If students do not suggest reading food labels, raise the idea.

EXPLORE

b. Pass out food labels and a copy of the food label record sheet to pairs of students. Ask: *What kind of information is given on the food labels?* Allow students time (10 to 15 minutes) to discuss the information given on the food labels and how it relates to the tests they have completed previously.

Nutrition Facts

Serving Size 2/3 cup (55g)
Servings Per Container 12

Amount Per Serving

Calories 210
   Calories from Fat 25

% Daily Value*

Total Fat 3g	**5%**
Saturated Fat 1g	**4%**
Polyunsaturated Fat 0.5g	
Monounsaturated Fat 1.5g	
Cholesterol 0mg	**0%**
Sodium 140mg	**6%**
Potassium 190mg	**5%**
Total Carbohydrate 44g	**15%**
Other Carbohydrate 23g	
Dietary Fiber 3g	**13%**
Sugars 18g	
Protein 5g	
Vitamin A	0%
Vitamin C	0%
Calcium	2%
Iron	6%
Thiamine	10%
Phosphorus	10%
Magnesium	10%

* Percent Daily Values are based on a 2000 calorie diet. Your daily values may be higher or lower depending on your calorie needs.

		Calories	2,000	2,500
Total Fat	Less than		65g	80g
Sat Fat	Less than		20g	25g
Cholesterol	Less than		300g	300g
Sodium	Less than		2400mg	2400mg
Potassium			3500mg	3500mg
Total Carbo			300g	300g
Dietary Fiber			25g	30g

Calories per gram:
Fat 9   •   Carbohydrate 4   •   Protein 4

EXPLAIN

c. Explain that starch and sugar are carbohydrates. The labels give the total amount of carbohydrates in one serving of the food, but not the specific amounts of starch or sugar. Also explain that people who study nutrients (called **nutritionists**) suggest the average amount of each nutrient a person should consume. This amount is called the *recommended daily allowance*, or RDA. Answer questions students might have, for example, about serving sizes or grams and milligrams.

ELABORATE

d. Tell students to examine the food labels and record on their record sheet the information given about carbohydrates (starch and sugar), fats, proteins, calcium, and vitamin C (the type of vitamin they have tested).

Food Label Record Sheet

Name of Food _____

Serving Size _____

Nutrient	Weight per Serving	Percentage of U.S.RDA
Carbohydrates		
Fats		
Proteins		
Minerals-calcium		
Vitamins-vitamin C		

e. Bring pairs of students together in groups of six. Ask students to compare the nutrition facts from their food labels and record sheets and to complete the food group facts chart illustrated:

FOOD GROUP FACTS CHART

Calories	Food highest in calories per serving:	Food lowest in calories per serving:
Carbohydrates	Food highest in carbohydrates per serving:	Food lowest in carbohydrates per serving:
Fats	Food highest in fats per serving:	Food lowest in fats per serving:
Proteins	Food highest in proteins per serving:	Food lowest in proteins per serving:
Calcium	Food highest in calcium per serving:	Food lowest in calcium per serving:
Vitamin C	Food highest in vitamin C per serving:	Food lowest in vitamin C per serving:

f. Assemble the class as a whole and discuss which kinds of food are high and low in basic nutrients.

9. HOW CAN STUDENTS PLAN A HEALTHY DAILY MENU FOR THEMSELVES? (5–8)

▶ *Teaching Background*

The U.S. Department of Agriculture (USDA) has replaced the Food Pyramid used for many years with an interactive website, called MyPyramid, found at http://MyPyramid.gov. This imaginative innovation can be valuable and fun for children and adults. Before teaching this lesson, you should explore the website for yourself. You will want, especially, to locate the MyPyramid Plan web page and find your own healthy eating plan.

Materials

- Computers connected to the Internet (ideally, one computer for each team of four students)

ENGAGE

a. Ask: *How can you plan a health daily menu for yourself?*

Tell students that from research findings and conclusions, nutritionists recommend the amount of each food group, including grains, vegetables, fruits, milk, and meat and beans, that people should include in their daily diets.

EXPLORE

b. Direct teams of students working at computers to the MyPyramid website, at http://MyPyramid.gov. Allow some time for students to explore the website. Tell students to locate the My Pyramid Plan web page and fill in the requested information. The computer will then display a My Pyramid Plan for recommended daily food requirements, based on the information submitted.

c. Tell students to fill in the following My Pyramid Plan chart to show their own daily requirements.

MY PYRAMID PLAN DAILY FOOD GROUP REQUIREMENTS

Food Group	Recommended Daily Amount	Estimated Food Group Amounts in Yesterday's Menu (breakfast, lunch, and dinner)	Goals for Tomorrow
Grains			
Vegetables			
Fruits			
Milk			
Meat and Beans			

d. Ask students to locate the Meal Tracking Worksheet on the website, access and review it, and then follow these steps.

1. Working individually, students should write down their breakfast, lunch, and dinner menus for yesterday or a typical day.

2. Using the My Pyramid Worksheet (Meal Tracking Worksheet), estimate the total amount of grains, vegetables, fruits, milk products, and meat and cheese they
ate on that day.
3. Set food goals for themselves for tomorrow.
4. Determine breakfast, lunch, and dinner menus that will help them meet their
food group goals.

EXPLAIN

e. Allow teams of students to present their findings and menu goals to the class as a
whole. Provide ample time for presentations, discussion, and questions from other students. Ask: *How close are the daily food choices in yesterday's menu to the recommenda-
tions of the pyramid?*

SECTION IV
Earth and Space Science Activities

Earth is the home planet of human beings, the only planet in the universe known to support life. Life is possible on the earth largely because of a set of linked factors, including the earth's position within the solar system, its size and mass, its structure and resources, its range of temperatures, its atmosphere, and its abundance of water.

Students in grades K–8 can begin to develop understanding of the earth as a set of closely interrelated systems by studying the geological structure of the earth; the atmosphere, climate, and weather of the earth; the earth's oceans; and the earth in the solar system.

I. STRUCTURE OF THE EARTH

Children explore the complexities of the earth as they study the properties of rocks and minerals, the crystalline structure of minerals, and the structure of the earth's surface.

A. PROPERTIES OF ROCKS AND MINERALS

▶ *Science Background*

A mineral is a solid element or compound that has a specific composition and a crystalline structure. There are many different minerals in and on the earth—for example, talc, calcite, quartz, fluorite, and diamond. Minerals can be distinguished by such properties as hardness, texture, luster, streak color, cleavage, density, crystalline structure, and chemical properties.

Rocks are composed of minerals. Waves, wind, water, and ice cause erosion, transport, and deposit of earth materials. Sediments of sand and smaller particles are gradually buried and are cemented together with dissolved minerals to form solid rock. Rocks buried deep enough may be re-formed by pressure and heat, melting and recrystallizing into different kinds of rock. Layers of rock deep within the earth may be forced upward to become land surfaces and even mountains. Eventually, this new rock will erode under the relentless, dynamic processes of the earth.[1]

---

[1]American Association for the Advancement of Science. 1993. *Benchmarks for Science Literacy* (New York: Oxford University Press); F. J. Rutherford & A. Ahlgren, 1990. *Science for All Americans* (New York: Oxford University Press).

Science Standards

All students should develop an understanding of

- properties of the earth's systems (K–4).
- structure of the earth's systems (5–8).

Concepts and Principles That Support the Standards

- The earth's materials are solid rocks and soils, water, and gases of the atmosphere (K–4).
- The varied materials have different physical and chemical properties (K–4).

Objectives

1. Describe properties of rocks and minerals, including texture, luster, color, cleavage, hardness, density, and crystalline structure.
2. Perform tests to determine the hardness of minerals and rocks.
3. Construct charts of the properties of a variety of minerals and rocks, and use the charts to identify specific minerals and rocks.

1. WHAT ARE ROCKS AND MINERALS LIKE? (2–5)

Materials

- Kits of rock samples, including such rocks as basalt, granite, limestone, marble, pumice, sandstone, shale, and slate
- Kits of mineral samples, including such minerals as feldspar, calcite, fluorite, gypsum, graphite, hematite, hornblende, magnetite, mica, and quartz

(Kits of rocks and minerals can be obtained from scientific supply houses such as Delta Education or Carolina Biological. For addresses, see Appendix C.)

ENGAGE

a. Ask: *Where do you find different kinds of rocks?* (At home, on the school campus, on the way to school) *How are the different rocks alike? How are they different? Where do you think the rocks originally came from?*

EXPLORE

b. Initially refer to both rocks and minerals as "rocks." Provide each small group with a mixture of samples of several different rocks. For example, select large and small samples of calcite, quartz, feldspar, talc, granite, sandstone, and magnetite. Let each student in the cooperative groups examine each rock. Ask the groups to discuss what is the same and what is different about the rocks. Students often describe rocks in imaginative detail: "This rock weighs three and a half crayons. This rock is shiny and has little ripples. This one is shaped like a loaf of bread and you can stand it on its end."

EXPLAIN

c. Ask: *What were some of the property words you used to describe the rocks?* (Words related to color, texture, relative shininess, relative weight, shape, etc.)
d. Explain that rocks can be described in terms of properties, such as shape, size, color, weight, or texture. All rocks are made of materials called *minerals* that have properties that may be identified by testing. Mineral properties include color, odor, streak, luster,

hardness, and magnetism. Rocks are made up of one or more minerals, so all of the specimens we looked at are rocks, even though some of them were made of just one mineral.

ELABORATE

e. Select four rocks that are similar in color, such as four black rocks. Place the rocks on a tray so that each student in the group can observe them. Tell each student to write down descriptions of the four rocks, without letting the other students in the group know which rocks they are describing. Ask them to take turns reading their description of one rock, while the other students try to determine which rock is being described.

EVALUATE

f. You can assess a student's level of development for the process skill of observing by comparing these indicators with evidence you observe in the classroom. As you progress down this list, when you reach a statement that you would answer negatively based on your observation of the student or when you reach a statement that is difficult to answer yes or no, you have found the student's level of development for the process skill of observing. By looking further down the list, you can see the next steps for the student's learning about how to observe. The list that appears below is adapted from the Exploratorium's Institute for Inquiry and based on Wynne Harlen's work.[2] The student:

1. can identify obvious differences and similarities between the rock samples.
2. makes use of several senses in exploring the rock samples.
3. identifies differences in detail between the rock samples.
4. identifies ways rock samples are similar, even if the ways they are different are more obvious.
5. uses his/her senses appropriately and use hand lenses or microscopes to see details on rock samples.
6. can distinguish from many observations of rock samples, those that are relevant to the task they are doing.

2. WHAT IS MEANT BY THE STREAK OF A MINERAL, AND HOW CAN WE TEST FOR IT? (2–5)

Materials

- Kits of mineral samples, including such minerals as feldspar, calcite, fluorite, gypsum, graphite, hematite, hornblende, magnetite, mica, and quartz (with identifing numbers 1–12 on the samples (e.g., in each kit the feldspar sample is labeled 1, etc.)
- Copies of Mineral Properties Chart
- Streak plates
- Colored pencils or crayons

ENGAGE

a. Display a set of minerals. Ask: *What are some ways these minerals are different from each other?* When color is mentioned, explain that in this investigation they will record information about the property of color for each of the minerals in their kit. Tell them

---

[2]Adapted from Chapter 9 of *Teaching, Learning and Assessing Science 5–12* by Wynne Harlen (Sage, 2000).

they will also test each mineral by scratching it on a streak plate, then record information about the color of the streak produced by each mineral.

EXPLORE

b. Provide each small group with a mineral kit and two streak plates.

c. Demonstrate how one stroke of the mineral across the porcelain plate will usually produce a streak.

d. Have the students begin a mineral properties chart as in the illustration. Children should start with a blank chart and fill in all parts, including the labeling of each column as they make observations and tests of each mineral in this and future activities. Use observed color and streak color as the first two properties on the chart.

Mineral Properties Chart							
Number of Mineral	**Observed Color**	**Streak Color**	**Feel**	**Hardness**	**Luster**		
1	green to white	grayish					
2			soapy	softer than a penny			
3					metallic		
4					dull		
5							
6							
7							
8							
9							
10							
11							
12							

e. Provide time for the groups to observe each rock to determine its color and record their findings in the Observed Color column, and to test each rock by scratching it on the streak plate, then record their findings in the Streak column on the chart.

EXPLAIN

f. Have groups share their data with the class. Discuss the ways each group's data was alike and different and the possible reasons for that. Point out differences in details of the descriptions presented by the groups. Ask: *In what ways might these details be helpful in identifying another sample that was the same mineral as one you have tested? Are there any ways the details might not be helpful?*

Ask: *Does just looking at the color a mineral give you enough information to identify it?* (not really) *Were there more than one black mineral sample in your kit?* (Yes) *Did the streak test help in any way to tell the black minerals apart?* (The streaks of the black minerals aren't the same so they help tell the black samples apart.)

g. Explain that color was probably one of the first properties you used to describe the minerals. However, *observable color* of a mineral is not a conclusive clue to its identity, because different samples of the same mineral may have different colors. The color of the powdered form of the mineral is more consistent than its observable color. Geologists obtain powdered forms of minerals by wiping them across a *streak plate*. That mineral property, called *streak*, is described in terms of the color of the streak of powdered mineral that is left on the streak plate.

Nature of Science

Ask: *Why should we record descriptions of rocks and minerals in a chart?* Explain that building a chart of mineral properties is a way to organize data. Charts of mineral properties help us to summarize observations and identify unknown minerals. Other ways to organize data and information include data tables, graphs, and classification systems. Scientists use all of these ways to display data in order to make it easier to analyze or make sense of.

ELABORATE

h. Distribute colored pencils and/or crayons to each group. Instruct the groups to look at the observable colors and streaks of their minerals again. This time they should use colored pencils or crayons to record their findings on their chart.

EVALUATE

i. During the Explore and Elaborate stages, interact with cooperative groups to formatively assess their color and streak descriptions of different minerals. The following checklist might be helpful in monitoring and record keeping:

☐ Data table is organized and appropriately labeled.
☐ Data are entered in correct cells of the data table.
☐ Color and streak are described in detail with words.
☐ Color and streak are represented by coloring.

3. HOW CAN MINERALS BE IDENTIFIED BY THE WAY THEY FEEL? (2–5)

Materials
  • Kits of mineral samples, including such minerals as feldspar, calcite, fluorite, gypsum, graphite, hematite, hornblende, magnetite, mica, and quartz
  • Mineral Properties Charts

ENGAGE

a. Ask: *How can the way a mineral feels be used to identify the mineral? What are some words that describe the way a mineral feels?* (Smooth, rough, rounded edges, and soapy.)

EXPLORE

b. Have students feel each mineral and record their descriptions in their charts. Encourage them to use as much detail as possible in their descriptions.

EXPLAIN

c. Bring the whole class together to discuss their findings. Write the descriptive words they have used on the board. Look for synonyms, and identify subtle differences in meaning among them. Work with the class to develop an operational definition of the "feel" of a mineral.

ELABORATE

d. Have students work with a partner. One partner should close their eyes or be blindfolded. The other partner should hand the non-seeing partner each mineral sample to describe by touch and write down the description the non-seeing partner suggested. Then the partners should switch roles, and repeat the activity.

    The partners should look over the lists that they made and discuss similarities and differences in the words used. Encourage them to also discuss if it was easier to make detailed observations with their sense of touch when their sense of sight could not be used.

EVALUATE

e. Check students' Mineral Properties Charts to formatively assess their ability to include detail about how minerals feel in their descriptions and drawings.

4. WHAT IS MEANT BY THE HARDNESS OF A MINERAL, AND HOW CAN WE TEST FOR IT? (2–5)

Materials

- Kits of mineral samples, including such minerals as feldspar, calcite, fluorite, gypsum, graphite, hematite, hornblende, magnetite, mica, and quartz
- Pennies
- Steel nails
- Mineral Properties Charts

ENGAGE

a. Ask: *Are the minerals in your kit equally hard? Which one seems hardest? Which one seems softest? How can you tell?*

EXPLORE

b. Demonstrate how to use a penny to gently scratch a soft mineral and a nail to gently scratch a mineral of medium hardness. Explain that students will classify minerals as *soft*, *medium*, and *hard* using a copper penny and a steel nail as standards:

- A soft mineral can be scratched by a penny.
- A mineral of medium hardness can be scratched by a nail, but not by a penny.
- A hard mineral cannot be scratched by a nail.

To prevent damage to minerals, encourage students to scratch gently.

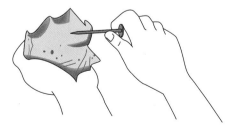

c. Have students test the hardness of each mineral in their charts. Tell students to add a "hardness" column to the mineral properties chart and to record the hardness of each mineral.

EXPLAIN

d. In a large group, ask students to report the results of their hardness tests. Work toward agreement in hardness test results, that is, they are classified as soft, medium, or hard based on the criteria given previously. Students may have to retest some mineral samples in order to reach consensus.

ELABORATE

e. You've classifed the minerals in your set into three groups soft, medium, and hard. Ask: *How could you put the minerals in order from hardest to softest?* Lead students to suggest that we could scratch two minerals together gently.

   Explain that the relative hardness of a mineral can be determined by a scratch test. The harder of two minerals will scratch the softer.

EVALUATE

f. To assess student understanding of the mineral property called hardness, have students respond to the following writing prompts in their science notebook.
   1. Mineral hardness is . . .
   2. I found the hardness of the minerals in my kit by . . . .

5. WHAT IS MEANT BY LUSTER, AND HOW CAN IT BE USED IN IDENTIFYING MINERALS? (2–5)

Materials

- Kits of mineral samples, including such minerals as feldspar, calcite, fluorite, gypsum, graphite, hematite, hornblende, magnetite, mica, and quartz
- Mineral Properties Charts
- Penlights or flashlights
- Overhead projector (optional)

ENGAGE

a. Hold a shiny mineral sample in the beam of light coming from an overhead projector or a flashlight, rotate it so it sparkles when viewed by the class. Ask: *What are some words you can use to describe the way light reflects from the surface of this mineral?*

EXPLORE

b. Have students hold each of their minerals up to the light or shine a flashlight on each one and describe in their own words the way each mineral looks in the light. Tell them to record their descriptions in their science notebooks.

EXPLAIN

c. In a large group, ask students to report their results. Write the words they use to describe luster on the board. Discuss the descriptive words (adjectives) that were used.

d. Tell students that *luster* refers to the way a mineral's surface reflects light. Explain that some minerals have a metal-like luster and are called *metallic*. Other minerals are *nonmetallic*. Some terms you could use to describe the nonmetallic luster of a mineral might be *dull, glassy, waxy, pearly,* and *shiny*. Write the italicized words on the board for future reference. Revisit the student's words and see if any of them are synonyms for the terms geologists typically use to describe luster.

   Find examples of things in the room, other than mineral samples, that have lusters that could be described with the terms listed above and use them for examples of the meanings of these terms.

ELABORATE   e. Have students label the next column of their Mineral Properties Chart, Luster. Instruct them to select the most appropriate scientific term describing luster for each of the mineral samples and write that term in the correct cell on the chart.

EVALUATE   f. To assess student understanding of the mineral property called luster, have students respond to the following writing prompts in their science notebook.
   1. A mineral's luster is a description of . . .
   2. I found the luster of the minerals in my kit by . . .

6. HOW CAN THE TRANSMISSION OF LIGHT THROUGH A MINERAL BE USED TO IDENTIFY THE MINERAL? (2–5)

Materials
- Kits of mineral samples, including such minerals as feldspar, calcite, fluorite, gypsum, graphite, hematite, hornblende, magnetite, mica, and quartz
- Mineral Properties Charts
- Flashlights or penlights
- Overhead projector (optional)
- Clear plastic wrap or a blank transparency for the overhead
- Wax paper
- Aluminum foil

ENGAGE   a. Hold common transparent (e.g., clear plastic), translucent (e.g., wax paper), and opaque (e.g., aluminum foil) materials to the lens of an overhead projector or flashlight. Ask: *How do these materials differ in the way they transmit light? Do the minerals in our kits also transmit light differently?*

EXPLORE   b. Have students shine a flashlight on each mineral and look to see how much light is transmitted. Students should record their findings for each of the numbered minerals in their science notebooks.

EXPLAIN   c. In a large group, ask students to report their findings. Then introduce the terms scientists use to describe materials that tranmit different amounts of light. Explain that materials can be *transparent*, with a lot of light shining through them; *translucent*, with a little light shining through; or *opaque*, with no light shining through. Ask: *How can the amount of light a mineral transmits help us in identifying it?* (Different minerals transmit different amounts of light.)

ELABORATE   d. Have students label the next column of their Mineral Properties Chart, Light Transmission. Instruct them to select the most appropriate scientific term describing light transmission for each of the mineral samples and write that term in the correct cell on the chart.

EVALUATE   e. To assess student understanding of the mineral property called light transmission have students respond to the following writing prompts in their science notebook.
   1. A mineral's light transmission is a description of . . .
   2. I found the light transmission of the minerals in my kit by . . .

7. WHAT CAN THE SHAPE OF A MINERAL TELL US? (2–5)

Materials
- Kits of mineral samples, including such minerals as feldspar, calcite, fluorite, gypsum, graphite, hematite, hornblende, magnetite, mica, and quartz
- Mineral Properties Charts
- Models of various geometric solids—cube, tetrahedon, sphere, etc. (as found in math kits)

ENGAGE
a. Display the models of geometric solids you have collected. Ask: *How are these shapes different? Do you know what any of these shapes are called? Do any of your minerals seem to have a characteristic shape?*

EXPLORE
b. Have students describe and sketch the shape of each mineral in their science notebooks. Circulate among cooperative groups to formatively assess the descriptions of shape entered in the chart. This will let you know what concepts should be addressed during the explain phase of the lesson. Work with individuals and small groups to suggest procedures and answer questions related to the shape property.

EXPLAIN
c. In a large group, ask students to report their findings. Then introduce the terms scientists use to describe the shapes of mineral samples. Tell students that the shape of a mineral is often a clue to its crystal-like structure. The shape of minerals might be described as like a cube, like a tilted box (e.g., calcite), having crystals, having masses that are not fully crystals, having thin layers (e.g., biotite), or having no special shape.

ELABORATE
d. Have students label the next column of their Mineral Properties Chart, Shape. Instruct them to use a term that was discussed to describe the shape for each of the mineral samples and write that term in the correct cell on the chart.

EVALUATE
e. Check students' Mineral Properties Charts to formatively assess their ability to include detail about mineral shape in their descriptions and drawings.

8. WHAT SPECIAL PROPERTIES DO DIFFERENT MINERALS HAVE? (2–5)

Materials
- Kits of mineral samples, including such minerals as feldspar, calcite, fluorite, gypsum, graphite, hematite, hornblende, magnetite, mica, and quartz
- Mineral Properties Charts
- Paper clips
- Conductivity testers (made from a battery, battery holder, bulb, bulb holder, and three wires)

ENGAGE
a. Ask: *Do any of your mineral samples attract iron or steel objects? How could you find out?* (Test if paper clips are attracted to any of the mineral samples.) *Do any of your mineral samples conduct electricity? How could you find out?* (Test them with the conductivity testers we used in our electricity unit.)

EXPLORE

b. Give each group several paper clips and a conductivity tester or the materials to construct one. Have students label the next column on their Mineral Properties Charts, Magnetic, and label the following column, Conducts Electricity. As they test each mineral for these properties students should write *Yes* or *No* in the appropriate cell on their Mineral Properties Chart to indicate if each mineral sample is magnetic (attracts the paper clips) and if each mineral sample conducts electricity (the bulb lights in the circuit tester when the mineral sample is placed between the ends of the two wires).

EXPLAIN

c. Bring the class together to share their findings about these two special mineral properties. Ask: *Did each group find the same mineral sample(s) were magnetic? Did each group find the same mineral sample(s) were conductors of electricity?* If not, have students complete the elaborate phase of this activity.

ELABORATE

d. Have groups re-test their samples to provide evidence for their data. Let other groups observe each other's evidence. If the results for a mineral are different from the group, discuss strategies for determining the reason for the surprising result, they apply those strategies.

EVALUATE

e. To assess student understanding of these two special mineral properties, have students respond to the following writing prompts in their science notebook.
   1. If a mineral is magnetic, it . . .
   2. If a mineral conducts electricity, it . . .

9. HOW CAN YOU IDENTIFY AN UNKNOWN MINERAL? (2–5)

Materials

- Kits of mineral samples, including such minerals as feldspar, calcite, fluorite, gypsum, graphite, hematite, hornblende, magnetite, mica, and quartz
- Mineral Properties Charts
- Streak plates
- Pennies
- Iron nails
- Paper clips
- Conductivity testers
- Flashlights or penlights

ENGAGE

a. Ask: *How can you use your mineral properties chart to identify a mineral sample?*

EXPLORE

b. Give students one or more of minerals 1–12 with the identifying number labels removed. Have students use their mineral properties charts to identify each mineral.

EXPLAIN

c. Ask: *What have you concluded about the identity of your unknown samples? How did you use observation, testing, and your charts to identify the unknown samples?*

ELABORATE

d. Provide students with a master chart of mineral properties. Instead of having letters related to the mineral sample properties, this chart lists the names of minerals and their properties. Have them label the next column on their Mineral Properties Chart, Mineral's Name. Challenge students to compare their data with the information on the master chart to figure out the names of each of the samples they have been testing.

e. Encourage students to use library and Internet resources to look up additional information and deepen their understanding about the minerals they have been investigating.

EVALUATE

f. As a self-assessment, if discrepancies between their chart and the master chart occur with any of the minerals, encourage students to make some fresh observations.

g. As a summative assessment, give each student four mineral samples labeled A, B, C, D. One sample should be a mineral not included on students' charts; the other three samples should be minerals that are included on their charts. Allow each student to use his or her completed Mineral Property Chart to determine the name of three of the minerals and to identify the one the student cannot name because it is new. On a sheet of paper, students should write their name and list the letters A, B, C, D. Beside each letter the name of a mineral or the word *new* should be written.

B. THE STRUCTURE OF MINERALS: CRYSTALS AND CRYSTAL FORMATION

▶ *Science Background*

Crystals are nonliving substances that form into rocklike bodies of various shapes. Crystals grow in size when more layers of the same substance are added on; the basic crystal shape, however, remains the same. The size of crystals is determined by differences in the rate of crystallization and in the length of time crystals have to form. If crystals are disturbed in the forming process, they will break apart into hundreds of microscopic pieces. Crystalline form is important in determining some of the properties of substances.

 NSES   Science Standards

All students should develop an understanding of

- properties of the earth's systems (K–4).
- structure of the earth's systems (5–8).

Concepts and Principles That Support the Standards

- Earth materials are solid rocks and soils, water, and gases of the atmosphere (K–4).
- The varied materials have different physical and chemical properties (K–4).

Objectives

1. Demonstrate and describe different kinds of investigations to grow crystals.
2. Describe how crystal size is affected by conditions during formation.
3. Distinguish between and describe the formation of stalactites and stalagmites.

1. HOW CAN SALT CRYSTALS BE GROWN? (3–6)

Materials

- Salt
- Tablespoon
- Jar lid
- Small glass
- Magnifying lens
- Water

ENGAGE

a. Guide students to examine a grain of salt through a magnifying lens. If a video microscope is available, use it to show the class salt grains under higher magnification by displaying the image on a TV or computer monitor or projecting it onto a screen. Ask: *What do you see? What does a salt grain look like? What are crystals? How are crystals formed?*

EXPLORE

b. Guide students to conduct these activities within their cooperative groups and to record the answers to the questions below in their science notebooks:
   1. Obtain a tablespoon of salt, a jar lid, and a small glass of water. Mix the salt into the glass of water. Stir the water well. Let the solution stand for a few minutes until it becomes clear.
   Ask: *What happens to the salt?*
   2. Very gently pour some of the salt solution into the jar lid. Put a piece of string in the solution, letting one end hang out, as in diagram (a). Let the solution stand for several days where the lid will not be disturbed.
   Ask: *What do you predict will happen to the salt solution?*

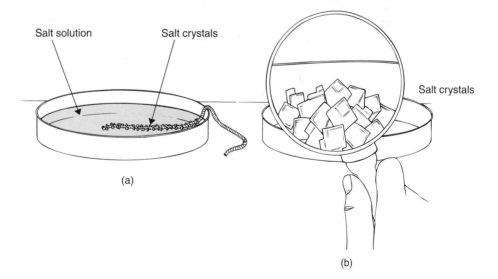

(a)

(b)

   3. After several days have passed, use your magnifying lens to look at the materials in the lid. Lift the string out of the jar lid. Examine the string with your magnifying lens. Describe what you see with the hand lens. See diagram (b).

EXPLAIN

    c. Bring students together for a whole class discussion about their findings. Have each group describe and show their results to the class. Ask: *How are the materials in the lid different from your original salt solution? Why do you now have a solid when you started out with a liquid? What name could you give to the formations in the lid?*

    d. Explain to the students that the salt dissolved in the water. When the salt water stood for several days, the water evaporated, leaving behind crystals of salt. Crystals are non-living substances found in nature that are formed in various geometrical shapes.

2. HOW CAN SUGAR CRYSTALS BE GROWN? (3–6)

Materials

- Tablespoon
- Jar lid
- Granulated sugar
- Small glass
- Water

ENGAGE

    a. Instruct students to examine grains of sugar through a magnifying lens. If a video microscope is available, use it to show the class salt grains under higher magnification by displaying the image on a TV or computer monitor or projecting it onto a screen. Ask: *What do you observe? How are sugar grains different from salt grains? How can we grow crystals of sugar?*

EXPLORE

    b. Students should conduct these activities in their cooperative groups and record the answers to the questions below in their science notebooks:

       1. Obtain a tablespoon of sugar, a jar lid, and a small glass of water. Be sure the tablespoon is clean. Mix a tablespoon of sugar into the glass of water. Stir the water well. Let the solution stand for a few minutes until it becomes clear. Ask: *What happens to the sugar? How is the sugar solution similar in appearance to the salt solution?*

       2. Very gently pour some of the sugar solution into the lid and let the solution stand undisturbed for several days. Ask: *What do you think might happen to the sugar solution?*

       3. After several days have passed, use your magnifying lens to look at the materials in your lid.

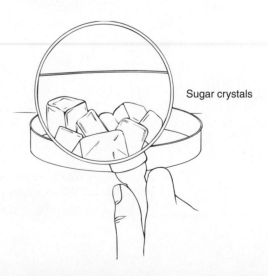

Sugar crystals

EXPLAIN

    c. Bring students together for a whole class discussion about their findings. Have each group describe and show their results to the class. Ask: *How are the materials in this lid different from your original sugar solution? How are the materials in this lid different from the salt crystals? How are they alike? What happened to the sugar solution?*

    d. Explain that when the sugar water stood for several days, the water evaporated, leaving behind sugar crystals.

3. WHAT ARE STALACTITES AND STALAGMITES, AND HOW ARE THEY FORMED? (3–6)

Materials

- Paper towel
- Epsom salt
- Spoon
- 30 cm (1 ft) of thick string
- Large tin can
- Two small jars or clear plastic cups
- Two heavy washers

ENGAGE

    a. Display a picture of the inside of a cavern showing stalactites and stalagmites. Ask: *Where do you think this picture was taken? How are rock formations like these formed?*

EXPLORE

    b. Allow students to carry out this investigation in cooperative groups:

       1. Fill the large tin can about three-quarters full of water. Add Epsom salt one spoonful at a time, stirring vigorously after each addition, until no more will dissolve.

Note: Epsom salt crystals will fall to the bottom of the can when no more will dissolve.

       2. Fill the two small jars or plastic cups with the Epsom salt solution and place the containers 5 cm (2 in.) apart on the paper towel. Tie a heavy washer to each end of the string. Place one washer in each of the small jars or paper cups.

Note: Arrange the string in the cups so that you have at least 5 cm between the string and the paper towel.

       3. Observe the jars or cups, the paper towel, the string, and the washer daily. Record the observations on a record sheet or in your science journals.

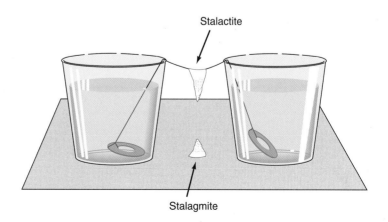

Stalactite

Stalagmite

EXPLAIN

    c. Bring the whole class together to discuss the results of the investigation. Ask: *What did you observe? What is the substance deposited on the string and on the paper towel? How did they get there? What is your evidence?*

    d. Help students learn the difference between stalactites and stalagmites. Point out that the deposits that hang down are called **stalactites** (*c* for ceiling), while those that point up are called **stalagmites** (*g* for ground).

          Ask: *Is the crystal formed on the string like a stalactite or a stalagmite? Why do you think so? Is the crystal formed on the paper towel like a stalactite or a stalagmite? Why do you think so?*

Nature of Science

    e. Children sometimes fail to understand the link between causes and effects because they think of an investigation in terms of its component parts rather than its interactions. Scientists use the notion of *system* to help them think in terms of components and interactions. Explain that a system is a collection of components that interact to perform some function. Examples of systems are a school system and the city water system.

          Thinking of an investigation as a **system** made up of parts that interact with one another can help to broaden children's thinking. Ask: *What are the components of our investigation system?* (Containers, Epsom salt, water, string, washers, paper towels) *How does each component interact with other components? What is your evidence?*

          By observing small systems, we can draw inferences about what happens in larger systems of the world. Ask: *How is what we observed like what might happen in a cavern in the earth?*

ELABORATE

    f. Encourage students to learn more about rock features in caverns and caves through library and Internet research. Each research group could prepare an educational brochure or commercial encouraging travel to a specific underground attraction. Through their research they will probably find that other underground features exist, including columns and helectites.

EVALUATE

    g. Before research begins, have the class help you develop a rubric describing the criteria and expectations for the brochures and commercials. These rubrics will guide student work and serve as a scoring guide when you assess their final products.

Stalactites and stalagmites in Mammoth Cave, Mammoth Cave National Park, Kentucky.

C. STRUCTURE OF THE EARTH'S SURFACE

▶ *Science Background*

The earth's surface is always changing. Waves, wind, water, and ice shape and reshape the earth's land surface by eroding rock and soil in some areas and depositing it in other areas, sometimes forming seasonal layers. Smaller rocks come from the breaking and weathering of bedrock and larger rocks. Soil is made partly from weathered rock, partly from plant and animal remains. Soil also contains many living organisms.[3]

NSES Science Standards

All students should develop an understanding of

- properties of the earth's systems (K–4).
- structure of the earth's systems (5–8).

[3]American Association for the Advancement of Science, 1993. *Benchmarks for Science Literacy* (New York: Oxford University Press).

NSES

Concepts and Principles That Support the Standards

- Soils have properties of color and texture, capacity to retain water, and ability to support the growth of many kinds of plants (K–4).
- Soils consist of weathered rocks and decomposed organic material from dead plants, animals, and bacteria. Soils are often found in layers, with each having a different chemical composition and texture (5–8).
- The surface of the earth changes. Some changes are due to slow processes, such as erosion and weathering, and some changes are due to rapid processes, such as landslides, volcanic eruptions, and earthquakes (K–4).

Objectives

1. Describe how germinating seeds and plants can naturally break up rocks and soil.
2. Demonstrate a procedure for determining the composition of soils.
3. Describe what might be found in soils.
4. Demonstrate a procedure to illustrate how the earth's surface forms layers.
5. Demonstrate, describe, and explain a procedure to illustrate how layers in the earth's surface might be observed.

1. HOW CAN LIVING THINGS PRODUCE FORCES THAT CAN CHANGE THE EARTH'S SURFACE? (K–4)

Materials

- Two plastic vials or medicine bottles with snap lids
- Dry bean seeds
- Water

ENGAGE

a. Display a large rock. Ask: *How could this rock be broken?* List students' suggestions on chart paper for use later in the lesson.

EXPLORE

b. Fill both of the vials or medicine bottles with as many dry beans as will fit. Add as much water as you can to one vial of beans. Snap the lids on both vials.
    Ask: *What do you think might happen to the two vials?*

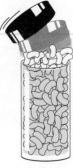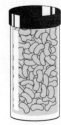

A Water   **B** No water

c. Observe both vials the next day.

EXPLAIN

d. Bring the class together for discussion. Ask: *What do you observe? Why do you think it happened?* Lead students to understand that in the container with water, the beans expanded and lifted the lid off. In the vial without water, there was no observable change.

e. Refer back to the chart developed during the engage phase of the lesson. Lead students to realize that all ideas on the list are related to force. Remind students that force is needed to make something move. Ask: *Was there force involved when the lid came off one of our containers? How do you know?*

Ask: *How could the force of germinating seeds and growing plants produce changes in the earth's surface?* Help students infer that swelling and growing plants change the land by breaking up rocks and soil just as the swelling beans lifted the vial's lid off.

ELABORATE

f. Ask students to find places on the school grounds or on concrete walks where plants grow through and crack rocks like this:

EVALUATE

g. Have students draw and write in their science notebooks about their observations during the explore and elaborate phases of the lesson. By looking over this work, you can formatively assess their observation and recording skills.

h. To assess their understanding of the concept that growing plants can affect the earth's surface, display the rock used during the engage phase of the lesson, then ask children to respond to the following questions:
   1. Could a plant break this rock?
   2. Why or why not?
   3. What evidence supports your answer?

2. WHAT IS IN SOIL? (3–6)

Materials

- Soil (from backyard)
- Alum
- Clear plastic vial with lid

ENGAGE

a. Ask: *What is in soil? How can we find out?*

EXPLORE

b. To observe different kinds of materials in backyard soil:
   1. Add about 1 inch of soil to a clear plastic vial with a lid (approximately 1 inch in diameter and 3 inches high).
   2. Add a pinch of alum to the soil. Tell the students that alum is a chemical used in making pickles. It is safe, but caution the students not to taste it.
   3. Fill the vial to the top with water, cover it, and shake it vigorously.
   4. Place the vial on the table and leave it there for the duration of the investigation.
   5. After several minutes, observe and record observations. The alum acts as a dispersing agent, helping the soil particles to break into smaller parts and settle out into layers. Students should observe sand at the bottom of the vial, silt above the sand, clay above the silt, water, and organic matter floating on the water.

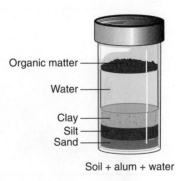

Organic matter
Water
Clay
Silt
Sand

Soil + alum + water

EXPLAIN

c. Ask: *From the results of your investigation, what do you conclude is in soil? Which particles do you think are larger: sand, clay, or silt? Why do you think so?*

ELABORATE

d. Ask: *How could you find out how much of each kind of material their is in soil?* Lead students to suggest measuring the layers that were formed during the Explore section of the lesson. Then provide rulers so they can measure the layers in their vial. Suggest that they display their finding using either a bar or pie graph. Then allow each group to share their findings with the class.

EVALUATE

e. Challenge each student to produce a visual representation of soil and its contents. Before they start, have them suggest criteria and expectations for this product, leading to a rubric that will guide them in their work and that you will use for assessing their products.[4]

---

[4]Adapted from GEMS (Great Explorations in Math and Science), 1994. *Terrarium Habitats.* Lawrence Hall of Science, Berkeley, CA.

....

3. WHAT IS CORE SAMPLING, AND HOW CAN WE USE IT TO INFER LAYERS IN THE EARTH'S CRUST? (3–6)

Materials

- Cupcakes
- Clear plastic straws
- Plastic knives

Preparation

In this activity, straws will be used to take core samples of layered cupcakes. Layered cupcakes may be made by the teacher or a parent volunteer as follows:

1. Use either different flavors or white batter mixed with food coloring.
2. Put batter in four layers in foil or paper cups.
3. Bake the cupcakes. Add frosting if desired.

ENGAGE

a. Show students a cupcake. Ask: *What do you think is inside the cupcake? How could we find out without eating it or cutting into it? How can scientists learn what's underground?*

EXPLORE

b. Provide groups of students one cupcake on a paper plate, five clear plastic straws cut into thirds, a plastic knife, drawing paper, and markers. Do *not* remove the foil or paper cup from the cupcake.
c. Instruct students to draw what they think the inside of the cupcake looks like.
d. Show and tell students how to take side "core samples," as in diagram (a):
   1. Carefully insert a straw into the side of the cupcake, rotate slightly, remove, and place sample on paper plate.
   2. Repeat with another straw.
e. Instruct students to take two side core samples of their cupcake. Ask: *Can you determine what the entire cupcake looks like with these two core samples? If not, what must you do?*
f. Instruct students to take three samples by inserting the straw straight down into the cupcake, as in diagram (b).

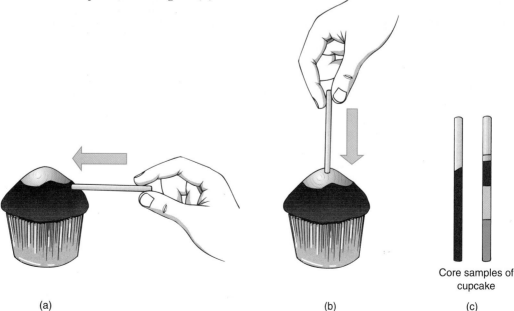

Core samples of cupcake

(a)   (b)   (c)

g. Compare these samples with those taken from the side, as in diagram (c).

h. Ask: *How are they different? Based on your core samples, what do you infer is inside the cupcake?* Instruct students to make drawings of what they now think the inside of the cupcake looks like.

EXPLAIN

i. Post the student drawings completed in step h of the lesson. Ask: *On what data did you base your drawing? How sure are you of the accuracy of your drawing? Why?*

j. Provide students this background information:

Geologists study the earth and use many devices to discover what is under the surface. **Core sampling** is done by putting hollow drilling tubes into the ground and extracting a sample of what the tubes went through.

k. Ask how does your straw sampling of the cupcake compare and contrast with core sampling done by geologists?

ELABORATE

l. Ask: *How could you find out what the inside of your cupcake looks like?* Tell students to use the plastic knives to cut down and separate the cupcakes into halves. Have them draw what the inside of the cup cake actually looks like. Ask: *How do your direct observations compare with your inferences and your drawings? Can geologists check the inferences they make from their core samples, the way you checked the inside of your cupcake? Why or why not?*

EVALUATE

m. To assess student understanding about the use of data from core sampling, show students pictures of cores from a different cupcake. Challenge them to draw what the inside of the cupcake looks like when sliced vertically through the center and horizontally through the center, based on the data. Then ask them to expain why they drew the inside of this cupcake the way they did.[5]

II. ATMOSPHERE, WEATHER, AND CLIMATE OF THE EARTH

Our spherical earth consists mostly of rock, with three-fourths of the planet covered by a thin layer of water and the entire planet blanketed by a thin layer of air called the *atmosphere*. Weather (in the short run) and climate (in the long run) involve the transfer of heat energy from the sun in and out of the atmosphere. The earth has a variety of climatic patterns, which consist of different conditions of temperature, precipitation, humidity, wind, air pressure, and other atmospheric phenomena. Water continuously circulates in and out of the atmosphere—evaporating from the surface, rising and cooling, condensing into clouds and then rain or snow, and falling again to the surface. The water cycle plays an important part in determining climatic patterns.

Children can begin to understand the atmosphere, water cycle, weather, and climate by engaging in inquiry activities related to evaporation and condensation, and observing and recording the weather on a regular basis. Emphasis should be on developing observation and description skills and forming explanations based on observable evidence.[6]

---

[5]Cupcake Geology activity in the Mesa Public Schools Curriculum Unit "Earthquakes" by JoAnne Vasquez.

[6]Adapted from *Science for All Americans, Benchmarks for Science Literacy*, and the *National Science Education Standards*.

A. THE WATER CYCLE

▶ *Science Background*

In the **water cycle**, water evaporates into the air as **water vapor**. As the air becomes laden with water vapor, the **relative humidity** of the air increases. When warm, moist air cools, it condenses as liquid water on available surfaces such as an iced tea glass, a bathroom mirror, or dust particles in the air.

NSES Science Standards

All students should develop an understanding of

- changes in the earth and sky (K–4).
- structure of the earth's systems (5–8).

Concepts and Principles That Support the Standards

- Water, which covers the majority of the earth's surface, circulates through the crust, oceans, and atmosphere in what is known as the *water cycle* (5–8).
- Water evaporates from the earth's surface, rises and cools as it moves to higher elevations, condenses as rain or snow, and falls to the surface where it collects in lakes, oceans, soil, and rocks underground (5–8).

Objectives

1. Observe and describe the disappearance of water that is left uncovered.
2. Define *evaporation* and explain that evaporated water has not disappeared but has changed into water vapor (a gaseous state) and has gone into the air.
3. Use the cohesive bond model of water developed in previous activities to explain what happens when a liquid evaporates.
4. Explain how interactions between a liquid and its environment may affect evaporation.
5. Define *condensation* and *dew point*.
6. Describe and demonstrate the conditions for condensation.
7. Construct and explain a model of the water cycle.

1. HOW MUCH WATER EVAPORATES FROM AN OPEN AQUARIUM, AND WHERE DOES IT GO? (K–4)

Materials

- Aquarium or other large, open container
- Measuring cup or graduated cylinder
- Water
- Masking tape or marking pen

Safety Precautions

When children work with water, cover their work tables, perhaps with newspapers. Have plenty of paper towels on hand to clean up water spills.

ENGAGE

a. Direct children's attention to the aquarium. Ask: Does the amount of water in the aquarium stay the same? How could we find out?

EXPLORE

b. Assist students to conduct this investigation:

1. Using masking tape or marking pens, mark the beginning water level of a classroom aquarium.

2. Check the water levels each morning. Using a measuring cup, add enough water to the aquarium to bring the water level back up to the original marks you made. Be sure the water added to the aquarium sits in a large open container for at least 24 hours so that chemicals such as chlorine will dissipate and the new water won't harm the fish.

3. Keep a record of how much water was added each day over a period of a week or two.

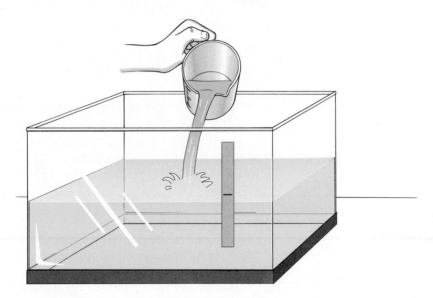

EXPLAIN

c. Remind the class that several weeks ago we asked the question: *Does the amount of water in the aquarium stay the same?* Ask: *What did we find out?* Discuss the record of how much water was added each day with the class. Ask: *Why did we need to add water? Was the amount of water we needed to add the same each day? Why or why not?*

d. Ask: *Where do you think the water that was missing from the aquarium went?* List students' suggestions on chart paper. They might suggest the following:

- The missing water soaked into the sand.
- The fish drank it.
- The custodian spilled it.
- It went into the air.

ELABORATE

e. Challenge the children to design fair tests (controlled investigations) to check their ideas. Depending on the age and experience of your class, you may want to do these investigations one at a time with the whole class or you may have groups working on different investigations simultaneously. In kindergarten, the plans will probably be formulated in a whole class discussion scaffolded with many strategic questions by the teacher. In higher grades, student groups might be expected to design their own investigation. Be sure children share their plans with you before they begin their investigation.

f. Remind students that in a controlled investigation, all variables are kept the same except one. Some summarized plans that represent controlled investigations follow:

1. To test if the water soaked into the sand, observe two aquariums with water and fish, one with and one without sand.
2. To test if the fish drank the water, compare one container with fish and one without. Both containers should be identical in every other way except one has no fish.
3. To test if the water went into the air, observe one container covered and one uncovered.

g. After the investigations are complete, ask: *What did you observe in your investigations? What can you conclude?* Discuss with the students how they can interpret the data from each of their experiments. For example, explain that the amount of the missing water was the same in aquariums with and without sand, so the water must not have soaked into the sand. There was a difference in the missing water only in the experiment in which one aquarium was covered and the other was not covered. Therefore, the cover must have prevented water from going into the air.

Discuss with the children how these experiments provide evidence that the water went into the air. Explain that the missing water does not just disappear; it changes into water vapor (a gaseous state) and goes into the air. Tell them that scientists call this process *evaporation*.[7]

EVALUATION

h. If student groups planned and conducted their own investigations, you could formatively assess their skill in planning and conducting investigations by applying indicators for assessing the development of process skills. The following indicators have been adapted from Wynne Harlen's work.[8] The indicators in the following checklist are arranged sequentially so the level of the process skills increases from the beginning to the end of the list.

Students

☐ develop a plan that is general but still useful (lacking detail or needing further thought.

☐ have an idea of the variable to be changed (the independent or manipulated variable) or what things should be compared.

☐ keep constant those variables (the controlled variables) that must be kept the same for a fair test.

☐ have some idea ahead of time what they will compare or measure (the dependent or responding variable) to find a result.

☐ select a realistic way of measuring or comparing things (the dependent or responding variable) to find a result.

☐ use procedures that ensure reasonably accurate results.

---

[7]Adapted from a variation of an SCIS activity developed by Herbert Thier.

[8]Adapted from Chapter 9 of *Teaching, Learning and Assessing Science 5–12* by Wynne Harlen (Sage, 2000).

2. HOW CAN YOU PROMOTE THE EVAPORATION OF WATER? (3–6)

Materials
- Various containers of various depths and sizes of openings
- Medicine droppers
- Construction paper
- Lamps with 60 watt bulb
- Water
- Straws

Safety Precautions

Caution the children not to touch the light bulb and electrical connections. For safety reasons, you may choose to demonstrate that water evaporates more quickly when it is heated.

ENGAGE

a. Ask: *What can you do to speed up the evaporation of water?*

EXPLORE

b. Form small groups of 3 or 4 students. Each group should have all of the materials listed previously. Tell the students to use these materials to try out different things that might speed up the evaporation of a drop of water on construction paper. Let them know that they will only have 20 minutes to explore.

c. In their science notebooks, students should create an I Notice/I Wonder chart. Throughout the exploration phase they should record things they observed (noticed) and questions (wonders) that come to mind as they explore the interactions of these materials with water.

EXPLAIN

d. Bring the class together to discuss their findings. Draw an I Notice/I Wonder chart on the board, then use it to consolidate the class's ideas. Ask the students to identfy the variables they changed to try to speed up evaporation, such as fanning, blowing, heating, being in the light, and spreading out the drop (surface area).

e. On a sticky note each student should write his or her name and list in order of preference the three variables he or she is interested in investigating. Then students should stick their notes on the board under the first variable on their list. The teacher can move notes around if needed to form workable cooperative groups for the next part of the lesson. As long as the teacher moves students to one of their choices, even if they don't get their first choice, the students still have input into the decision.

ELABORATE

f. In their new groups, ask students to develop a question that can be investigated relating to the variable their group has chosen. Remind them that it is important to only change one variable, so that they have a fair test (controlled experiment). Each group should share its question with the class for a discussion to determine if all of the suggested questions can be investigated. If necessary, the class can help reword any questions so they can be investigated.

In their new groups, students develop the procedure for their investigation. Once the teacher approves their plan, they may begin their investigation.

After experimenting, collecting data, analyzing it, and drawing conclusions, students should prepare and present a summary of their findings for the class.

EVALUATE

g. To assess student understanding of how different variables affect the speed of evaporation, challenge students to develop a plan for a system to evaporate a liter of water as quickly as possible. The plans should include a description of the system, the purpose of each of its parts, an explanation of why it was designed this way, supported by evidence from the class's prior investigations, and a labeled sketch of the system.

3. HOW FAST DOES WATER IN A WET SPONGE EVAPORATE? (3–6)

Materials

- Meterstick or wire coat hanger
- Paper clips
- Sponge
- Masking tape or marking pens

ENGAGE

a. Ask: *How can we determine the rate of evaporation of water in a wet sponge?*

EXPLORE

b. Assist students to set up and conduct this investigation:
   1. Using a meterstick or wire coat hanger and paper clips, build either of the balances shown.

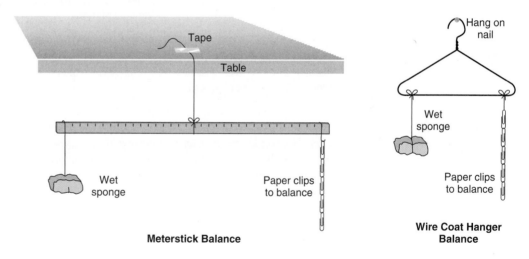

Meterstick Balance

Wire Coat Hanger Balance

   2. Soak a piece of sponge until it is very wet, but not dripping. Hang the sponge with an S-shaped paper clip or string to one end of the balance. Add paper clips to the other end until the balance is level. Ask: *How many clips did it take?*
   3. Every 15 minutes, check to see if the balance is level. Ask: *What do you see happening after several observations? Why do you think the paper clip end of the balance is lower?*
   4. Keep a written record of what happens.
   5. At each 15-minute observation, take off and record how many paper clips must be removed to keep the balance level.

6. When the sponge is dry, take your written observations and plot a line graph with the data. Set up your graph like the one that follows.

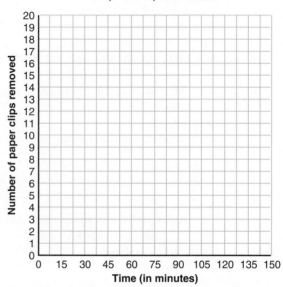

EXPLAIN

c. Bring the class together to compare the result from each group. Ask: *What were you measuring? How did you measure it? What does the graph tell you about the rate of evaporation of the water in a wet sponge?*

ELABORATE

d. Ask: *What are some variables that might affect how quickly the water in the sponge evaporates? How could you set up an experiment to test the effect of these variables on evaporation?*

e. Some variables that might affect the rate of evaporation are type of liquid (water vs. alcohol), temperature of the liquid (hot vs. cold), air temperature (hot vs. cold), wind velocity (no wind, moderate wind, strong wind), and relative humidity (dry day vs. moist day). Guide students in designing investigations, gathering data, and recording and graphing the results in the same way as they did previously.

f. Ask: *What did you observe in your investigations? What do you conclude?*

EVALUATE

g. To assess student understanding of variables that affect evaporation, have students respond to this writing prompt:

How do your findings from your investigation relate to each of these situations?

• Water evaporates faster from your hands when you vigorously rub them together.

• A blow dryer can be used to dry your hair faster.

• Your hair dries faster on a dry day than on a wet one.

• A wet towel dries faster if it is spread out rather than crumpled in a ball.

4. WHAT IS CONDENSATION? HOW DOES IT OCCUR? (3–6)

Materials

- Clean, empty vegetable or fruit cans
- Water
- Ice

ENGAGE

a. Hold up a cold soda can. Drops of water will probably appear on the outside surface of the can. Ask: *What do you see on the outside of this soda can? Where do you think these droplets came from?*

EXPLORE

b. Provide each group two identical, empty vegetable cans. Give students these instructions:
   1. Add the same amount of water to each can so that they are about three-fourths full.
   2. Place ice in one of the cans so that the water is almost to the top of the can.
   3. Stir the water in each can.
   4. Observe the outside of each can.

EXPLAIN

c. Ask: *What happened to the outside of each can as you stirred the water?* (Moisture collected on the outside of the container with ice water.) *What conditions were necessary for the water to appear on the outside of the can?* (The can had to be cool.) *Where did the water come from?*

d. If students suggest that cold water soaked through the can, ask: *How could we test this hypothesis?*
Hint: You might put food dye in the water and then observe to see if any of the food coloring actually soaked through the can.
   Ask: *People often say that a glass of ice water is sweating; why is this explanation incorrect?*

e. Provide this explanation of condensation:

When water evaporates, it goes into the air as water vapor. If moisture-laden air comes into contact with a surface that is cool enough, then water vapor condenses (changes from a gas to a liquid) from the air and collects on the cool surface.

ELABORATE

f. Ask: *What is the source of the warm, moist air in each of these examples of condensation? What is the surface on which water condenses in each case?* Allow students to use library and Internet resources to confirm their answers.

- Formation of clouds. (Warm, moist air in the atmosphere rises and cools. As the water vapor cools, it condenses on dust particles.)
- Dew. (Warm, moist air is cooled as it mixes with cooler air near the surface of the earth. As the water vapor cools, it condenses on the grass and other surfaces.)

- Vapor trails. (Warm, moist air from the exhaust of a jet mixes with cooler air high in the atmosphere. As the water vapor cools, it condenses on dust particles in the atmosphere.)
- Moisture on bathroom mirrors after a hot shower. (Warm, moist air produced during the hot shower condenses on the cooler bathroom mirror.)

EVALUATE

g. To check student understanding about the concept of condensation, ask students to use the Frayer model, a graphic organizer that helps students develop their vocabularies.

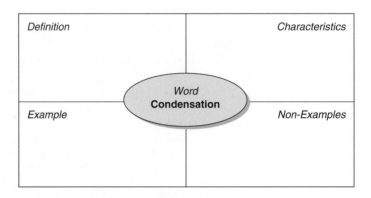

5. HOW CAN EVAPORATION AND CONDENSATION BE USED TO DESALINATE SALT WATER? (3–5)

Materials

- Salt
- Water
- Tablespoon
- Small weight (rock)
- Large sheet of black construction paper
- Large clear plastic bowl
- Plastic wrap
- Large rubber band
- Small glass custard cup

ENGAGE

a. Ask: *How can evaporation and condensation be used to remove the salt from salt water?*

EXPLORE

b. This activity may be done individually or in groups of two to four:
   1. Pour 3 tablespoons of salt into a large clear plastic bowl, add water to a depth of about 2 to 3 cm, and stir until all the salt is dissolved.
   2. Place the small glass cup in the water in the center of the bowl, as in the diagram.
   3. Cover the large bowl with plastic wrap and fasten the wrap with a large rubber band.
   4. Place a weight (small pebble) on top of the plastic wrap directly above the custard dish, as shown in the diagram.

5. *Caution:* Make certain that the plastic wrap sticks tightly to the sides of the bowl and that the large rubber band keeps it sealed when the pebble is placed on the wrap.
6. Carefully place the bowls in direct sunlight on a sheet of black construction paper, making sure the custard cup is directly under the weight pushing down on the plastic wrap.

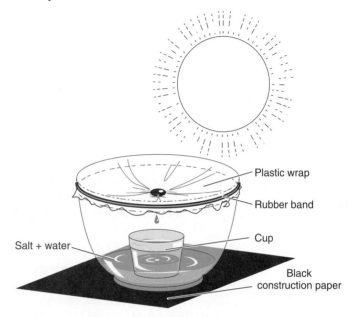

7. Record your observations every day in your observation journal.
8. After about a week, take off the plastic wrap and taste the water in the custard cup.

c. Bring the class together to discuss the changes they observed over the week. Ask:

Why do you think you were told to cover the salt water with plastic wrap? (To keep the water in the system)

Why do you think you were told to put the bowl on black construction paper? (To absorb sunlight and warm the system)

How does the water in the custard cup taste? (Like pure water)

Where did the water in the custard cup come from? (It condensed on the plastic wrap, then dripped into the custard cup.)

What happened to your salt solution? (Its surface got gradually lower in the bowl.)

Where did the water in the bowl go? (It evaporated into the air above the bowl and under the plastic wrap, then condensed on the plastic wrap and dripped into the custard cup.)

What is left in the bottom of the large bowl? (Depending on how much water is left, either salt crystals or very salty water)

▶ *Science Background*

Water in a saline solution absorbs the sun's energy and evaporates, leaving the salt behind. The water vapor contains no salt, so when it condenses on the cool surface of the plastic wrap and drips from the lowest point, only water falls into the cup. This system for removing salt from salt water is called a solar still.

6. WHAT IS THE TEMPERATURE AT WHICH CONDENSATION TAKES PLACE? (3–6)

Materials
- Clean, empty cans
- Ice
- Thermometers

ENGAGE

a. Ask: *How can we find out how cold a surface has to be before water vapor condenses on it?*

EXPLORE

b. Give students these instructions:
   1. Fill an empty can about three-fourths full of tap water at room temperature.
   2. Place a thermometer in the water and read the temperature.
   3. Add about one-fourth can of ice to the water.
   4. Stir the ice and water and read the temperature every 2 minutes.
   5. Carefully observe the outside of the can. At the first sign of condensation, read the temperature of the cold water. Wiping the outside of the can occasionally with a brown paper towel will aid in determining when condensation first forms on the can.

EXPLAIN

c. Instruct groups to record on the board the temperature at which condensation first occurred. Note discrepancies among the data collected. According to the *Benchmarks for Science Literacy*, when students arrive at very different measurements of the same thing, "it is usually a good idea to make some fresh observations instead of just arguing about who is right" (American Association for the Advancement of Science, 1993, *Benchmarks For Science Literacy*. New York: Oxford University Press, p. 10).

d. Explain that the temperature at which condensation will form on a cool surface is called the *dew point*. The dew point depends on the relative humidity of the air—that is, on the relative amount of moisture already in the air.

B. WEATHER

▶ *Science Background*

The components of weather are temperature, precipitation, humidity, wind, air pressure, clouds, and other atmospheric phenomena. These weather conditions can be readily observed and recorded by children. By keeping a weather journal during the year, students can discover weather patterns and trends, though they may not be consistent. Younger students can draw daily weather pictures of what they see; older students can make charts and graphs from the data they collect using simple weather instruments.

Science Standards

All students should develop an understanding of

- properties of the earth's systems (K–4).
- structure of the earth's systems (5–8).

Concepts and Principles That Support the Standards

- Water circulates through the crust, oceans, and atmosphere in what is known as the water cycle (5–8).
- The atmosphere is a mixture of gases that include water vapor (5–8).
- Clouds, formed by the condensation of water vapor, affect weather and climate (5–8).
- Global patterns of atmospheric movement influence local weather (5–8).

Objectives

1. Name and measure such components of weather as temperature, wind direction and speed, air pressure, and precipitation.
2. Describe patterns and trends in local weather conditions.
3. Construct a variety of weather instruments.
4. Name and describe different types of clouds, and explain how clouds are formed.

1. HOW CAN WE DESCRIBE THE WEATHER? (K–3)

Materials

- Thermometers

ENGAGE

a. Ask: *What is our weather like today?* Record the words students use to describe the weather (*cold, hot, warm, muggy, cloudy, rainy, windy,* etc.).

EXPLORE

b. Ask: *If we wanted to compare the weather today with the weather on another day, what would we record about today's weather?* Most children see weather forecasts on television. They are beginning to learn that weather controls much of their lives, from the clothes they wear to the games they play. Through discussion, lead children to consider these variables related to weather: temperature, cloud cover, wind, humidity, and rain or snow (precipitation).

c. Construct a bulletin board depicting a large weather chart similar to the one shown. Encourage children to make daily observations of weather conditions and to make entries on the class weather chart.

Day / Date	MON	TUES	WED	THURS	FRI	MON	TUES	WED	THURS	FRI	MON	TUES	WED	THURS	FRI
Temperature															
Clouds	○	○	○	○	○	○	○	○	○	○	○	○	○	○	○
Wind	|	|	|	|	|	|	|	|	|	|	|	|	|	|	|
Other	▭	▭	▭	▭	▭	▭	▭	▭	▭	▭	▭	▭	▭	▭	▭
Student's Name															

EXPLAIN

d. Examine the weather chart with the children. Discuss the kinds of things children might do that would be affected by the weather. If they play outside, what would they wear: warm clothes, rain gear? Discuss the weather conditions for several days in a row.

e. Ask: *What patterns in the weather do you see? How has the temperature changed from day to day? How is the weather today different from last summer? last winter?* Count the number of cool days, warm days, cloudy days, clear days, rainy days, and dry days to help find patterns in the weather.

ELABORATE

f. Ask: *What is the weather like in other regions? How would weather conditions affect life in other regions?* Using the Internet, find and chart daily weather conditions in other regions and countries around the globe.

2. HOW DOES TEMPERATURE VARY FROM PLACE TO PLACE AND DURING THE DAY? (2–4)

Materials
- Thermometers

ENGAGE

a. Ask: *How does the temperature vary from place to place? Is the temperature the same inside and outside the classroom? Is the temperature the same everywhere on the school grounds? Is the temperature the same in the shade and the sun? How could we find out?*

EXPLORE

b. Guide students to measure and compare the temperature at various locations: near the floor and near the ceiling of the classroom, inside and outside the classroom, in the sun and in the shade, and at different places on the school grounds.

EXPLAIN   c. Have students share their findings with the class. Discuss the differences in the temperatures at different locations and the possible reasons for these differences.

ELABORATE   d. Ask: *Is the temperature the same throughout the day?* Allow students to measure the outside temperature every hour. Discuss the temperature differences that are observed.

EVALUATE   e. To assess student understanding about the reasons for different temperatures at different places and at different parts of the day, ask students to respond to the following multiple choice questions and give reasons for their answers:

    1. Where would you expect it to be cooler on a sunny day?
      A. in the shade
      B. in the sun

    2. On a sunny day, when would you expect the outside temperature to be highest?
      A. early in the morning
      B. mid-morning
      C. noon
      D. late afternoon
      E. just before sunset

3. HOW CAN YOU MAKE A WIND VANE, AND HOW IS IT USED TO DETERMINE WIND DIRECTION? (3–6)

Materials
- Scissors
- Construction paper
- Drinking straw
- Pencil with eraser
- Straight pin
- Glass bead
- Empty thread spool
- A 30 cm square piece of corrugated cardboard
- Electric fan

ENGAGE   a. Ask: *How can you tell the direction the wind is blowing?*

Construct   b. To make a wind vane, follow these directions:
    1. Cut an arrow-shaped point and tail fin from construction paper, as shown in the diagram.
    2. Attach the point and tail fin to the straw by cutting notches in both ends of the straw and gluing the cutouts in place.
    3. Attach the straw to a pencil by sticking the straight pin through the middle of the straw, through a glass bead, and into the pencil eraser. Make sure the straw can swing easily in all directions and is balanced.
Note: Move the pin in the straw until it balances with arrow and tail attached.

4. Glue the empty thread spool to the center of the corrugated cardboard. Mark north, south, east, and west on the cardboard as shown in the diagram.

5. When the glue has dried, push the pencil into the hole of the spool and check to see that the straw moves easily. You now have a wind vane.

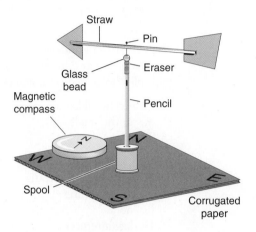

Straw

Pin

Eraser

Glass bead

Magnetic compass

Pencil

Spool

Corrugated paper

EXPLORE

c. Turn on the fan to produce a breeze so that you can test your wind vane. Notice what happens when you place your wind vane in the air flow 2 to 3 meters from the fan.

EXPLAIN

d. Ask: *What do you see happening to the arrow?* (It turns.) *Why do you think the arrow turns this way?* (The tail of the arrow is larger than its point so the tail gets pushed away from the wind source.) *From which direction is the wind blowing?* (From the direction of the fan) *How do you know?* (The arrow on the wind vane is pointing toward the fan.)

The arrow will swing around until the point faces the direction from which the wind is blowing. This direction then becomes the wind's name. Ask: *How would you name this wind?* (It would be called a "fan wind," because it comes from the direction of the fan.)

ELABORATE

e. Carefully take your wind vane outdoors and line up the north label on your wind vane with the north on a magnetic compass. If the wind is strong, tape the cardboard to a horizontal surface or weight it down with something heavy.

f. Ask: *What do you see happening to the arrow?* (It turns to point into the wind.) *From which direction is the wind blowing?* (Answers will vary but should be the compass direction toward which the arrow points.) *How do you know?* (The arrow points toward the direction from which the wind blows.) *What would you name this wind?* (It would be named for the compass direction the arrow points.)

g. Ask: *Does the wind always blow from the same direction? How could we find out?*

h. Keep a record of wind observations three times a day for 1 week. Make sure to record the data on a chart.

After 1 week, do you detect

any pattern of winds during the day?

any pattern of winds from day to day?

any prevailing or consistent direction from which the wind blows?

any correlation between wind direction and weather conditions, such as temperatures, humidity, clouds, and so on?

i. Check local TV weather and newspapers for wind direction. *How do your data compare? If they differ, why do you think so?*

EVALUATE

j. To assess student understanding about how to use a wind vane to determine wind direction, ask students to respond to the following related items.

The arrow of the wind vane is pointing to the west.

1. From what direction is the wind blowing?
   A. North
   B. South
   C. East
   D. West

2. What should this wind be called?
   A. a north wind
   B. a south wind
   C. an east wind
   D. a west wind

3. Why did you select that name?
   A. Because winds are named for compass directions
   B. Because winds are named for the direction from which they are blowing
   C. Because winds are named for the direction toward which they are blowing

▶ *Science Background*

Wind, or moving air, brings about changing weather conditions. A **wind vane** is an instrument that shows the direction from which the wind is blowing. Winds are named for the direction from which they blow. For example, a north wind is blowing from the north to the south. An **anemometer** is an instrument that measures wind speed.

4. HOW CAN YOU MEASURE HOW FAST THE WIND BLOWS? HOW DOES WIND SPEED VARY WITH LOCATION AND TIME? (3–6)

Materials

- Long sewing needle
- Red marking pen
- 30 cm of monofilament nylon line
- Protractor
- Ping-Pong ball
- Bubble level (hardware store)
- Glue
- Tongue depressor
- Cardboard

Preparation

For teachers only: Thread a sewing needle with a 30 cm monofilament line, push the needle through the Ping-Pong ball, and knot and glue the end of the line to the Ping-Pong ball.

Safety Precautions

Use caution when pushing the needle through the Ping-Pong ball.

ENGAGE

a. Ask: *How can we measure how fast the wind blows?*

CONSTRUCT

b. Either the teacher or students should follow these directions to make an anemometer:
   1. Glue the other end of the line that is attached to the Ping-Pong ball to the center of a protractor. With the marking pen, color the line red.
   2. Glue a bubble level to the protractor as shown in the diagram.
   3. Glue a tongue depressor to the protractor as a handle. You now have an anemometer to measure wind speed.
   4. When the glue is dry, turn on the fan to produce a breeze so that you can test your anemometer.

EXPLORE

c. To take readings of the wind's speed, follow these directions:
   1. In the wind, hold the protractor level using the tongue depressor handle.
   2. Keep the protractor level by making sure the bubble is centered in the bubble level.
   3. Observe any swing of the Ping-Pong ball and string and see what angle the string makes on the protractor. For instance, in the diagram the string moved to approximately 65 degrees.

Bubble level

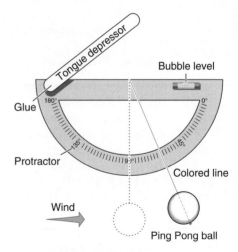

d. Explore how the angle of the string holding the Ping-Pong ball changes when you hold your anemometer different distances from the fan and in different positions in the breeze coming from it. Record your findings on a data table.

EXPLAIN

e. Invite students to describe their anemometers and explain how they work. Have them share their findings. Ask: *Where do you think the wind speed was greatest?* (Answers will vary.) *What evidence do you have to support your answer?* (It was where the Ping-Pong ball blew up at the greatest angle.) What have you measured? (angle of the string) *How do you think the angle of the string relates to the wind speed?* (The smaller the angle on the protractor crossed by the string, the greater the wind speed.)

f. Explain that the following table relates the wind speed to the angle of the string on the anemometer. Have students use the table to determine the wind speeds at the places they collected data in the fan's breeze.

Protractor Anemometer Wind Speeds			
String Angle	Wind Speed (Miles per Hour)	String Angle	Wind Speed (Miles per Hour)
90°	0	50°	18.0
85°	5.8	45°	19.6
80°	8.2	40°	21.9
75°	10.1	35°	23.4
70°	11.8	30°	25.8
65°	13.4	25°	28.7
60°	14.9	20°	32.5
55°	16.4		

ELABORATE

g. At different times over the next few days, use your anemometer in various spots on your school grounds and then refer to the chart to find the wind speed.

   After you have tested the wind speed in different places on your school grounds, record the data on a chart like this one.

Date
Time
Protractor angle
Wind speed
Wind direction

h. Guide students to use their charts to answer these questions:
   Where does the wind blow the fastest on your school grounds?
   Does wind blow faster at ground level or at higher levels?
   Is there a place where wind blows faster, such as between two buildings or at a corner of two wings of a building? Why?

EVALUATE

i. To assess student understanding of how to determine wind speed with the anemometer, have students respond to the following item.

   1. Max is holding his anemometer at 5:00 p.m. outside of his house. The string crosses the protractor at the 80° mark. Based on the table, what is the approximate wind speed?
   A. 5 miles per hour
   B. 8 miles per hour
   C. 32 miles per hour
   D. 80 miles per hour

5. HOW CAN YOU MEASURE RELATIVE HUMIDITY AND HUMIDITY CHANGES? (3–6)

Materials

- Two thermometers
- Wide cotton shoelace
- Small dish of water
- Empty milk carton
- Thread
- Piece of cardboard

ENGAGE

a. Ask: What is humidity? How can it be measured?

Construct

b. Give students these instructions:
   1. Obtain an empty milk carton, two identical thermometers, a cotton shoelace, and some thread. *Note:* The two thermometers should register the same temperature before the shoelace is placed over one of them; otherwise, the difference in readings must be considered a constant that is part of all computations.
   2. Cut a 10 cm section from the cotton shoelace and slip the section over the bulb of one of the thermometers. Tie the shoelace section with thread above and below the bulb to hold the shoelace in place. Thread the other end of the 10 cm section through a hole in the milk carton and allow it to rest in water inside the milk carton.
   3. Attach both thermometers to the milk carton as shown in the diagram.

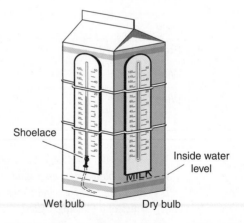

Shoelace

Inside water level

Wet bulb   Dry bulb

EXPLORE

c. Ask: *What do you think might happen to the thermometer with the wet shoelace? Why do you think so?*
d. When their shoelace is wet, tell students to fan it with a piece of cardboard for 1 minute. Then have them check the temperature readings of the two thermometers.

EXPLAIN

e. Tell the class that they have built **hygrometers**— instruments that measure the relative humidity in the atmosphere.
f. Have each student group post their results on a class chart for all to see. Discuss the data. Ask: *How do you account for the difference in readings between the thermometer with the shoelace (called the "wet bulb") and the one without the shoelace (called the "dry bulb")?*

g. Explain that when the shoelace is wet, the evaporation of the water results in a cooling of the wet-bulb thermometer, whereas the dry-bulb thermometer continues to read the temperature of the air around it. Ask: *Why do you think you were asked to fan the wet-bulb thermometer?*

h. Demonstrate how to use the relative humidity table provided. To locate the relative humidity on the table, find the temperature of the dry-bulb thermometer on the y-axis (vertical axis) and the difference between the readings of the two thermometers on the x-axis (horizontal axis). The example described after the following table shows a dry-bulb temperature of 76°F, a difference of 8°F (wet-bulb, 68°F), and a relative humidity of 67%.

FINDING RELATIVE HUMIDITY IN PERCENT
Difference in degrees between wet-bulb and dry bulb thermometers

Air temperature (reading of dry-bulb thermometer) in degrees fahrenheit

	1	2	3	4	5	6	7	8	9	10	11	12	13	14	15	16	17	18	19	20	21	22	23	24	25	26	27	28	29	30
30°	89	78	68	57	47	37	27	17	8																					
32°	90	79	69	60	50	41	31	22	13	4																				
34°	90	81	72	62	53	44	35	27	18	9	1																			
36°	91	82	73	65	56	48	39	31	23	14	6																			
38°	91	83	75	67	59	51	43	35	27	19	12	4																		
40°	92	84	76	68	61	53	46	38	31	23	16	9	2																	
42°	92	85	77	70	62	55	48	41	34	28	21	14	7																	
44°	93	85	78	71	64	57	51	44	37	31	24	18	12	5																
46°	93	86	79	72	65	59	53	46	40	34	28	22	16	10	4															
48°	93	87	80	73	67	60	54	48	42	36	31	25	19	14	8	3														
50°	93	87	81	74	68	62	56	50	44	39	33	28	22	17	12	7	2													
52°	94	88	81	75	69	63	58	52	46	41	36	30	25	20	15	10	6													
54°	94	88	82	76	70	65	59	54	48	43	38	33	28	23	18	14	9	5												
56°	94	88	82	77	71	66	61	55	50	45	40	35	31	26	21	17	12	8	4											
58°	94	89	83	77	72	67	62	57	52	47	42	38	33	28	24	20	15	11	7	3										
60°	94	89	84	78	73	68	63	58	53	49	44	40	35	31	27	22	18	14	10	6	2									
62°	94	89	84	79	74	69	64	60	55	50	46	41	37	33	29	25	21	17	13	9	6	2								
64°	95	90	85	79	75	70	66	61	56	52	48	43	39	35	31	27	23	20	16	12	9	5	2							
66°	95	90	85	80	76	71	66	62	58	53	49	45	41	37	33	29	26	22	18	15	11	8	5	1						
68°	95	90	85	81	76	72	67	63	59	55	51	47	43	39	35	31	28	24	21	17	14	11	8	4	1					
70°	95	90	86	81	77	72	68	64	60	56	52	48	44	40	37	33	30	26	23	20	17	13	10	7	4	1				
72°	95	91	86	82	78	73	69	65	61	57	53	49	46	42	39	35	32	28	25	22	19	16	13	10	7	4	1			
74°	95	91	86	82	78	74	70	66	62	58	54	51	47	44	40	37	34	30	27	24	21	18	15	12	9	7	4	1		
76°	96	91	87	83	78	74	70	67	63	59	55	52	48	45	42	38	35	32	29	26	23	20	17	14	12	9	6	4	1	
78°	96	91	87	83	79	75	71	67	64	60	57	53	50	46	43	40	37	34	31	28	25	22	19	16	14	11	9	6	4	1
80°	96	91	87	83	79	76	72	68	64	61	57	54	51	47	44	41	38	35	32	29	27	24	21	18	16	13	11	8	6	4
82°	96	91	87	83	79	76	72	69	65	62	58	55	52	49	46	43	40	37	34	31	28	25	23	20	18	15	13	10	8	6
84°	96	92	88	84	80	77	73	70	66	63	59	56	53	50	47	44	41	38	35	32	30	27	25	22	20	17	15	12	10	8
86°	96	92	88	84	80	77	73	70	66	63	60	57	54	51	48	45	42	39	37	34	31	29	26	24	21	19	17	14	12	10
88°	96	92	88	85	81	78	74	71	67	64	61	58	55	52	49	46	43	41	38	35	33	30	28	25	23	21	18	16	14	12
90°	96	92	88	85	81	78	74	71	68	64	61	58	56	53	50	47	44	42	39	37	34	32	29	27	24	22	20	18	16	14

Example:
Temperature of dry-bulb thermometer 76°
Temperature of wet-bulb thermometer 68°
The difference is 8°

Find 76° in the dry-bulb column and 8° in the difference column. Where these two columns meet, you read the relative humidity. In this case, it is 67%.

ELABORATE

i. Take readings on your hygrometer every day for 2 weeks and record your findings. Also try readings in different places.

j. Discuss the data groups have collected. Ask: *What patterns have you discovered? Using your hygrometer, can you predict which days are better for drying clothes outside?*

k. Use library and Internet resources to find the answer to this question: *How is relative humidity used by weather forecasters to predict weather?*

EVALUATE

1. To check student understanding about how to use the hygrometer and the Finding Relative Humidity in Percent chart to measure relative humidity, have students answer the following items.

   1. On the hygrometer the wet-bulb thermometer reads 66°F and the dry-bulb thermometer reads 84°F. What is the relative humidity?
      A. 18%
      B. 38%
      C. 66%
      D. 84%

   2. *Explain how you determined the relative humidity from the data given in the previous problem.*

► *Science Background*

Air contains moisture (from evaporated water from the ground, rivers, lakes, and oceans). Air pressure and temperature affect the amount of moisture air can hold at any given time. Relative humidity is the amount of water vapor actually contained in volume of air divided by the maximum amount that could be contained in the same volume.

III. THE EARTH'S OCEANS

Our earth has been called *the water planet*. Children are naturally drawn to water. "Whether they are playing in a pond, chasing waves at the beach, or splashing in a rain puddle on a city street, children are entranced by water" (Valerie Chase, 1997, *Living in Water*. Baltimore: National Aquarium in Baltimore, p. 1).

The earth's water is found in oceans, lakes, rivers, ponds, and streams; in ground water systems; and in ice and water vapor forms. Water circulates through the crust, atmosphere, and oceans of the earth in the *water cycle*. Rain falling on land collects in rivers and lakes, soil, and porous layers of rock, and much of it flows back to the oceans.

More than 97% of all the water on the earth is salt water in ocean basins. Oceans, as well as the land, are contained within the crust of the earth. Oceans cover 71% of the earth's surface, with land covering 29%. There are four oceans on the earth: Pacific Ocean, Atlantic Ocean, Indian Ocean, and Arctic Ocean. The Antarctic Ocean is included with the Pacific, Atlantic, and Indian Oceans. Seas, gulfs, and bays are all parts of oceans that are partially enclosed by land.

Plants and animals survive in the ocean, on the ocean floor and ocean trenches, or on rocky shores, because they have adapted to the conditions of these tremendously different habitats. For example, plants and animals on the seashore must resist battering ocean waves or find security in crevices and fissures. Most of the animals on sandy shores live below the surface. A sandy beach may appear lifeless, but when the tide rolls in, the inhabitants spring into action and an astounding variety of life is revealed.

 Science Standards

All students should develop an understanding of

• structure of the earth's systems (5–8).

NSES

Concepts and Principles That Support the Standards

- In the course of the water cycle, water evaporates from the earth's surface, rises and cools as it moves to higher elevations, condenses as rain or snow, and falls to the surface where it collects in lakes, oceans, soils, and underground (5–8).
- Water is a solvent. As it passes through the water cycle, it dissolves minerals and gases and carries them to the oceans (5–8).
- Oceans have a major effect on climate, because water in the ocean holds a large amount of heat (5–8).

Objectives

1. Demonstrate that the water pressure in a body of water increases with depth.
2. Demonstrate and explain that the buoyant force of salt water is greater than the buoyant force of fresh water.
3. Compare the surface area of the earth that is ocean with that which is land.
4. Compare the amount of water in the oceans with the total amount of water in the earth system.
5. Identify a variety of foods that contain nutrients from ocean organisms.
6. Describe and explain the effects of pollution on life in water.

1. WHAT PART OF THE EARTH'S SURFACE IS COVERED BY OCEANS? (3–6)

Materials

- Inflatable globe (preferably showing natural land features rather than political boundaries)

ENGAGE

a. Hold up the inflatable globe. Ask: *What is this globe a model of?* (Earth) *How is it like the real earth and how is it different? What is shown on the globe's surface?* (Land and oceans) *About how much of the earth is covered by oceans? How could we use the globe to find out?*

EXPLORE

b. Tell the class we need to collect data by using a sampling method. Help the students follow these steps:
    1. Show the class a two-column table with the headings "Ocean" and "Land."
    2. Select a student to be the record keeper.
    3. Instruct one student to toss the inflatable globe to another student.
    4. The person who catches the globe will look to see if his or her right thumb is on an ocean or land part of the globe's surface and report this information to the record keeper.
    5. The record keeper will make a tally mark in the appropriate column on the table.
    6. Then the inflatable globe should be tossed to another student and the process repeated.
    7. Continue for a total of 100 tosses.

EXPLAIN

c. Ask: *How many times out of 100 tosses was the catcher's right thumb on an ocean area?* (Approximately 70 times) *How many times out of 100 tosses was the catcher's right thumb on a land area?* (Approximately 30 times)

d. Ask: *Why do you think the catcher's right thumb was on an ocean area more often than on a land area?* (Because more of the surface of the inflatable globe is ocean area so there is more chance of the catcher's right thumb being on an ocean.) Discuss the term *percent* with the class. *What percent of the times was the catcher's thumb on an ocean area?* (The answer should be close to 70%.) *What percent of the times was the catcher's thumb on a land area?* (Answer should be close to 30%.)

ELABORATE

e. Challenge the class to find out what percent of the earth's surface is covered by oceans using their textbook or other references. (70%) Ask the class to explain how well and why this sampling technique worked to estimate the relative amount of land and ocean on the earth's surface.

2. WHAT PART OF THE EARTH'S WATER IS IN THE OCEANS? (3–8)

Materials
- Six 2-liter bottles
- Graduated cylinders
- Permanent marker
- Colored water

ENGAGE

a. Ask: *What part of the earth's water is in the oceans? How could we make a model to show this?*

EXPLORE

b. Conduct this teacher demonstration:
   1. Show the class a 2-liter bottle labeled "All Earth's Water" filled with 2,000 ml of colored water. Tell them this represents all the water on the earth.
   2. Then display five other 2-liter bottles containing the following volumes of colored water on a table in front of a sheet of chart paper: Bottle A, 1,944 ml; Bottle B, 1,750 ml; Bottle C, 1,400 ml; Bottle D, 1,000 ml; Bottle E, 700 ml.
   3. Tell the students that one of these bottles represents the amount of water in the earth's oceans.
   4. Ask students to vote for the one they think represents the water in the earth's oceans by writing the letter of their choice on a Post-It note. Have the students stick their Post-It in a column above the bottle that matches the letter they chose.

EXPLAIN

c. Tell the class they have just created a histogram of their ideas. Ask: *Which bottle do most of you think represents the water in the earth's oceans? How do you know? How could we find out which bottle best represents the amount of water in the earth's oceans?*

d. Ask groups of students to decide what information they would need and how they would make the bottle that represents the water in the earth's oceans. After they have had some discussion time, provide the information that 97.2% of the earth's water is in the oceans. You might also reveal that the bottle labeled "All Earth's Water" contains 2,000 ml of colored water.

ELABORATE

e. Allow groups to use colored water, graduated cylinders, and a 2-liter bottle to create a model that represents the amount of water in the oceans.

f. Encourage groups to compare their completed model with the "All Earth's Water" bottle. Ask each group to explain to the class how they decided how much water to put in the bottle and how they carried out their idea.

g. Based on the models constructed by the groups, ask them to vote again (this time by a show of hands) for the lettered bottle that they think best represents the amount of water in the earth's oceans. (They should select bottle A.) Ask: *Are you surprised by how much of the earth's water is in the oceans? Do you think that the oceans are an important part of our planet? Why?*

h. Ask students to list the places that water is found in the earth's system. Answers might include lakes, rivers, ponds, oceans, puddles, in the soil, underground, in the air as water vapor, in clouds as water droplets, frozen in ice caps and glaciers, and so on. Challenge them to find out how much of the earth's water is found in each and to create a visual representation of their findings. They might make a model or a circle graph.[9]

EVALUATE

i. The products from the elaborate phase of the lesson could be assessed with the help of the following rubric.

Criteria	Developing	Proficient	Exemplary
Accuracy of data	Some data is inaccurate	All data is accurate	All data is accurate and sources for data are listed
Places water is found	Less than 8 places are listed with data	At least 8 places are listed with data	More than 8 places are listed with data
Visual representation	Graph or model does not show correct proportions or is not labeled to show what parts of the graph or model represent each water place	Model, circle graph, or bar graph shows relative proportions of water in different places	Meets Proficient expectations and includes % of water on earth for each place

3. DO OBJECTS FLOAT DIFFERENTLY IN SALT WATER THAN IN FRESH WATER? (4–6)

Materials

- Two raw eggs
- Two clear glass containers
- Box of kosher or pickling salt, which can be purchased in many supermarkets. When dissolved in water, this salt produces a clear solution. Table salt can be substituted, but it makes a cloudy rather than a clear solution
- Large container for mixing concentrated salt water

---

[9]Information relating to this investigation is available at http://www.sea.edu/12lessonplans/K12WatersEarth.htm.

Preparation

For this teacher demonstration, you will need a mixture of concentrated salt water for one container and an equal amount of fresh water for the other container. To prepare for the demonstration, follow these steps:

1. Prepare the salt water by mixing one part salt with four parts cool water in a large container. For example, if you use 300 ml cups (10 oz), add half a cup of salt to 2 cups of water. Stir the salt-water mixture thoroughly until the salt dissolves.
2. Pour concentrated salt water into one container and put an equal amount of fresh water in the other container.

ENGAGE

a. Show the students the two containers of water without discussing their contents. Ask: *Do you think an egg will float in water?*

EXPLORE

b. Put an egg in each container. Have students record their observations and questions on an I Notice / I Wonder chart in their science notebooks.

EXPLAIN

c. Ask: *What did you observe?* Discuss students' observations with them. Ask: *Why do you think the egg floated in one container of water and sank in the other one?* Through questioning and discussion, lead students to understand that salt water is denser than fresh water. The denser salt water was able to support the egg. Ask: *Would it be easier for you to float in a fresh water lake or in the ocean? Why?*

ELABORATE

d. Ask: *How much salt will need to be added to fresh water to increase its density so that it will support an egg?*
e. Place an egg in the fresh water. Add salt a spoonful at a time, stirring the water, until the egg rises and floats. Count the number of spoonfuls of salt needed. Measure the volume of salt added and compare it to the original volume of the water.[10]

4. WHAT AFFECTS THE PRESSURE OF A STREAM OF WATER? (3–5)

Materials

- Plastic gallon milk jug
- Water
- Nail or pencil

ENGAGE

a. Ask: *If the side of a plastic milk jug were punctured with very small holes (one above another) and the jug were then filled with water, what do you think would happen to the water? How would the water pour out of the holes?*

---

[10]For additional information on this activity, see Science and Technology for Children (STC), 1995. *Floating and Sinking: Teacher's Guide.* Carolina Biological Supply Co., Burlington, NC.

EXPLORE

b. Prepare and perform this teacher demonstration for students:
    1. Obtain a clean, plastic, 1-gallon milk jug.
    2. About 4 cm from the bottom of the milk jug, puncture a very small hole with a pencil or nail. Puncture three additional small holes 1 cm apart, vertically, above the first hole as in the diagram. Put masking tape over the holes.
        Note: Do not make the holes too large.

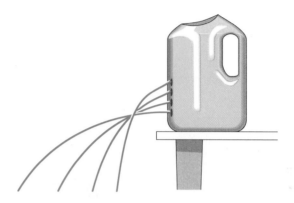

    3. Fill the container half full with water. Hold the plastic jug over a sink, large basin, or tub, and remove the masking tape as shown.
c. Ask: *What do you notice about the way the water comes out of the holes? Which stream went the greatest distance? Which stream went the least distance?*

EXPLAIN

d. Ask: *Why do you think the water comes out of the holes like this?*
e. Ask: *If the jug were filled closer to the top with water, do you think there would be a difference in the way the water comes out?* Tape over the holes, refill the jug until the water is within a centimeter of the top, and remove the tape. Ask: *What do you notice about the way the water comes out of the holes? What difference did you notice in the way the water came from the holes of the jug when there was less water and when there was more water in it?*
f. Ask: *What can you conclude about how water pressure varies with depth?*

ELABORATE

g. Ask: *What results do you think you would get if you used a quart, half-gallon, or 2-gallon container? Try it and record your findings.*

5. WHAT FOODS CONTAIN PRODUCTS FROM THE OCEAN? (4–6)

Materials

- Food product labels
- Grocery store advertisements
- Sorting mats and transparency with a Venn diagram as shown

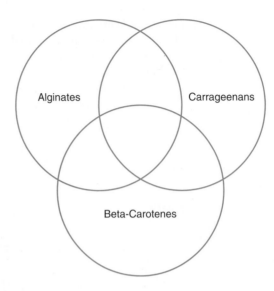

Preparation

Several weeks before this lesson, ask your students and colleagues to collect the ingredient lists from the following products they might use at home: brownie mix, cheese, chocolate milk, coffee creamer, cottage cheese, egg substitute, evaporated milk, frozen foods and desserts, frozen yogurt, ice cream, infant formula, margarine, mayonnaise, multiple vitamins, pet food, pudding, relishes, salad dressing, sauces and gravies, sour cream, toothpaste, whipped topping, whipping cream, and yogurt. Provide a box for collection of the labels and containers in your classroom.

ENGAGE

a. Distribute the grocery store advertisements to the class and encourage them to look them over. Ask: *Do you eat anything that comes from the ocean?* (Students will probably suggest fish, shrimp, clams, etc.) *What do these products eat?* (Students will probably say other smaller animals in the ocean.) *Are there plants in the ocean?* (Students will probably say seaweed or algae.) *Do some of the animals in the ocean eat the ocean plants? Do you eat any of the ocean plants?* (Some students may know that seaweed is used to wrap sushi.)

EXPLORE

b. Guide students to collect data following these procedures:
   1. With students working in small groups (four students per group is best), distribute to each group at least 10 ingredient lists from different products from the collection box. The groups do not need to have the same assortment of ingredient lists.
   2. Provide each group with a copy of the Venn diagram. Give the students a few minutes to look at their materials. Suggest that they use the Venn diagram to organize their ingredient lists based on the presence of alginates, carrageenans, and beta-carotenes.
   3. If students need assistance, display the transparency of the Venn diagram on the overhead projector and model the procedure. Ask a student to read an ingredient list to look for any or all of these ingredients. Then write the name of the product in the appropriate segment of the Venn diagram. Do several more examples if necessary.
   4. Each group should write the names of each of the products for which they have an ingredients list on their Venn diagram. If you want them to include more product names, they can switch label sets with another group.

EXPLAIN

c. Ask the groups to share their findings with the class. Have them describe what the product names in each segment of the Venn diagram have in common.

d. Ask if anyone knows what these ingredients are. Then tell the students that each of these ingredients comes from seaweeds, which are large forms of marine algae that grow in coastal waters around the world. The three terms on the Venn diagram refer to compounds extracted from each of the three main kinds of marine algae: brown, red, and green. Alginates come from brown algae. They make water-based products thicker, creamier, and more stable. In ice cream, they prevent the formation of ice crystals. Carrageenans come from red algae. They are used in stabilizing and gelling foods, cosmetics, pharmaceuticals, and industrial products. Beta-carotene comes from green algae. It is a natural pigment that is used as yellow-orange food coloring and may help prevent certain types of cancers.

ELABORATE

e. Challenge students to find other products that contain these ingredients in their pantries or at the grocery store. Bring samples of edible seaweed such as nori, kombu, dulse, and kelp to class for students to observe. Explain that these marine algae are used in many Asian cuisines, often as wrappers for rice, meat, and vegetables (sushi). Using proper sanitation precautions, offer samples of the edible seaweed to students who wish to try it.[11]

6. WHAT ARE SOME EFFECTS OF WATER POLLUTION? (3–8)

Materials

- For each group, four quart-sized or 2-liter clear containers (plastic soda bottles, food jars with covers, etc.)
- Tap water aged for 3 to 4 days
- Soil and/or gravel from an aquarium or pond
- Water with algae and other aquatic microorganisms from a freshwater aquarium or a pond
- Measuring cups and spoons
- Plant fertilizer
- Hand lenses for each group
- Liquid laundry detergent (not green)
- Motor oil
- Vinegar

Preparation

Two weeks in advance of conducting this activity, four jars should be set up by you and designated student helpers for each cooperative group of students:

1. Fill four containers one-third full with aged tap water, add 4 cm of pond soil or aquarium gravel, and then fill the rest of the jar with pond water and algae.
2. Add 1 teaspoon of plant fertilizer to each jar, stir well, and loosely screw on the jar covers.
3. Put the jars near the window in good, indirect light or under a strong artificial light.
4. Label the jars A, B, C, and D.

---

[11]Adapted from two Internet lessons: "There Are Algae in Your House!" from the Ocean Planet website of the Smithsonian (http://oceancolor.gsfc.nasa.gov/seaWIFS) and "Is There Seaweed/Algae in Your Food?" from Neptune's website (http://pao.cnmoc.navy.mil/educate/Neptune/lesson/social/algae.htm).

ENGAGE

a. Ask: *What things do people do, sometimes unknowingly, that result in water pollution? How can water pollution affect water environments in ways that are detrimental to the organisms that live in or depend on the water?*

EXPLORE

b. Guide students to conduct this investigation:
    1. Provide each group of students the four jars that were set up 2 weeks earlier. The jars contain pond water, algae, pond soil or aquarium gravel, and fertilizer.
    2. Instruct the groups to observe and describe on their record sheets how each jar looks. Make sure students use hand lenses.

RECORDING OBSERVATIONS		
Date _____ Observers'/Recorders' Names _____		
Jar	Observation Before Additive	Observation After Additive
A		
B		
C		
D		

3. Students should add 2 tablespoons of detergent to jar A, enough motor oil to cover the surface of jar B, and 1/4 to 1/2 cup (250 ml) of vinegar to jar C. Jar D will not have any additive and will be the control. See the diagram.

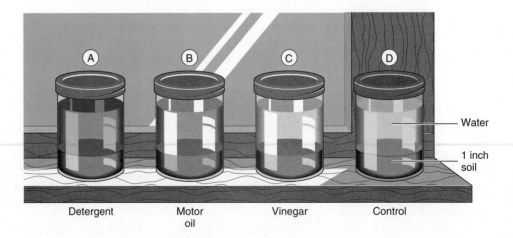

4. Students should loosely cover the jars and return them to the light as before.
5. Ask: *What do you think might happen in each of the jars?*
6. Provide time for students to observe and record their observations two to three times a week. After 4 weeks, groups should summarize their observations.

EXPLAIN
    c. Ask: *What changes did each jar go through? Why do you think jars A, B, and C went through such changes?*

ELABORATE
    d. Guide students to related readings in texts or online that provide further information about the effects of these pollutants on water and on organisms exposed to the polluted water.

    e. Ask:
      How could you apply these findings?
      How might you set up activities to try to reverse the effects of the pollutants used in jars A, B, and C?
      Where in everyday life do we see the effects of water pollution like that in jars A, B, and C? How could these effects be prevented?

7. HOW CAN WE TRY TO REVERSE THE EFFECTS OF AN OIL SPILL? (3–8)

Materials
- Aluminum pan
- Motor oil
- Feathers
- Paper towels
- Dishwashing liquid
- Four hard-boiled eggs
- Paper plate
- Very large rubber band
- Turkey baster

ENGAGE
    a. Ask:
      How difficult do you think it is to clean up an oil spill? How do you think it could be done?
      What is the most effective way to clean up an oil spill?
      What devastating effects does an oil spill have on the environment?

EXPLORE
    b. Fill an aluminum pan half full of water, cover the water surface with motor oil, and use it for the following parts of the activity.

    c. Feathers in an oil–water mix. Leave feathers in the oil–water mix for several minutes. Remove the feathers. Ask: *How do you think we might remove oil from the feathers?* Try wiping the feathers with paper towels. Ask: *Did wiping with paper towels remove all the oil?* Try cleaning the feathers with dishwashing liquid. Ask: *Which method of cleaning the oil off the feathers was better? What other ways might we try to remove the oil from feathers?* Try them.

    d. Eggs in an oil–water mix. Put four hard-boiled eggs (with shells on) into the oil–water mix and then remove one egg at a time after each of these intervals: 15 minutes, 30 minutes, 60 minutes, and 120 minutes. Ask: *What happens to the eggs?* Try removing the oil from the eggs with the methods you used for the feathers. After cleaning the oil off the eggs, crack and remove the shells. Ask: *Did the oil get inside the egg that was in the oil for 15 minutes? the one for 30 minutes? the one for 60 minutes? the one for 120 minutes?* Record your findings. Ask: *If oil did get into the egg, can it be removed?*

e. Removing or containing oil. Using the following materials, how might you remove or keep the oil from spreading: paper towel, dishwashing liquid, turkey baster, large rubber band? Lay a paper towel on the surface of the oil and let it stay for 3 minutes. Remove the paper towel and put it on the paper plate. Ask: *What do you see happening to the paper towel and oil?* Add more motor oil, if needed, and spread a very large rubber band on the top of the oil. Ask: *What happens to the oil?* Using the turkey baster, try to remove the oil. Ask: *What happens to the oil?* Replace the oil into the pan of water. Add several drops of dishwashing liquid. Ask: *What happens to the oil?* Ask: *Which method was best for removing the oil? Which method was best for keeping the oil together in one place?*

EXPLAIN

f. Ask: *What possible problems and adverse effects might result when chemicals are used to remove oil from animals in a real oil spill? How might an oil spill in Alaska affect people in the continental United States? Sometimes oil spills are purposely set on fire. What adverse effects might this have on the environment?* Lead students to understand that oil spills adversely affect land and water plants and animals directly by coating them with oil, often leading to their deaths. In addition, an oil spill affects future plant and animal life by destroying eggs and interfering with plant reproduction. Sometimes, the procedures used to reverse oil spills can interfere with environmental interrelationships, especially when chemicals are used.

Additional Activities Related to Oceans

Scientific study of the oceans bridges many science disciplines. Marine biologists monitor animals and plants that live in ocean habitats. Some chemists investigate mineral content and salinity levels of oceans. Physical oceanographers study wave and tidal action. Meteorologists observe weather systems affected by ocean currents. Therefore, many of the activities from previous sections could be included in a study of the oceans.

- Activities on the water cycle, such as "How Much Water Evaporates from an Open Aquarium, and Where Does It Go?" (p. A-219), "How Can You Promote the Evaporation of Water?" (p. A-222), and "What Is Condensation? How Does It Occur?" (p. A-225) can contribute to an understanding of how water circulates between land, the atmosphere, and bodies of water.
- Activities on aquariums, including "How Can We Construct an Aquarium Habitat?" (p. A-158), "What Can We Observe in an Aquarium?" (p. A-160), and "What Environmental Factors Affect Life in an Aquarium Habitat?" (p. A-181) involve simulations of marine environments.
- "How Can Salt Crystals Be Grown?" (p. A-209) could help to explain formation of sea salt and the increased salinity of some tidal pools. "How Can Evaporation and Condensation Be Used to Desalinate Salt Water?" (p. A-226) further explores the nature of salt water.

IV. VIEWING THE SKY FROM EARTH

A. POSITIONS AND MOTIONS OF THE SUN, MOON, AND STARS

▶ *Science Background*

Beyond the earth's atmosphere, other objects are visible in the earth's sky. The brightest and most noticeable of these is our sun, the star at the center of our solar system. Energy from the sun heats both the ocean and land, drives the process of photosynthesis enabling plants to produce food, and illuminates our world during the daytime. Our moon appears about the size of the sun in our sky, though it does not shine as brightly. Rather than producing its own light, the moon is visible because of reflected sunlight. Other planets in our solar system are also visible in the earth's sky. Mercury, Venus, Mars, Jupiter, and Saturn appear at times in the night sky, looking like bright, non-twinkling stars.

Objects in our sky appear to move because the earth rotates on its axis once every 24 hours, the period known as 1 day. Though it appears that the sun, moon, planets, and most of the stars rise in the east and set in the west, it is really the earth's turning that is responsible for this apparent motion. Polaris, the North Star, because of its unique location directly above the earth's north pole, appears to remain stationary in the sky for viewers in the northern hemisphere.

NSES Science Standards

As a result of their science activities, all students should develop an understanding of

- objects in the sky (K–4).
- changes in the earth and sky (K–4).
- the earth in the solar system (5–8).

Concepts and Principles That Support the Standards

- The sun, moon, and stars all have properties, locations, and movements that can be observed and described (K–4).
- The sun has a pattern of movement through the sky. It appears to move across the sky in the same way every day, but its path slowly changes during the season (K–4).

Objectives

1. Observe and describe properties, locations, and movements of the sun, moon, and stars in the sky.
2. Describe the apparent daily motion of the sun across the sky and discuss how this motion varies during the year.
3. Compare and contrast the apparent motion of the sun across the sky with the apparent motion of the moon across the sky.
4. Observe, describe, and name the moon's phases as they change during the month, and explain why this happens.
5. Use compass directions and angles to describe the position of objects in the sky.

1. WHAT CAUSES SHADOWS? (K–2)

Materials
- Overhead projector
- Projection screen or blank wall

ENGAGE
a. Ask: *How are shadows formed?*

EXPLORE

b. Turn on the overhead projector so that it illuminates the projection screen or blank wall. Select several students to stand between the projector and the screen (facing the screen). Ask: *What do you see on the screen?* (Shadows) *What causes these shadows?*

c. Ask: *What is necessary for a shadow to form? If we didn't have the light from the overhead or the students standing here, would there be a shadow on the screen? How could we find out?* Students may suggest having the volunteer students move out of the light or turning off the overhead. Try these things and any other suggestions from students.

EXPLAIN

d. Ask: *When were shadows produced? What did they look like? What two things must you have to create a shadow?* Lead the children to the realization that in order to have a shadow, there must be a light source and an object to block the light. Encourage them to develop an operational definition of a shadow as dark area caused by the blocking of light.

2. HOW CAN SHADOWS BE CHANGED? (K–2)

Materials

- Flashlight
- Two large sheets of white paper
- Scissors
- Plastic funnel
- Pencil or crayon

ENGAGE

a. Ask: *Are shadows of the same object always the same size and shape?* Encourage students to share their ideas.

EXPLORE

b. Working with a partner, students should put a funnel on a large sheet of white paper. Suggest that they use the flashlight to make a shadow of the funnel on the paper. Encourage them to try shining the flashlight from different positions. Ask: *How does the shadow change?*

c. Suggest that students do the following to record the size and shape of two shadows. One student should shine the flashlight on the funnel while the other one traces and cuts the shadow shape out with the scissors, in this sequence:

1. First, while holding the flashlight low and to the side, trace and cut out the shadow of the funnel. Label it "low."

2. Next, switch roles with your partner. Put a new piece of white paper under the funnel, hold the flashlight high, and then trace and cut out the shadow of the funnel. Label it "high."

3. Compare the size and shape of the two cutout shadows.

EXPLAIN

d. Ask: *Are both of your shadow shapes the same?* (No) *How are they different?* (They are different sizes and shapes.) *Which one is longer?* (The one labeled "low" is longer.) *Which one is shorter?* (The one labeled "high" is shorter.) *What caused the difference in shapes?* (The position of the light source.) Try to lead the students to the conclusion that the position of the light source affects the shadow's size and shape. When the light source is low, shining on the object from the side, the shadow is long and when the light source is high, shining down on the object from above, the shadow is short.

ELABORATE

e. Ask: *What happens to the shadow if you move the light source in an arc from one side of the object, over it, and to the other side of the object?* This simulates the apparent motion of the sun in the sky and provides background experience for future activities.

EVALUATE

f. To see if students understand the relationship between the position of a light source and the length and direction of the shadow of a wooden block on a table, have students match the following statements:

Position of light source
1. Light is directly above the block.

2. Light is on the table on the right side of the block.
3. Light is above the table to the right side of the block.
4. Light is on the table on the left side of the block.
5. Light is above the table to the left side of the block.

Length and direction of shadow
A. Very long shadow to the left of the block.
B. Very long shadow to the right of the block.
C. Medium-long shadow to the right of the block.
D. No shadow, or very short shadow all around the block.
E. Medium-long shadow to the left of the block.

3. HOW DO SHADOWS CAUSED BY THE SUN CHANGE DURING THE DAY? (K–4)

Materials

- Flagpole or fence post
- Sidewalk chalk
- Paint stirrers (to use as stakes in the lawn)

ENGAGE

a. Ask: *Do you think that shadows outdoors change during the day? How might we find out?*

EXPLORE

b. On a sunny day, take the class outside to the flagpole or a fence post early in the morning. Ask: *Does the flagpole or fence post have a shadow? How could we mark the position of this shadow?*

c. Show the students the sidewalk chalk and paint stirrers if they need a hint. Have the students identify the "end" of the shadow, that is, the part cast by the top of the flagpole or the fence post. If the end of the shadow falls on concrete, sidewalk chalk can be used to mark its position. If the end of the shadow falls on grass, a paint stirrer can be used as a stake to mark its position. Record the time of the observation either in chalk on the concrete or with pencil on the paint stirrer. Throughout the day, about once each hour if possible, return to the flagpole or fence post with the class to mark the shadow's current position.

EXPLAIN

d. After making the final afternoon observation, ask: *What did you find out about how the shadow changed during the day?* (It started out long on that side, then got shorter, then got longer on the other side.) *Why do you think the shadow changed in this way?* (Because the sun seemed to move across the sky.) *How did the position of the sun change during our observations today?* (Indicating directions, lead students to understand that it started out low over there in the morning, moved higher in the sky around noon, then kept moving that way in the afternoon.) Develop the concept that the sun appeared to move from east to west in the sky during the day and that caused the size, shape, and direction of the shadow to change over time.

ELABORATE

e. Ask: *Do you think the flagpole or fence post shadow will change the same way tomorrow? next week? next month? How could we find out?* Assist the students in continuing their investigation of shadow positions throughout the school year and help them look for patterns in their findings.

EVALUATE

f. To check student understanding about how shadows change throughout the day have them fill in the blanks in the following story.

Early in the morning the sun is low in the _____.
When I am outside early on a sunny morning my shadow is _____ and points toward the _____.
During the morning the _____ rises higher in the sky.
My shadow gets _____.
My shadow is _____ at noon when the sun is almost _____.
During the afternoon my shadow becomes _____.
In the evening the sun is low in the _____.
My shadow is _____ and points toward the _____.

4. HOW CAN SHADOWS TELL YOU WHEN IT IS LOCAL NOON? (4–6)

Materials

For each small group of students

- Long nail
- Hammer
- Sheets of white paper (8.5 × 11 inches)
- Rectangular board big enough to hold the paper
- Pencil
- Clock or watch
- Metric ruler

ENGAGE

a. Ask: *On a sunny day, at what time are shadows the shortest? How could we find out? How does the position of the sun in the sky relate to the length of the shadow cast by an object?*

EXPLORE

b. Put a piece of paper in the middle of the board. Hammer the nail into the board and paper as shown, making sure the nail will not easily come out of the board.

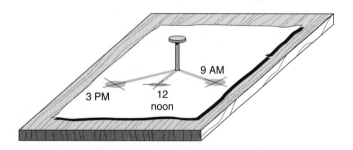

c. Late in the morning about 10:30, place the board where it will get sunlight until about 2:00 in the afternoon. Do not move the board during your observations. Every half hour or at shorter intervals, draw an X at the end of the shadow cast by the nail. Beside the X, note the time of each observation.

d. Upon returning to the classroom, carefully measure the distance between each X and the nail to the nearest millimeter. Create a data table that shows the time of the observation and the length of the corresponding shadow. Construct a line graph to represent these data. The manipulated or independent variable, "time of observation," should be plotted on the x-axis; the responding or dependent variable, "shadow length," should be plotted on the y-axis.

EXPLAIN

e. Ask: *Did the shadow length change during your observation period? When was it shortest? When would you expect to have the shortest shadow?* (When the sun was highest in the sky) Explain that "local noon" occurs when the sun is at its highest point above the horizon for a given day. Local noon does occur in the middle of the day at a given location, but because time zones cover large geographic areas, local noon probably does not occur exactly at 12:00 noon according to your accurately set clock. Daylight savings time, which shifts the time by 1 hour during certain months of the year, also affects the clock time that local noon occurs. Ask: *Is local noon exactly at 12:00 noon on the clock at our location? How do you know?*

ELABORATE

f. Ask: *Do you think local noon will occur at the same time tomorrow at this location? How could we find out? How could you modify your observations to be more certain of the actual time of local noon? Do you expect students in other towns to find the same time for local noon at their location? Why or why not? How could you find out?* (Students might suggest sharing data electronically with schools in other geographic areas.)

5. WHY IS THERE DAY AND NIGHT? (2–4)

Materials

- Styrofoam ball (about the size of a baseball)
- Craft stick and brad for each small group
- Lamp with a bright bulb (at least 100 watts)
- Globe
- Room that can be darkened
- Small lump of sticky tack

ENGAGE

a. Ask: *What do you think causes day and night? Does every place on earth have daytime or nighttime at the same time?*

EXPLORE

b. Distribute a ball, craft stick, and brad to each small group. Demonstrate how to assemble these parts as shown.

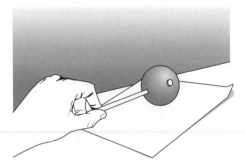

c. Have the students hold the ball by the craft stick. Then darken the room lights and turn on the bright light. Tell students to discover what they can about the way the ball is lit and record observations about their ball. The following questions might guide their thinking: *How much of the ball is lit up? Is the brad in the lit part? If not, what can you do to the ball to move the brad to the lit part? If you became tiny and were on the brad on the lit side of the ball, would you be able to see the bright light bulb? If you were tiny and were on the brad on the unlit side of the ball, would you be able to see the bright light bulb?*

EXPLAIN

d. Ask the class to share their observations of the balls in the bright light.

e. Show the globe to the class. Ask: *What is the globe a model of?* (Earth) *How is the globe like the earth? How is it different?* Place the lamp several meters from the globe and darken the room. Then, turn on the bright bulb. Ask: *What do you think the bright bulb is a model of?* (The sun) *How is the bright bulb like the sun? How is it different? Is the entire globe lit by the bright light? How much of it is lit?* (One half) *Which half?* (the half toward the bright light) *How does this model now show day and night?* (The lit side of the earth is having daytime, and the unlit side is having nighttime.) *What happens when I turn the globe?* (The places that are lit change.) *Are the same places on the earth having daytime when the globe is turned?* (No)

f. Stick the small lump of sticky tack on the globe to mark the location of your school. Ask: *Is it day or night where the sticky tack is? What could I do to the globe so that the sticky tack is having daytime, then nighttime, then daytime, and so on?*

g. Slowly spin the globe on its axis in a counterclockwise direction as viewed from above the north pole. As the sticky tack moves from darkness into the light, explain to the students that this is sunrise for the people at that location. When the sticky tack is in the center of the lit side of the globe, with the light shining directly onto it, it is noon for the people at that location. When the sticky tack moves from the lit to the unlit area, it is sunset. When the sticky tack is in the center of the unlit area, on the side of the earth away from the sun, it is midnight.

EVALUATE

h. Check for student understanding of why we have day and night by having students respond to the following multiple-choice item:

   1. We have day and night because:
      A. The earth turns once on its axis each day.
      B. The sun travels around the earth once each day.
      C. The earth travels around the sun once each day.
      D. The sun turns on and off, it shines during the day but is dark during the night.

6. HOW DOES THE APPEARANCE OF THE MOON'S SHAPE CHANGE OVER TIME? (2–4)

Materials
- Black construction paper
- Soft white chalk

ENGAGE

a. Distribute materials to the students. Give them 5 minutes to draw the shape of the moon. Post the pictures for all to see. Ask: *Are all the drawings the same shape?* (No) Sort them so that similar shapes are grouped together. Ask representatives from each group to tell why they drew the moon the way they did. Ask: *Can everyone's drawing be correct even if they are different shapes?* (Yes) *How can this be?* (The moon doesn't always appear the same shape.) *How could we find out how the appearance of the moon's shape changes over time?* (Hopefully, someone will suggest observing and recording the moon's appearance in the sky for a week or so.)

EXPLORE

b. Have the students take home a large sheet of black construction paper and some white chalk, then observe the moon daily for a week. They should divide their paper into eight equal rectangles as shown.

Moon Calendar by Suzy	11/5	11/6	11/7
11/8	11/9	11/10	11/11

Students can use the first rectangle for the title and their name and the remaining seven spaces for their daily observations. It is best to begin this assignment several days after new moon when fair weather is expected—the waxing crescent moon should be visible in the western sky shortly after sunset. Assuming it is clear, the moon should be visible in the evening sky for the next week. If there is an overcast night, students should indicate on their chart that the sky was cloudy.

EXPLAIN

c. At the end of the observation period, students should bring their moon calendars to class to share and compare. Ask: *How did the moon's shape seem to change during the week?* Have them see if everyone's observations supported the same conclusions. Ask: *Did more of the moon appear to be illuminated each night?* Tell the students that the apparent shape of the moon is known as its phase. Use a chart like this to introduce the names of the phases. Challenge the students to identify which phases they observed.

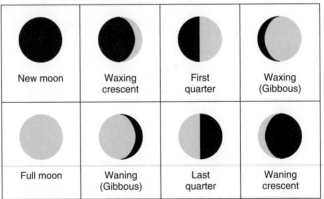

New moon	Waxing crescent	First quarter	Waxing (Gibbous)
Full moon	Waning (Gibbous)	Last quarter	Waning crescent

Phases of the Moon as Seen From the Earth

ELABORATE

d. Ask students to predict what the moon will look like for the next few days, then make observations to check their predictions.

An ongoing Moonwatch Bulletin Board[12] could be maintained in your classroom. Each night, have three students draw the shape of the moon on an index

---

[12]For additional details on moon watches, see G. Robert Moore, "Revisiting Science Concepts," *Science and Children* 32(3), November/December 1994, 31–32, 60.

card. Have the three students compare their drawings and arrive at one drawing that represents their observations. Post the drawing on the appropriate month/date cell on the bulletin board calendar. As a pattern develops, have the class predict the next day's moon phase.

7. WHY DOES IT APPEAR THAT THERE ARE PHASES OF THE MOON? (4–6)

Materials
- Styrofoam ball (about the size of a baseball) and a craft stick for each student
- Lamp with a bright bulb (at least 100 watts)
- A room that can be darkened

ENGAGE

a. Ask: *What are moon phases? Why does the moon have phases?*

EXPLORE

b. Use some simple objects to create a model that shows the cause of the moon's phases as viewed from the earth. In this model a styrofoam ball represents the moon, a bright lightbulb represents the sun, and your head represents the earth. Your eyes will see the view of the moon phase from the earth.

c. Insert the craft stick into the styrofoam ball to act as a handle. Hold the moon ball in your left hand with your arm outstretched. Ask: *How much of the moon ball can you see at one time?* Darken the room. Ask: *Is it easy to see the moon ball? Is any part of it illuminated?* Turn on the bright lightbulb to represent the sun. Look at the moon ball from several angles. Ask: *Is part of it illuminated now? How much of the moon ball is illuminated at the same time?* Describe the location of the lit part in relation to the bright light.

d. The moon orbits around the earth each month. To simulate this in your model, stand facing the bright light, hold the moon ball in your left hand so that the moon ball appears to be a little to the left of the lightbulb. Ask: *Is a lit area visible on the moon ball when it is in this position?* Describe it. (The right edge of the moon ball is illuminated in a narrow crescent shape.) Slowly turn to your left, keeping your arm holding the moon ball outstretched. Watch how the illuminated part of the moon ball varies as its position changes. If the moon ball goes into the shadow cast by your head, just lift the moon ball a little higher so the light can reach it. Move the moon ball around its orbit several times. Look for patterns in the way it is illuminated.

EXPLAIN

e. Have a class discussion about the questions posed in the explore phase of the lesson. Lead the students to an understanding of the following concepts.
   1. The moon does not produce its own light; it reflects light from the sun.
   2. Half of the moon, that half facing the sun, is illuminated at any given time.
   3. We can only see half of the moon's surface at any given time, the half that is facing the earth.
   4. Depending on the relative positions of the earth, sun, and moon, only part of the illuminated moon's surface may be facing the earth, so we see phases of the moon.

ELABORATE

f. Have the students complete an illustration showing the apparent moon phase when the moon is at various positions in its orbit around the earth. This illustration is really a two-dimensional model to explain why the moon appears to have phases. A completed illustration might look something like the following diagram.

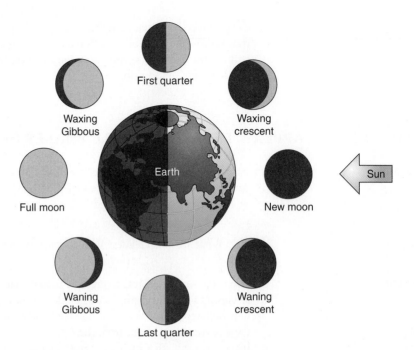

EVALUATE

g. To assess student understanding about why the moon has phases, have students answer the following questions.

   1. If the moon is full, it will rise in the east as the sun
      A. rises in the East.
      B. sets in the East.
      C. rises in the West.
      D. sets in the West.
   2. If the moon is between the earth and the sun, its phase will be:
      A. new.
      B. crescent.
      C. gibbous.
      D. full.
   3. Which of the following statements best describes why the moon has phases when viewed from the earth?
      A. The earth's shadow creates the moon's phases.
      B. How much of the illuminated half moon we see from the earth depends on the relative position of the earth, moon, and sun.
      C. Different parts of the moon emit light at different times of the month.
      D. Clouds in the earth's atmoshere block parts of the moon from our view.

8. HOW CAN WE DESCRIBE POSITIONS OF OBJECTS IN THE SKY? (4–6)

Materials

• Cardinal direction signs
• Ten index cards each labeled with a large number from 1 to 10
• Masking tape or sticky tack
• Adding machine tape
• "Handy Angle Measurements" sheet

Preparation

Post cardinal directions—north, south, east, and west—on the classroom walls. Post the 10 index cards at various locations on the walls and ceiling of the classroom. Put a strip of adding machine tape all the way around the room at the students' seated eye level. This represents the horizon.

ENGAGE

a. Ask: *How could you explain to someone where to look for a particular object in the sky? What kinds of measurements and units might be helpful?* Ask several students to describe the location of something in the classroom. Discuss alternative approaches.

EXPLORE

b. Point out the cardinal directions signs posted in the room. Distribute copies of the "Handy Angle Measurements" sheet shown. Demonstrate how to extend your arm, and discuss the angles represented by the different parts of the hand. Mention that the adding machine tape around the room represents the horizon, the starting point for their angle measurements. Ask the students to try to measure the angle from the horizon line to the point straight overhead using an outstretched arm and clenched fist. It should take approximately nine fists, since the angle from the horizon to the point overhead (zenith) is 90 degrees and each fist represents about 10 degrees.

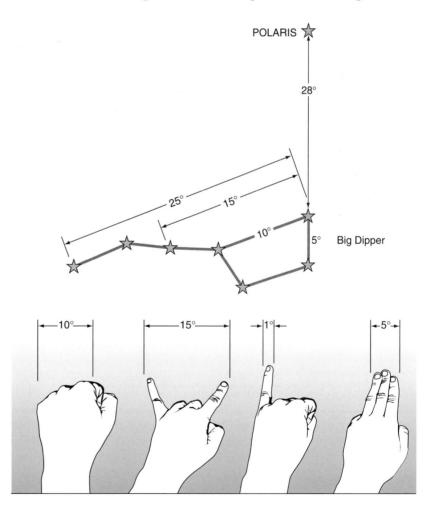

c. Have the students number from 1 to 10 on a sheet of paper. Ask them to use cardinal directions and angle measurements to describe the position of each index card number posted in the room, from their seat.

Note: Because the cards are relatively close to the observers, the observing position will affect the results. Do not expect students in different parts of the room to have the same direction and angle measurement for each card.

EXPLAIN

d. Ask: *How were you able to describe the positions of the index cards?* (By finding the direction to look and measuring how high above the horizon with my outstretched hand)

   Could you use this same technique to describe the position of objects in the sky? What would you need to know to be successful? (Cardinal directions)

Safety Precautions

Caution students to never look directly at the sun. The sun is very bright. Looking at it could cause blindness. Only use this technique to describe the location of the moon, stars, planets, and so on.

ELABORATE

e. Apply this measuring technique to describing the position of the moon in the sky. Find out how the moon moves across the sky during the night. Determine the cardinal directions around your observation point. A compass, street map, or locating Polaris (the North Star) should help.

f. Record your observations in a data table like the one shown.

Time of Observation	Direction	Angle Above the Horizon
7:30 p.m.		
8:00 p.m.		
8:30 p.m.		
9:00 p.m.		
9:30 p.m.		
10:00 p.m.		

Observe and record the position of the moon at half-hour intervals. Describe how the moon moves during the night. Develop an investigation to determine how the position of the moon at a given hour changes from night to night. Ask: *What did you find?*

g. If you live in the northern hemisphere, you can determine your latitude by measuring the position of Polaris above the horizon. Polaris is the end star in the handle of the Little Dipper. The pointer stars of the Big Dipper are helpful in finding Polaris. Polaris is *not* the brightest star in the sky. To find it, face the northern horizon. Look for the patterns shown in the Handy Angle Measurement diagram. The orientation of the Big Dipper will vary, but its pointer stars always point toward Polaris. Decide which star is Polaris. Determine how many degrees it is above the horizon using the Handy Angle Measurement technique. That number of degrees should be the same as the latitude of your observation position. Note the position of Polaris relative to objects on the ground (trees, houses, etc.). Try finding Polaris several hours later. Ask: *Is it still in the same angle above the horizon? Is it still in the same place relative to the objects on the ground?*

You might notice that while Polaris is in the same location, the nearby star patterns have seemed to move in a counterclockwise direction around Polaris. Activity 5, Making a Star Clock in the GEMS (Great Explorations in Math and Science) Module *Earth, Moon, and Stars*, is a good activity related to the motion of the circumpolar constellations (those around the pole).[13]

B. MODELS OF THE SOLAR SYSTEM AND THE EARTH-MOON SYSTEM

▶ *Science Background*

Our solar system includes the sun (our star), eight planets, and numerous smaller bodies including Pluto, asteroids, and comets that orbit the sun. The four planets closest to the Sun—Mercury, Venus, Earth, and Mars—are known as the inner planets. The other four planets—Jupiter, Saturn, Uranus, and Neptune—are known as the outer planets. Pluto lost its status as a planet in 2006 when 424 astronomers at the International Astronomical Union meeting voted to change the definition of the term *planet*.

The earth-moon system is unique in the solar system. Other planets have moons, but the earth is the only planet with just one very large moon. Although much smaller than the sun, our moon appears about the same size in our sky. This is because it is much closer to the earth.

Science Standards

All students should develop an understanding of

- the earth in the solar system (5–8).

Concepts and Principles That Support the Standards

- The earth is the third planet from the sun in a system that includes the moon, the sun, seven other planets and their moons, and smaller objects, such as dwarf planets, asteroids, and comets (5–8).
- The sun, an average star, is the central and largest body in the solar system (5–8).
- Models can represent the real world, making abstract concepts more concrete (5–8).

Objectives

1. Demonstrate and describe a scale model of our solar system.
2. Name the planets in order of size.
3. Name the planets in order of distance from the sun.
4. Demonstrate and describe a model of the earth-moon system.

---

[13]For many good astronomy activities, see GEMS (Great Explorations in Math and Science), 1986. *Earth, Moon, and Stars*, by Cary I. Sneider. Lawrence Hall of Science, Berkeley, CA.

1. HOW SPREAD OUT ARE THE PLANETS IN OUR SOLAR SYSTEM? (3–6)

Materials

- Ten sentence strips, each labeled with one of the solar system bodies (Sun, Mercury, Venus, Earth, Mars, Jupiter, Saturn, Uranus, Neptune, Pluto)

ENGAGE

a. Ask students to draw a picture showing what they know about the orbits of the planets around the sun in our solar system. To assess students' prior knowledge, ask: *How many planets did you include? Could you name the planets? Do you think you placed the planets in the right order from the sun? Are the orbits of the planets all the same distance apart? What is a scale model? Was your drawing a scale model? Why or why not?*

EXPLORE

b. Select 10 students to represent the major bodies in the solar system. Give each of them a labeled sentence strip to hold.

    Select a starting place at one edge of the playground or at the end of a very long hall. Instruct the sign holding students to follow these instructions for constructing the model solar system.

1. The "sun" stands at one end of the area.
2. Mercury takes 4 small steps from the sun.
3. Venus takes 3 small steps outward from Mercury.
4. Earth takes 2 small steps beyond Venus.
5. Mars takes 5 small steps beyond Earth.
6. Jupiter takes 34 small steps beyond Mars.
7. Saturn takes 40 small steps beyond Jupiter.
8. Uranus takes 90 small steps beyond Saturn.
9. Neptune takes 100 small steps beyond Uranus.
10. Pluto takes 88 small steps beyond Neptune.

c. Tell the class that the positions of the students with the signs represent the average distance between the planets' orbits. With the holders remaining in their places and holding up their signs, all the students should observe the spacing and think about these questions: *Which planets' orbits are closest together? Which ones are really spread out? Are the planets' orbits spaced at equal distances from the sun?*

EXPLAIN

d. Upon returning to the classroom, discuss the students' responses to the questions. Important ideas to emerge from the discussion include the following:

- The first four planets—Mercury, Venus, Earth, and Mars—do not have much distance between their orbits. These planets are known as the *inner planets.*
- The rest of the planets—Jupiter, Saturn, Uranus, and Neptune—have rather large distances between their orbits. These planets are known as the *outer planets.*
- Pluto, once considered a planet, was reclassified as a dwarf planet in 2006. Pluto's average distance from the sun is represented in the model we created on the playground.

e. Explain that the planets are not usually lined up as in our model. The model does not show the actual positions of the planets, just the relative spacing of their orbits.

EVALUATE

f. To assess student knowledge of the relative positions of the planets in our solar system, have students respond to the following items.

   1. List the planets in order by their distance from the sun.

   2. Which of the following statements best describes the location of the planets in our solar system?

     A. The planets are all lined up in a straight line.

     B. The planet's orbits are equal distances apart.

     C. The inner planets' orbits are closer together than the orbits of the outer planets.

     D. The planets are all the same distance from the sun.

2. HOW DO THE PLANETS IN OUR SOLAR SYSTEM COMPARE IN SIZE? (5–8)

Materials

- Butcher paper
- Pencils
- Markers
- Scissors
- Metersticks
- Metric rulers or metric tapes

ENGAGE

a. Cut out a circle with a diameter of 5.6 cm to represent Earth. Show the circle to the class. Ask: *If we made a scale model of the planets in our solar system, how big would each planet be if Earth was this big?*

EXPLORE

b. Have the class count off by sevens. Tell each of the "ones" to draw a circle to represent Mercury in this model. Each of the "twos" should draw Venus to this scale, and so on. When the models showing student's prior knowledge are cut out, ask all the "ones" to bring their Mercury circles to the front of the room. Compare the range of sizes represented and how these circles compare with the Earth circle. Ask: *What does this tell us about what these people know about the size of Mercury compared to Earth?* Repeat this procedure with each of the other number groups and their cutout planets. You will probably be able to conclude that as a class we really are not sure how the planets compare in size.

c. Tell the class that the diameter of the Earth circle in our model is 5.6 cm. Measure its diameter so they can confirm its size. Tell them that you will give each person the diameter measurement of their planet, so that they can make an accurate scale model for our solar system models. The following table includes the data:

Group Number From Counting Off	Planet	Diameter in Centimeters
Ones	Mercury	2.1
Twos	Venus	5.3
Threes	Mars	3.0
Fours	Jupiter	62.6
Fives	Saturn	52.8
Sixes	Uranus	22.4
Sevens	Neptune	21.7

It may be necessary to review the meaning of the term *diameter*—the distance across the circle through the center. If students are reminded that diameter = 2 × radius, they might realize that if they find the radius (half of the diameter) of their circle and swing the radius around a center point, they will get a circle of the proper diameter. This technique is especially useful for the big planet circles.

d. After each circle is cut out, it should be labeled with the name of the planet it represents. Students should have the diameter of their planet circle checked for accuracy by at least two other students and make any necessary corrections.

e. Encourage students to get into solar system groups of eight so that there is one model of each planet in their group. Provide each group with a 5.6 cm diameter Earth circle. Challenge the groups to use their models to make a list of the planets in order of size from smallest to largest.

EXPLAIN

f. Ask: *How did you compare the planets' sizes?* (We made scale models.) *Are our models the actual sizes of the planets?* (No. They are much smaller, but are "to scale" so they can be compared.) You may want to explain that in our model 1 cm = approximately 2,285 km. At this scale, the diameter of the sun would be approximately 6 meters. Perhaps you could draw a circle with a diameter of 6 meters on the playground so they could see how big the sun is compared to the planets. Ask: *Do our models show the actual shapes of the planets?* (No. Planets are spheres, not circles. We made a two-dimensional rather than a three-dimensional model.)

g. Ask: *What did you learn about the relative sizes of planets?* (They vary greatly in size.) *What was the order of the planets from smallest to largest diameter?* (Mercury, Mars, Venus, Earth, Neptune, Uranus, Saturn, Jupiter)

ELABORATE

h. Ask students to make up comparison questions about the relative diameters of the planets, for example: *Which planet has a diameter about half Earth's diameter?* (Mars) *How many Earth diameters would fit in one Jupiter diameter?* (11) Have them challenge each other to find the answers using the scale models as an aid.

EVALUATE

i. To assess student knowledge of the relative sizes of the planets in our solar system, have students respond to the following items.

1. List the planets in our solar system in order from smallest to largest.   .

2. Which of the following statements best describes the relative sizes of the planets in our solar system?

A. All of the planets in our solar system are about the same size.

B. The inner planets are all much smaller than the outer planets.

C. The further a planet is from the sun, the larger it is.

D. The further a planet is from the sun, the smaller it is.

3. HOW COULD YOU MAKE A SCALE MODEL OF THE EARTH AND MOON? (5–8)

Materials

- Basketball
- Volleyball
- Softball
- Baseball
- Tennis ball
- Golf ball
- Ping-Pong ball
- Piece of rope 7.28 meters long
- Metric rulers

ENGAGE

a. Hold up the basketball. Tell the class that in our model of the earth and moon, it will represent the earth. Display the other balls. Ask: *Which ball would you select to represent the size of the moon in our model?* Record responses on a histogram on the board. *What would we need to know to determine which ball best represents the size of the moon when the earth is the size of a basketball?* (The actual diameter of the earth and the moon)

EXPLORE

b. The diameter of the earth is 12,756 km and the diameter of the moon is 3,475 km. Ask: *What information do we need to collect about the balls to select the best ball to represent the moon?* Have the students get into small groups to come up with a plan to determine which ball would represent the moon. Carry out your plan.

EXPLAIN

c. Ask: *Which ball did your group select to be the best moon ball if the earth is the size of the basketball?* (The tennis ball is best, because the earth's diameter is about 3.7 times the diameter of the moon, and the basketball's diameter is about 3.7 times the diameter of the tennis ball.)

Ask: *What procedures did your group use to solve this problem?* (Measured the balls, used ratios, etc.) This might be an appropriate time for a review about ratios and proportions. *What is the scale of this model?* (1 cm on this model = approximately 530 km in reality)

ELABORATE

d. Ask: *If we use the basketball to represent the earth and the tennis ball to represent the moon, how far apart should they be held to represent the actual distance between the earth and the moon?* Ask a student to hold the basketball to represent the earth. Start with the tennis ball close to the basketball and slowly walk away. Ask the students to tell you when you should stop. As different groups of students or individuals tell you the distance is right, stick a piece of tape on the wall or floor to show the distance they predicted. After all have expressed their ideas, move back close to the basketball. Give the student holding the basketball one end of the 7.28 meter rope. Slowly unwrap the rope as you retrace your steps away from the basketball. When you get to the end of the rope, hold up the tennis ball. Now the model represents the relative sizes of the earth and the moon and how far they are apart. The actual distance from the earth to the moon is approximately 384,000 km. The moon is approximately 30 earth-diameters from the earth.

Appendixes

Safety Requirements and Suggestions for Elementary and Middle School Inquiry Activities

Consult your state's classroom safety and health manual for specific state policies, requirements, and suggestions.

Safety Guidelines for Teachers

1. Review science activities carefully for possible safety hazards.
2. Eliminate or be prepared to address all anticipated hazards.
3. Consider eliminating open flames; use hot plates where possible as heat sources.
4. Be particularly aware of possible eye injuries from chemical reactions, sharp objects, small objects such as iron filings, and flying objects such as rubber bands.
5. Consider eliminating activities in which students taste substances; do not allow students to touch or inhale unknown substances.
6. Warn students of the dangers of electrical shock; use small dry cells in electrical activities; be aware of potential problems with the placement of extension cords.
7. Maintain fair, consistent, and strictly enforced discipline during science activities.
8. Instruct students in the proper care and handling of classroom pets, fish, or other live organisms used as part of science activities.
9. Instruct students to report immediately to the teacher
   - any equipment in the classroom that appears to be in an unusual or improper condition,
   - any chemical reactions that appear to be proceeding in an improper way, or
   - any personal injury or damage to clothing caused by a science activity, no matter how trivial it may appear.
10. Post appropriate safety rules for students in the classroom, review specific applicable safety rules before each activity, and provide occasional safety reminders during the activity.

Safety Rules for Students

1. Always follow the safety procedures outlined by your teacher.
2. Never put any materials in your mouth.
3. Avoid touching your face, mouth, ears, or eyes while working with chemicals, plants, or animals.
4. Always wash your hands immediately after touching materials, especially chemicals or animals.
5. Be careful when using sharp or pointed tools. Always make sure that you protect your eyes and those of your neighbors.
6. Wear American National Standards Institute approved safety goggles (with Z87 printed on the goggles) whenever activities are done in which there is a potential risk to eye safety.
7. Behave responsibly during science investigations.

REFERENCES

The University of the State of New York, *Elementary Science Syllabus*, 49, 1985, Albany, NY: The State Education Department, Division of Program Development; Ralph E. Martin, Colleen Sexton, Kay Wagner, and Jack Gerlovich, *Teaching Science for All Children*, 1994, Boston: Allyn & Bacon; Full Option Science System (FOSS) Teacher's Guides, 1994, Washington, DC, National Academies of Science.

Measuring Tools, Measuring Skills

In elementary and middle school science and mathematics, students should have many opportunities to

- use a variety of types of measuring instruments;
- measure length, area, volume, mass, and temperature; and
- make comparisons using different systems of units.

Metric Prefixes

milli = .001 (one thousandth)
centi = .01 (one hundredth)
kilo = 1000 (one thousand)

Measuring Length
Length is a linear measure.

Metric Units

millimeter = 0.001 meter (one-thousandth of a meter; the thickness of about 20 pages)
centimeter = 0.01 meter (one-hundredth of a meter; width of a little fingernail)
kilometer = 1000 meters (about 10 city blocks)

Some Conversions

1 inch = 2.54 centimeters
1 centimeter = 10 millimeters
100 centimeters = 1000 millimeters = 1 meter
1 meter = 39.37 inches = 3.28 feet
1000 meters = 1 kilometer = 0.621 mile
100 meters = 109 yards
1 yard = 3 feet

Use the ruler to convert lengths between units.

1 in. = _____ cm = _____ mm
3 in. = _____ cm = _____ mm
10 cm = _____ mm = _____ in.
140 mm = _____ cm = _____ in.

Use the ruler to measure lengths.

Length of dollar bill = _____ in. = _____ cm = _____ mm
Diameter of quarter = _____ in. = _____ cm = _____ mm
Thickness of quarter = _____ in. = _____ cm = _____ mm

Measuring Area
Area is a surface measure.

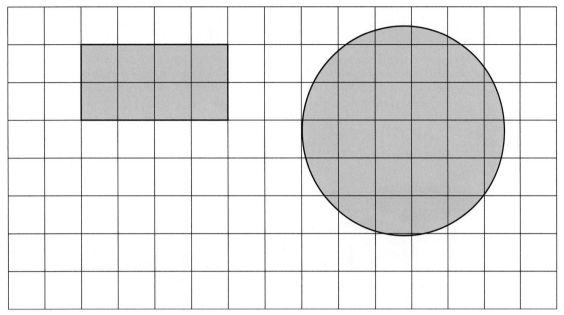

The area of each small square in the figure is 1 square centimeter = 1 cm².

Determine the area of the shaded rectangle

- by counting squares. _____
- by formula ($A = L \times W$). _____

Determine the area of the shaded circle

- by counting squares. _____
- by formula ($A = \pi r^2$). _____

Measuring Volume
Volume is three-dimensional.

1 cubic centimeter (cm³ or cc) is the volume of a cube that is 1 centimeter on each side.

Some Conversions

1 cm³ = 1 cc = 1 milliliter (ml)
1000 cm³ = 1000 ml = 1 liter
1 liter = 1.06 quarts

Determine the volume of the large solid in the figure

- by counting unit cubes.
- by using the formula, $V = L \times W \times H$. _____

Estimate the volume of a golf ball in cubic centimeters. A golf ball has a diameter of about 4 cm.

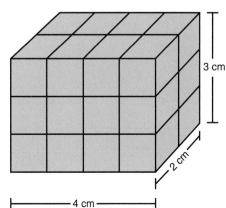

[*Answer*: Estimate how many unit cubes (1 cm³) might fit inside a golf ball if it were hollow. A good estimate of its volume might be between 25 and 40 unit cubes. By formula, the volume of a golf ball is about 33.5 cm³.]

Measuring Mass and Weight

Mass is a measure of the amount of matter in an object and, also, a measure of the inertia of an object. Mass is measured in grams, milligrams, or kilograms using a balance. Weight is a measure of the gravitational pull on an object, measured with a spring scale. Mass and weight are not the same thing, but the weight of an object can be found from its mass.

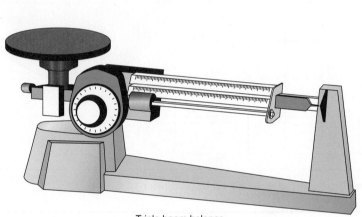

Triple beam balance

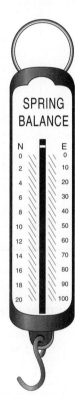

Spring scale

Some Conversions

> 1000 grams (g) = 1 kilogram (kg)
> 1 milligram = 0.001 gram (one-thousandth of a gram)
> 1 gram = 1000 milligrams (mg)
> 1 kg-mass weighs 2.2 pounds on the surface of the earth

Some Masses and Weights

> Mass of nickel = 5 g
> Mass of small child weighing about 60 pounds on earth = 27.3 kg (divide 60 by 2.2)
> Weight on moon of small child of mass 27.3 kg = 10 pounds (1/6 of weight on earth)

Food labels tell how many grams and milligrams of different substances are in a food product.

Measuring Temperature

Temperature is a measure of how hot or cold a substance is. Temperature is measured with a thermometer in degrees Celsius or degrees Fahrenheit.

Some Equivalent Temperatures: Use the Fahrenheit/Celsius thermometer to convert from one temperature unit to the other.

Boiling point of water	100°C = _____ °F
Normal body temperature	_____ °C = 98.6 °F
Room temperature	22°C = _____ °F
Freezing point of water	0°C = _____ °F
Slush of crushed ice, water, and ice cream salt	_____ °C = 10°F
A really cold day in Alaska	_____ °C = −15°F

Nutrition Facts

Serving Size 2/3 cup (55g)
Serving Per Container 12

Amount Per Serving

Calories 210
    Calories from Fat 25

% Daily Value*

Total Fat 3g	**5%**
Saturated Fat 1g	**4%**
Polyunsaturated Fat 0.5g	
Monounsaturated Fat 1.5g	
Cholesterol 0mg	**0%**
Sodium 140mg	**6%**
Potassium 190mg	**5%**
Total Carbohydrate 44g	**15%**
Other Carbohydrate 23g	
Dietary Fiber 3g	**13%**
Sugars 18g	
Protein 5g	
Vitamin A	0%
Vitamin C	0%
Calcium	2%
Iron	6%
Thiamine	10%
Phosphorus	10%
Magnesium	10%

* Percent Daily Values are based on a 2000 calorie diet. Your daily values may be higher or lower depending on your calorie needs.

	Calories	2,000	2,500
Total Fat	Less than	65g	80g
Sat Fat	Less than	20g	25g
Cholesterol	Less than	300g	300g
Sodium	Less than	2400mg	2400mg
Potassium		3500mg	3500mg
Total Carbo		300g	300g
Dietary Fiber		25g	30g

Calories per gram:

Fat 9   •   Carbohydrate 4   •   Protein 4

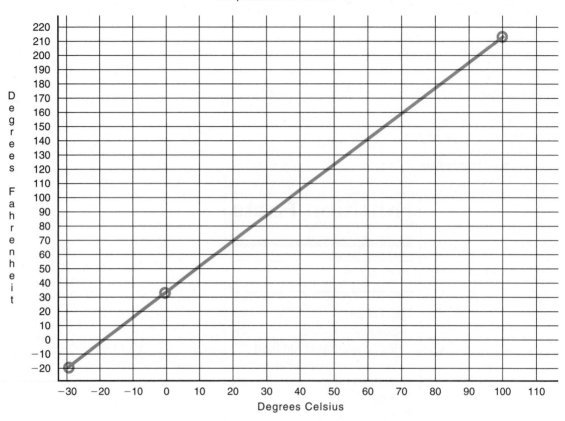

Temperature in °C and °F

Use the graph to find equivalent temperatures.

0°C   = _____ °F
212°F = _____ °C
40°F   = _____ °C
180°F = _____ °C
50°C   = _____ °F

Selected Sources of Science Supplies, Models, Living Things, Kits, and Software

Brock Optical

Microscopes—rugged enough for small children
E-mail: magiscope@aol.com
URL: http://www.magiscope.com

Carolina Biological Supply Company

Instructional materials for all sciences; Science and Technology for Children (STC) guides and materials
E-mail: carolina@carolina.com
URL: http://www.carolina.com

Delta Education

Materials, kits, and activities for hands-on science programs, including FOSS, SCIS 3+, and DSMIII (Delta Science Modules)
E-mail: ecurran@delta-edu.com
URL: http://www.delta-education.com

Discovery Scope

Small, handheld microscopes
E-mail: dscopes@aol.com
URL: http://www.discoveryscope.net

Educational Innovations

Heat-sensitive paper, UV-detecting beads, Cartesian diver, super-absorbent polymers, and other science supplies
E-mail: info@teachersource.com
URL: http://www.teachersource.com

Educational Products, Inc.

Science fair display boards and materials
E-mail: kdavis@educationalproducts.com
URL: http://www.educationalproducts.com

ETA/Cuisenaire

Hands-on science materials
E-mail: info@etacuisenaire.com
URL: http://www.etacuisenaire.com

Fisher Science Education

Instructional materials for all sciences
E-mail: info@fisheredu.com
URL: http://www.fisheredu.com

Forestry Suppliers, Inc.

Orienteering compasses, water, soil, and biological test kits, tree borers, soil sieves, rock picks, weather instruments, and other materials for interdisciplinary science teaching
E-mail: fsi@forestry-suppliers.com
URL: http://www.forestry-suppliers.com

Ken-A-Vision Manufacturing Co., Inc.

Microscopes
E-mail: info@ken-a-vision.com
URL: http://www.ken-a-vision.com

Lab-Aids, Inc.

Single-concept hands-on kits for chemistry, biology, environmental science, and earth science
E-mail: customerservice@lab-aids.com
URL: http://www.lab-aids.com

Learning Technologies, Inc.

Portable planetariums and other materials for astronomy teaching
E-mail: starlab@starlab.com
URL: http://www.starlab.com

Mountain Home Biological

Living materials, barn owl pellets, skull sets
E-mail: mtnhome@gorge.net
URL: http://www.pelletlab.com

NASCO

Science materials and supplies
E-mail: info@enasco.com
URL: http://www.nascofa.com

National Gardening Association

GrowLab guides for kids' gardening, professional development materials on plant science
E-mail: MK@garden.org
URL: http://www.kidsgardening.com

NSTA Science Store

Books, posters, software, CD-ROMs
URL: http://www.nsta.org

Ohaus Corporation

Balances and measurement aids
E-mail: cs@ohaus.com
URL: http://www.ohaus.com

Pitsco LEGO Educational Division

LEGO construction kits, model hot air balloons, educational technology products
E-mail: pitsco@pitsco.com
URL: http://www.pitsco-legodacta.com

Rainbow Symphony, Inc.

Lesson kits for the study of light and color, specialty optics materials, diffraction gratings, 3-D lenses, solar eclipse safe-viewing glasses
E-mail: kathy@rainbowsymphony.com
URL: http://www.rainbowsymphony.com

Sargent-Welch

GEMS materials, materials for all sciences
E-mail: Sarwel@Sargentwelch.com
URL: http://www.Sargentwelch.com

TOPS Learning Systems

Science lessons using simple available materials
E-mail: tops@canby.com
URL: http://www.topsscience.org

Source: Compiled by authors from advertisements and Web searches.

Selected Science Education Periodicals for Teachers and Children

American Biology Teachers

National Association of Biology Teachers
http://www.nabt.org/

Audubon Magazine

National Audubon Society
http://www.Audubon.org/nas/

Journal of Research in Science Teaching

National Association for Research in Science Teaching
http://www.narst.org

National Geographic

National Geographic Society
http://www.nationalgeographic.com/

National Geographic Kids

National Geographic Society
http://www.nationalgeographic.com/kids/

Natural History

American Museum of Natural History
http://www.amnh.org/naturalhistory/

Ranger Rick

National Wildlife Federation
http://www.nwf.org

School Science and Mathematics

School Science and Mathematics Association
http://www.ssma.org

Science

American Association for the Advancement of Science
http://www.aaas.org

Science and Children

National Science Teachers Association
http://www.nsta.org

Science Education

John Wiley & Sons
http://www.wiley.com

Science Scope

National Science Teachers Association
http://www.nsta.org

Scientific American

http://www.sciam.com

Sky and Telescope

Sky Publishing Corp.
http://www.skyandtelescope.com

Super Science (for grades 3–6)

Scholastic
http://teacher.scholastic.com

The Science Teacher

National Science Teachers Association
http://www.nsta.org

Your Big Backyard

National Wildlife Federation
http://www.nwf.org/kidszone/

Professional Societies for Teachers of Science, Science Supervisors, and Science Educators

American Association for the Advancement of Science (AAAS)

http://www.aaas.org

American Association of Physics Teachers (AAPT)

http://www.aapt.org/

American Chemical Society (ACS)

http://www.acs.org/

Association for Educators of Teachers of Science (AETS)

http://theaste.org/

Association for Supervision and Curriculum Development (ASCD)

http://www.ascd.org/

Council for Elementary Science International (CESI)

http://unr.edu/homepage/crowther/cesi. html

International Society for Technology in Education (ISTE)

http://www.iste.org/

National Association of Biology Teachers (NABT)

http://www.nabt.org/

National Association of Geoscience Teachers (NAGT)

http://www.nagt.org/

National Geographic Society (NGS)

http://www.nationalgeographic.com

National Science Education Leadership Association (NSELA)

http://www.nsela.org

National Science Teachers Association (NSTA)

http://www.nsta.org

National Wildlife Federation (NWF)

http://www.nwf.com/

School Science and Mathematics Association (SSMA)

http://www.ssma.org

Contemporary Elementary Science Projects and Programs

Name	Grades	Contact Information	Characteristics
AIMS	K–9	AIMS Educational Foundation http://www.aimsedu.org	*Activities Integrating Math and Science* are hands-on activities that supplement science programs; available as content-themed or state-specific collections of student and teacher pages; supported by professional development workshops; strong math integration, especially in areas of organization and graphing of data.
Bottle Biology	K–8	Department of Plant Pathology, College of Agricultural and Life Sciences, University of Wisconsin, Madison Available from NSTA Science Store http://www.nsta.org	*Bottle Biology* is an ideas book for exploring environmental interactions using soda bottles and other recyclable materials. The book contains more than 20 scientific investigations using bottle constructions, including the Ecocolumn, the Predator-Prey Column, the Niche Kit, and the TerrAqua Column.
BSCS Science Tracks: Connecting Science and Literacy	K–5	Biological Science Curriculum Study, Attn: BSCS Science Tracks, 5415 Mark Dabling Blvd., Colorado Springs, CO 80918-3842 http://bscs.org Available from: Kendall/Hunt Publishing http://www.kendallhunt.com	*BSCS Science Tracks: Connecting Science and Literacy* is a comprehensive, modular, kit-based elementary science program. Developed with the help of NSF funding it features: standards-based content, teaching, and assessment; the 5-E learning cycle; guided inquiry; focus on conceptual understanding; collaboration; student journals and continuous assessment.
FOSS	K–8	Lawrence Hall of Science, University of California, Berkeley http://www.lhs.Berkeley.edu Available from: Delta Education http://www.delta-education.com	*Full Option Science System* is an inquiry-based science program, funded in part by the NSF. This comprehensive, modular, kit-based program features: developmentally appropriate materials and concepts; informative teacher guides, FOSS Readers that provide reading in the content area practice through a variety of literary genres; suggestions for science notebooking; and newly developed formative assessment tools.
GEMS	K–10	Lawrence Hall of Science, University of California, Berkeley http://www.lhs.Berkeley.edu/	*Great Explorations in Math and Science* includes more than 70 teacher guides and handbooks. Materials kits for the stand-alone and supplementary units can be purchased. Easy to use, well organized teacher guides, support teachers with limited science background. Typical units can be completed in 2 to 4 weeks.
GrowLab	K–8	National Gardening Association Burlington, VT http://kidsgardening.com	*GrowLab: Activities for Growing Minds* is an innovative curriculum guide to support plant-related instruction though indoor gardening. Activities are inquiry-based and follow GrowLab's version of the 5-E instructional model. A workshop toolkit titled, *Growing Science Inquiry*, was also developed with the support of NSF.
Insights	K–6	EDC Center for Science Education http://cse.edc.org Available from: Kendall/Hunt Publishing Company http://www.kendallhunt.com	*Insights: An Inquiry-Based Elementary School Science Curriculum* is designed to meet the needs of all children in grades K–6 while specifically addressing urban students. Insights is a core curriculum of seventeen, 6- to 8-week kit-based modules. This NSF supported program focuses on key science concepts, creative and critical thinking, problem solving through experiences in the natural environment, developing positive attitudes about science, bridging science concepts to current social and environmental events; and integration with language arts and mathematics.

Name	Grades	Contact Information	Characteristics
Peaches	Preschool	Lawrence Hall of Science, University of California, Berkeley http://www.lhs.Berkeley.edu	*Preschool Explorations for Adults,* Children, and Educators in Science consists of 10 teacher's guides for children's activities and teacher workshops. Topics include Ant Homes Under the Ground, Homes in a Pond, and Ladybugs.
SAVI/SELPH	3–8	Lawrence Hall of Science, University of California, Berkeley http://www.lhs.Berkeley.edu	*Science Activities for the Visually Impaired/Science Enrichment for Learners with Physical Handicaps* is an interdisciplinary, multi-sensory science enrichment program designed to be used with students who are blind or visually impaired, physically disabled, learning disabled, hearing impaired, or developmentally delayed. There are nine modules, each focusing on a specific content area; teacher guides to the activities; teacher preparation videos; and specially designed equipment that allow students with disabilities full access to science investigations.
SCIS 3(+)	K–6	Lawrence Hall of Science, University of California, Berkeley http://www.lhs.Berkeley.edu Available from: Delta Education http://www.delta-education.com	*Science Curriculum Improvement Study,* one of the elementary science projects developed with NSF support in response to the launch of Sputnik, is now available (after multiple revisions) as SCIS 3(+). Its modules are organized around a hierarchy of science concepts. Science process skills are integrated into the materials centered modules, which use an inductive instructional approach at the three-phase learning cycle which evolved into the 5-E instructional model.
Seeds of Science	2–5	*Seeds of Science/Roots of Reading,* Lawrence Hall of Science, University of California, Berkeley, CA 94720 seeds@berkeley.edu Available from: Delta Education http://www.delta-education.com	*Seeds of Science/Roots of Reading* is a research-based, field-tested curriculum that integrates inquiry science with content-rich literacy instruction. This developing project, funded in part by the NSF, addresses the urgent need for materials that help students make sense of the physical world while addressing foundational dimensions of literacy. The program will include 12 concept-focused, kit-based modules two text series: a collection of integrated science and literacy units, and a parallel collection of literacy units. Both series feature delightful 4-color student books that are central to each of the units.
STC	1–8	National Science Resources Center, Smithsonian Institution Available from: Carolina Biological Supply Company http://www.carolina.com	*Science and Technology for Children* is a comprehensive, modular, kit-based science program featuring inquiry-centered science education curricula that can be used by school districts to construct core instructional programs. Developed using a rigorous research and development process, STC modules provide age-appropriate opportunities for children to expand their conceptual understanding of important science concepts, acquire problem-solving and critical-thinking skills, and develop positive habits of mind toward science.
The Young Scientist Series	Preschool	Education Development Center, Inc. Available from: Redleaf Press http://www.redleafpress.org	*The Young Scientist Series* is an NSF supported science curriculum for children who are three to five years old. Each of the three teacher's guides (*Discovering Nature with Young Children, Building Structures with Young Children, and Exploring Water with Young Children*) provides background information and detailed guidance for incorporating science into preschool programs using materials typically found in an early-childhood classroom.